CONSTITUTION OF INDIA AND PROFESSIONAL ETHICS

CONSTITUTION OF INDIA
AND
PROFESSIONAL ETHICS

M. Raja Ram
Assistant Professor
Department of Mechanical Engineering
S.J.C. Institute of Technology
Kolar District, Karnataka.

PUBLISHING FOR ONE WORLD
NEW AGE INTERNATIONAL (P) LIMITED, PUBLISHERS
(formerly Wiley Eastern Limited)
New Delhi • Bangalore • Chennai • Cochin • Guwahati • Hyderabad
Jalandhar • Kolkata • Lucknow • Mumbai • Ranchi
Visit us at www.newagepublishers.com

Published by New Age International (P) Ltd., Publishers
First Edition: 2008

ISBN (10): 81-224-2253-5

ISBN (13): 978-81-224-2253-5

Rs. 110.00

C-07-10-2064

Printed in India at Ajit Press, Delhi.
Typeset at Laser Craft, Delhi.

PUBLISHING FOR ONE WORLD

NEW AGE INTERNATIONAL (P) LIMITED, PUBLISHERS
(formerly Wiley Eastern Limited)
4835/24, Ansari Road, Daryaganj, New Delhi - 110002
Visit us at **www.newagepublishers.com**

Preface

Constitution of India and Professional Ethics is a compulsory subject prescribed to all the undergraduate Courses. The subject has been introduced at degree level by almost all universities in the country. This is very important subject, where every citizen must understand our Constitution and its components. Also, the detailed discussion on Professional Ethics is there, specifically for engineering profession students. This improves the ethical standards in the profession.

However, it is expected that this book may help the students who are preparing for their Competitive Examinations (All India/State Services Examinations). A large collection of Multiple Choice Questions is given for all the chapters where the students can get all possible questions. In these questions, the first choice i.e., 'a' is correct answer and the student will be knowing the possible other choices.

M. Raja Ram

Acknowledgement

Sincere Pranams to our Gurujis, Sri Sri Sri Balagangadharanatha Mahaswamiji and Sri Sri Nirmalanandanatha Swamiji.

- ❖ My heartfelt thanks to Dr. H.S. Ningappa, Principal, for his encouragement during preparation of this book.
- ❖ I feel extremely grateful to Dr. T. Munikenche Gowda, Professor & Head, Department of Mechanical Engineering, and to all my colleagues, for their moral support.
- ❖ I sincerely thank Dr. Y.M. Reddy, Ex-Principal, Sri Siddhartha Institute of Technology, Tumkur for his comments and for thorough cross-checking the contents.
- ❖ I am very grateful to all those who have helped in this preparation. Some have contributed directly, while many indirectly. This note of thanks may not be exhaustive but I extend my heartfelt gratitude to all those who helped me in bringing out this book.
- ❖ I would like to thank my family members who supported and encouraged constantly with their whole-heart and borne the late nights and early mornings and my needed demands with patience and kindness.
- ❖ All Suggestions for improving the contents of the book would be warmly appreciated.

M. RAJA RAM

Gandhiji's Talisman

I will give you a Talisman. Whenever you are in doubt or when the self becomes too much with you, apply the following test:

Recall the face of the poorest and weakest man whom you may have seen and ask yourself if the step you contemplate is going to be of any use to him. Will he gain anything by it? Will it restore him to a control over his own life and destiny? In other words, will it lead to Swaraj for the hungry and spiritually starving millions?

Then you will find your doubts and your doubts and your self melting away.

--- M.K. Gandhi

Contents

1.	**Preamble of Indian Constitution**	**1–10**
2.	**Fundamental Rights**	**11–15**
3.	**Directive Principles of State Policy**	**16–18**
4.	**Fundamental Duties**	**19–20**
5.	**Union Government**	**21–29**
6.	**State Government**	**30–33**
7.	**Constitutional Provisions**	**34–37**
8.	**Emergency Provisions**	**38–40**
9.	**Electoral Process**	**41–43**
10.	**Basics of Engineering Ethics**	**44–47**
11.	**Responsibility of Engineers**	**48–52**
12.	**Honesty, Integrity and Reliability**	**53–56**
13.	**Risk, Safety and Liability in Engineering**	**57–59**
	Annexure —Multiple-Choice Questions	**60–167**
	Special Annexure	**168-196**
	Annexure: Code of Ethics	**197-208**
	References	**209**
	Unsolved Sample Question Paper–I	**211**
	Unsolved Sample Question Paper–II	**219**
	Answers to Unsolved Sample Paper–I & II	**235**

1

Preamble of Indian Constitution

Government: A country has a definite boundary. The people residing in the country are its citizens. To ensure a peaceful and orderly life in the country, an organization is required. Such an organization is called the Government. It organizes the people and looks after their welfare. How is a government formed? What are its powers, functions and organs? What are the rights of the citizens? Answers to these questions are found in a document known as the "Constitution".

Constitution: The word 'Constitution' is developed from the word 'Constitute', which means 'to frame or to establish or to compose'. According to the Oxford English Dictionary, 'Constitution' means a 'system', according to which the laws and principles of the state is governed. It is a set of fundamental rules according to which the government of a state functions. It is a document which contains the rules and regulations guiding the administrations of a state. It defines the relationship between the rulers and the ruled and how rulers are created in the country. It may be written, or unwritten as in the case of Great Britain. It explains the powers belonging to the government, the fundamental rights of the citizens and the relationship between the citizens and the government. It upholds the principle that all citizens are equal before the law. Any law which is not in accordance with the constitution becomes invalid.

It is a document which is the supreme law of the land. It has derived from a Latin word 'salus populi suprema lex' meaning 'welfare of the people is the supreme law'. Hence, the Constitution of India is a public document which is considered as the voice of the people. It is the document having a legal sanctity. Constitution is an important instrument which confers powers, rights, functions, principles, restrictions and obligations on the part of individuals, states and everybody who are the citizens of India. The purpose of the Constitution is to maintain harmonious relations between the individuals and the states on the one hand and between the different organs of the government on the other. The Constitution reflects the will and wish of the people.

There are THREE pillars of the Constitution: Legislature, Executive and Judiciary. This is known as 'Doctrine of Separation of Power' (Lord Montesquieu). There are TWO types of Constitution: Rigid and Flexible Constitution.

Few other Definitions of Constitution

- The way of life the state has chosen for itself—Aristotle
- It is the collection of principles according to which the powers of the government, the rights of the governed and the relation between the two are adjusted—Woolsey
- It is that body of rules, or laws written or unwritten which determines the organization of government, the distribution of power to the various organs of the government and the general principles on which these powers are to be exercised—Gilchrist

- It consists of those of its rules or laws which determine the form of the government and the respective rights and duties of the citizens towards the government—Lord Bryce
- It is the rules which govern the state—Maciver

Framing of Indian Constitution: World War II in Europe came to an end on 09th May, 1945. In July, a new government came to power in the United Kingdom. The new British government announced its Indian policy and decided to convene a constitution drafting body. Three British cabinet members were sent to find a solution to the question of India's Independence. This team of ministers was called the Cabinet Mission. The Cabinet Mission discussed the framework of the constitution and laid down in some detail the procedure to be followed by the Constitution Drafting Body.

The Constitution of India was drawn up by a Constituent Assembly (established in accordance with the Cabinet Mission plan) initially summoned on 09th December, 1946, under the Presidentship of Sachidananda Sinha, for undivided India in the Constitution Hall (now it is called as Central Hall of Parliament House). On 01st July, 1947, the British Parliament passed the 'Indian Independence Act', to divide into India and Pakistan. With the partition of India, the representatives of East Bengal, West Punjab, Sindh and Baluchistan, N-W Frontier Province and the Sylhet district of Assam, which joined Pakistan, ceased to be members of the Constituent Assembly.

On 14th August, 1947, the Constituent Assembly met again as the Sovereign Constituent Assembly for the dominion of India under the Presidentship of Mr. Sinha. On the demise of Mr. Sinha, Dr. Rajendra Prasad became the President of the Constituent Assembly (11th December, 1946). A Draft Constitution was published in February 1948. 284 out of 299 members appended their signature to the Constitution and finally adopted it on 26th November, 1949. It came to effect on 26th January, 1950. The Constituent Assembly took almost three years (two years, eleven months and eighteen days to be precise) to complete its historic task of Drafting the Constitution for Independent India. During this period, it held eleven sessions covering a total of 166 days. Of these, 114 days were spent on the consideration of the Draft Constitution. Its sessions were open to the press and the public.

Draft Constitution and Drafting Committee

The work started with the presentation of the 'Objective Resolution' moved on 13th December, 1946 by Pandit Jawaharlal Nehru and was adopted on 22nd January, 1947. The Committee for scrutinizing the Draft Constitution and suggesting Amendments was formed on 29th August, 1947. The Draft was readied by February, 1948. The Constituent Assembly met thrice to read the Draft clause-by-clause in November, 1948, October, 1949 and November, 1949. After the third reading, it was signed by the President and adopted on 26th November, 1949. In fact, a Committee on Rules of Procedure was in place as early as December, 1946 under the Chairmanship of Dr. Bhimrao Ramji Ambedkar and Members were: Alladi Krishnaswami Ayyar, N. Gopalaswami Ayyangar, Dr. K.M. Munshi, Syed Md. Saadulla, B.L. Mitter (was replaced by N. Madhava Rao) and D. P. Khaitan (was replaced by T.T. Krishnamachari).

The Drafting Committee studied the constitutions of number of countries like France, Canada, USA, Switzerland, etc. and gathered the best features and adopted them for the realization of the aspirations of the people of India in our Constitution. The result of it was that we have one of the best constitutions of the world today. The Indian Constitution closely follows the British Parliamentary Model but differs from it; the Constitution is Supreme, not Parliament. So, the Indian courts are vested with the authority to adjudicate on the constitutionality of any law passed by the Parliament. Few like,

British Constitution

- Parliamentary form of Government
- The idea of Single Citizenship

- The idea of the Rule of Law
- Institution of Speaker and his/her Role
- Law-making procedure

United States Constitution

- Charter of Fundamental Rights, which is similar to US's Bill of Rights
- Federal Structure of Government
- Power of Judicial Review and Independence of the Judiciary

Irish Constitution

- Constitutional Enunciation of the Directive Principles of State Policy

French Constitution

- Ideals of Liberty, Equality and Fraternity

Germany Constitution

- Proclamation of Emergency

Japanese and Chinese Constitution

- The idea of the Fundamental Duties

Canadian Constitution

- A Quasi-federal form of Government (a Federal system with a strong Central Government)
- The idea of Residual Powers

Australian Constitution

- The idea of the Concurrent List
- Freedom of trade and commerce within the country and between the states

Soviet Constitution

- The Planning Commission and Five-year Plans

The Constitution has provided Provisions and the Procedures for the Amendment. The Parliament only can amend laws in the Constitution. Parliament has powers to make new Provisions or to cancel the Provisions which are against the welfare of the public and can even correct the Provisions, which are known as Amendments.

The Constitution consists of the following: (1) The Preamble; (2) Parts/Chapters I to XXII covering Articles/Clauses 1 to 395; (3) Schedules 1 to 8 and (4) An Appendix and totaling 1,17,369 words in its English language version. Today, it has XXVI Parts, 445 Articles and 12 Schedules and has undergone 92 Amendments.

On 26th January 1950, the Constitution of Independent India was adopted. The Constitution declared India as a Republic. This day is observed every year as the Republic Day and celebrated as National Festival. As provided in the Constitution, the first General elections were held during 1951-52. And the first elected body (Parliament) with two Houses, namely, Rajya Sabha and Lok Sabha, came into existence in May 1952.

Nehru's Objectives Resolution

- India is an Independent, Sovereign, Republic;
- India shall be Union of erstwhile British Indian territories, Indian States, and other parts outside British India and Indian States as are willing to be apart of the Union;
- Territories forming the Union shall be autonomous units and exercise all powers and functions of the government and administration, except those assigned to or vested in the Union;
- All powers and authority of sovereign an Independent India and its constitution shall flow from the people;
- All people of India shall be guaranteed and secured social, economic and political justice; equality of status and opportunities before law; and fundamental freedoms—of talk, expression, belief, faith, worship, vocation, association and action—subject to law and public morality;
- The minorities, backward and tribal areas, depressed and other backward classes, shall be provided adequate safeguards;
- The territorial integrity of the republic and its sovereign rights on land, sea and air shall be maintained according to justice and law of civilized nations; and
- The land would make full and willing contribution to the promotion of the world peace and welfare of mankind.

Main/Salient Features of Indian Constitution

1. **Written and Lengthiest:** It is written one and is also the lengthiest in the world.
2. **Preamble:** At the beginning, there is a Preamble, which is important in several aspects. It narrates the ideals (Justice, Equality, Individual Dignity, Fraternity and National Unity) and aspirations of the Indian people.
3. **Republic:** India is a Republic. As a Republic, people have a right to form their own government and to elect the head of the government.
4. **Government of the People:** It upholds a form of government which is of the people, by the people and for the people. People have the right to elect their own rulers.
5. **Fundamental Rights and Duties:** It has given six Fundamental Rights to the citizens. The government cannot take away any of these rights. When these rights are violated, the Judiciary would come to the rescue of the citizens. In addition to the Fundamental Rights, it has stated eleven Fundamental Duties to be performed by the citizens.
6. **Secularism:** As per the principle of secularism, the government must be impartial towards all the religions followed by its citizens. There shall be no 'State Religion'. At the same time, the government guarantees freedom of faith and worship to all citizens. However, the government has the right to restrict religious freedom when it disturbs public peace, as well as law and order.
7. **Independent and Impartial Judiciary:** Under the democratic system, all citizens are equal before the law. There cannot be different sets of laws for the different groups of people. The judiciary is expected to provide justice to all the sections of the society. Therefore, the Judiciary is given adequate powers.
8. **Universal Adult Franchise:** The system of election of representatives by all the adults of a country is called as Universal Adult Franchise. In India, an adult means one who is above the age of 18 years.
9. **Equal Rights to Women:** Here, both men and women have been given equal rights. The exploitation of women is considered an offence. Both get equal pay for equal work.

10. **Eradication of Untouchability:** It has prohibited the practice of untouchability in the country. The practice is deemed a crime and offenders can be punished.
11. **A Welfare State:** A State which aims at providing social and economic security to all its citizens is known as a Welfare State. Social security must be provided to the citizens so that they would live a peaceful life. They should have employment and adequate income, food, clothes, shelter and health care. The aged and destitute must get proper protection. It protects the weaker sections from exploitation, and provides equal social, economic and political opportunities to all citizens.

THE CONSTITUTION OF INDIA

1. We, **The People of India**, having solemnly resolved to constitute India into a
2. **Sovereign,**
3. **Socialist,**
4. **Secular,**
5. **Democratic**
6. **Republic** and to secure to all its citizens;
7. **Justice**, social, economic and political;
8. **Liberty** of thought, expression, belief, faith and worship;
9. **Equality** of status and of opportunity; and to promote among them all;
10. **Fraternity** assuring the dignity of the individual and the unity and integrity of the Nation;

In our Constituent Assembly this twenty-sixth day of November, 1949, do Hereby Adopt, Enact and give to ourselves this Constitution.

The Preamble of Our Constitution

It has great significance/importance that we should try to understand it.

✓ The Preamble begins with "We, the People of India" which means that the Constitution derives its authority from the people of India. So the ultimate source of all power is vested in the people. The sovereignty of the nation belongs to the people.

✓ Before Independence, we were under the British Rule. The Queen of Britain was the Sovereign Head of the State and we had no power to make law. Now the President is the Head of our State/Nation and the Sovereign power belonging to the State/Nation is vested in our Parliament, which represents the people of India, who are the masters of their own destiny. SOVEREIGN means the independent authority of the State. It means that is has the power to legislate on any subject; and that it is not subject to the control of any other State or External Power. That means, the word 'Sovereign' means supreme or independent. India is internally and externally sovereign-externally free from the control of any foreign power and internally, it has a free government which is directly elected by the people and makes laws that govern the people.

✓ The word 'SOCIALIST' was added to the Preamble by the 42nd Amendment Act of 1976. It implies social and economic equality. Social equality in this context means the absence of discrimination on the grounds of caste, colour, creed, sex, religion, language, etc. Under social equality, everyone has equal status and opportunities. Economic equality means that the government will endeavor to make the distribution of wealth more equal and provide a decent standard of living for all. India has adopted a mixed economy and the government has framed many laws to achieve the aim of socialism, such as the Abolition of Untouchability and Zamindari, The Equal Wages Act and The Child Labor Prohibition Act.

- ✓ The word 'SECULAR' was inserted into the preamble by the 42nd Amendment Act of 1976. Ours is Secular, which means that the State has no official religion. Here, all religions are equal. The freedom to follow any religion is guaranteed by the Constitution. Every person has the right to preach, practice and propagate any religion one chooses. The government must not favour or discriminate against any religion. It must treat all religions with equal respect. All citizens, irrespective of their religious beliefs are equal in the eyes of law. No religious instruction is imparted in government or aided schools.
- ✓ India is a DEMOCRACY. The people of India elect their governments at all levels (Union, State and Local) by a system of Universal Adult Franchise. Every citizen of India, who is 18 years of age and above and not otherwise debarred by law, is entitled to vote. Every citizen enjoys this right without any discrimination on the basis of caste, creed, colour, sex, religion or education. Elections are conducted once in five years to elect our representatives or Head of State (President) and the Executive. The various policies of the State are decided by them.
- ✓ As opposed to a monarchy, in which the Head of the State is appointed on hereditary basis for a lifetime or until he abdicates from the throne, DEMOCRATIC REPUBLIC is an entity in which the Head of the State is elected, directly or indirectly, for a fixed tenure. The President of India is elected by an Electoral College for a term of five years. It means a Government of the people, by the people and for the people (Abraham Lincoln - famous speech at Gettysberg).
- ✓ Our Constitution assures us the Justice: Social, economic and political through various measures of laws; and there is no scope for exploitation of weaker sections of the society or women. Social justice means that the state will treat all citizens as equal and will not discriminate between them on the basis of religion, caste, gender, race, status or place of birth. Economic justice means that the state will attempt to reduce the economic disparities between rich and the poor and will try to bring about equality in incomes. Political justice means that the state assures all people equal opportunities to participate in political activities.
- ✓ Our Constitution assures liberty to one and all. No one is arrested without the consent of law. All laws are equal and all are equal before law.
- ✓ Our Constitution has upheld Equality. So, there is no scope for inequality based on race, religion, language, sex, etc. practice of Untouchability is prohibited and it is a crime.
- ✓ Barker calls FRATERNITY as principle of cooperation. It includes a bunch of rights to share and enjoy the common resources and services of the nation, like, education, police, health and other services.

Purpose of the Preamble

- It indicates the source from which the Constitution came i.e., THE PEOPLE OF INDIA.
- It declares the rights and freedom which are assured to all the citizens of the country.

Different Models in the World

India is one of the biggest democracies in the world. We have democratic system of administration for over the last 50 years. Today, there are two types of democracies in the world. One is direct as in Switzerland; and the other is indirect or representative form of government. In direct democracy (City of Athens in Ancient Greece), all the people would assemble at a place and through mutual and direct discussions, decided the policies. In Indirect democracy, the formation of government is directly elected by the representatives.

India has adopted the British model of Parliamentary form of Government. But, we have no Crown as the Head of the State and we have a written Republican Constitution. Further, both India and USA are democratic in their system. But USA is having a Presidential form of government, while India is having a Parliamentary form of Government. Also, there are different kinds of democracies. For example, in Pakistan, they have a 'Guided Democracy' which is subjected to military administration. Myanmar (Burma) and Sri Lanka also have different types of democracies. Former Soviet Union and the present peoples China have what is called as 'People's Democracy', but in practice they are totalitarian. Also, we find constitutional monarchies in Japan and England but they are fully democratic.

Basic Structure of the Constitution

1. **Federal Structure:** The Constitution of India is based on a federal structure. That it is to say there exists both State and Central forms of Governments. But though it has federal structure, it is also has some unitary features. That is the Central Government is the Supreme Law making authority in the country.
2. **Supremacy of the Constitution:** All the authorities derive their powers, rights, duties and obligations from the Constitution.
3. **Distribution of Powers:** The distribution of power for running the country effectively has been done on the Principle of 'Doctrine of Separation of Power'. As the wording are there 'power corrupts and absolute power corrupts absolutely'. The distribution has been done in the following basis:
   - Legislature—to make/enact the laws
   - Executive—to implement the laws (constitutes of government machinery like police, public servants, etc.
   - Judiciary—to interpret/enforce the laws and constitution.

Schedules

Schedules can be added to the Constitution by Amendment. The 12 Schedules in force covers: The designations of the States and Union Territories; emoluments for high-level officials; forms of oaths/affirmations; allocation of the number of seats in the Rajya Sabha (Council of States—the Upper House of the Parliament) per state or Union Territory; provisions for the Administration and control of Scheduled Areas and Scheduled Tribes (areas and tribes needing special protection due to disadvantageous conditions); Provisions for the administration of tribal areas in Assam; the Union (Central) Government, State, and Concurrent (dual) lists of responsibilities; The official languages; land and tenure reforms; the association of Sikkim with India; anti-defection Provisions for Members of Parliament and Members of the State Legislatures; rural development; and urban Planning.

Amendments (Methods)

- By simple majority of the Parliament: Here, amendments can be made by a simple majority of members present and voting, before it sending it for the President's assent.
- By special majority of the Parliament: Here, Amendments can be made by a two-third majority of the total number of members present and voting which should not be less than the majority of the total membership of the House.
- By special majority of the parliament and ratification of at least half of the state legislatures by special majority. After this, it is sent to the President for his assent.

An amendment to the Constitution is taken very seriously, and needs at least two-thirds of the Lok Sabha and Rajya Sabha to pass it. The Constitution of India is one of most frequently amended constitutions in the world.

Indian Freedom Movement (1857 to 1947)

- 1857-58: First War of Indian Independence.
- 1858: British Crown takes over the Indian Government—Queen Victoria's Proclamation.
- 1861: Indian Councils Act—Indian High Courts Act—Indian Penal Code.
- 1877: Delhi Durbar— The Queen of England proclaimed Empress of India.
- 1878: Vernacular Press Act.
- 1881: Factory Act—Rendition of Mysore—Mysore state restored to its original ruler.
- 1885: Indian National Congress—First Meeting.
- 1892: Indian Council Act to regulate Indian Administration.
- 1899: Lord Curzon becomes Governor and Viceroy.
- 1905: First Partition of Bengal.
- 1906: Formation of the Muslim League.
- 1908: Newspapers Act.
- 1909: Minto-Morley Reforms.
- 1911: King George V and Queen Mary hold Durbar in Delhi. Partition of Bengal annulled to create the Presidency of Bengal. The Imperial Capital shifted from Calcutta to Delhi.
- 1914: The First World War begins.
- 1915: Defence of India Act.
- 1916: Congress had entered into Pact with Muslim League (called Lucknow Pact).
- 1917: Annie Besant becomes President of Indian National Congress.
- 1918: World War I ends.
- 1919: Rowlatt Act intended to perpetuate extraordinary powers enjoyed by Government during the war provokes country-wide protests. The massacre at Jalianwallabagh. Ali brothers and Maulana Abul Kalam Azad started Khilafat Movement (for restoring the Turkish Khalifate) with Gandhiji's support. Perfect Hindu-Muslim Accord. Montague-Chelmsford Reforms offer limited Provincial autonomy to the Indians.
- 1920: Congress okays Non-Cooperation Movement and Khilafat Movement. Students leave colleges, lawyers leave practice. Bonfire of British clothes, etc. to show popular dissatisfaction with the Reforms.
- 1921: Moplah (Muslim) rebellion in Malabar. Visit of the Prince of Wales.
- 1922: Civil Disobedience Movement. Congress makes Gandhiji a sole leader of Bardoli Satyagraha. Outburst of violence at Chauri Chaura leading to suspension of the Movement by Gandhiji.
- 1923: Swarajya Party started by C.R. Das and Motilal Nehru. Swarajists propose to enter the Councils and wreck the government from within. Khilafat Movement fizzles out as Kemal Pasha declares Turkey a secular state. Hindu-Muslim riots.
- 1925: Death of C.R. Das.
- 1926: Lord Reading expounds to the Nizam what paramountcy implies. Royal Commission on Agriculture. Factories Act.
- 1927: Indian Navy Act. Simon Commission appointed.
- 1928: Simon Commission comes to India. Boycott by all parties. All parties' Conference. Muslim leaders leave the Conference.

- 1929: Lord Irwin, Viceroy of India, promises Dominion Status for India. Lahore Session of the Congress asks for Independence. On the midnight of 31st December, Pandit Jawaharlal Nehru, President of the Congress, hoists the National Flag at Lahore.
- 1930: 26th January observed as Independence Day all over India. Civil Disobedience Movement continues. Gandhiji goes walking from Sabarmati Ashram to Dandi, a Salt Satyagraha (on 12th March - 241 mile footmarch with 79 followers). Repression let loose by the government. First Round Table Conference. Sir John Simon Commission's / Statutory Commission's Report published.
- 1931: Gandhi-Irwin Pact. Second Round Table Conference.
- 1932: Suppression of Congress Movement. Third Round Table Conference. The Communal Award. Poona Pact.
- 1933: White Papers on Indian reforms.
- 1934: Civil Disobedience Movement called-off.
- 1935: Government of India Act.
- 1936: Death of King George V. Accession and Abdication of Edward VIII. Accession of George VI.
- 1937: Inauguration of Provincial Autonomy. Congress Ministers formed in a majority of the Provinces.
- 1938: Resignation of Congress Ministers. Political deadlock in India.
- 1939: Beginning of World War II.
- 1942: Sir Stafford Cripps Mission to India. Both Congress and Muslim League refuse Cripps offer. Congress adopts Quit India Resolution (08th August). It gave slogan 'Do or Die'. Congress Leaders arrested and Congress declared as Illegal body (09th August). Netaji Subhash Chandra Bose forms the Indian National Army (INA) in Malaya, with the help of Japanese. He inaugurates the Government of Free India at Singapore.
- 1943: Bengal famine; Lord Wavell, the Viceroy and Governor General of India. Wavell's proposals for a settlement fall through as Congress and Muslim League could not agree.
- 1945: The Indian National Army under Bose surrenders to the British after collapse of Japan. National Army personnel tried for treason in India.
- 1946: Demonstrations against the trial of the INA men. The ratings of the Royal Indian Navy rise in open mutiny (18th February). Cabinet Mission in India (19th February). Cabinet mission announces its plans for an Interim Government and a Constituent Assembly. The Interim Government is to be formed by reconstituting Viceroy's Executive Council. Both Congress and Muslim League reject the proposal. Later the Congress accepts it. So the Interim Government is formed by inducting Congress nominees only. The Muslim League takes umbrage and starts direct action. Muslims attacks Hindus in Calcutta and the rest of the Bengal. Hindus retaliate. Riots breakout. Viceroy persuades the Muslim League to come in. But the League declines to join the Constituent Assembly unless the demand for a separate state—Pakistan—is conceded.
- 1947: All India Congress Committee accepts partition of India by a majority vote of 99 in favor and 52 against the resolution (06th January). The British Prime Minister Clement Attlee announces in the House of Commons that the British would leave India by a date not later than June, 1948 (20th February). Lord Louis Mountbatten declares the British decision on partition (02nd June). Indian Leaders accept Lord Mountbatten's decision on partition (03rd June). India is divided and Pakistan is created with full independence (14th August). India is declared independent of British Rule with New Delhi as Capital, Jawaharlal Nehru is sworn in the first Prime Minister by Lord Mountbatten, the Governor General of India (15th August).

Principles of Democracy

(1) Principle of liberty; (2) Equality; (3) Public Welfare; (4) Rule by the people; (5) Government by majority; (6) Public criticism of Government; (7) Democracy as a way of life; (8) Recognizing human dignity and universal brotherhood; (9) Tolerance; (10) Common way of life; (11) Social Justice; (12) Opportunity for individual development; (13) Constitutional rule; (14) Decentralization or separation of power; (15) Legislature representing the public opinion; (16) Existence of political parties; and (17) Election by adult franchise.

Values of Democracy

(1) Administration is in the hands of the people; (2) Adult Franchise system enables good government; (3) There is no scope for domination of any race, religion or language because all are equal ; (4) Legislatures are constituted by the elected representatives and people are obedient to the decisions taken by them; (5) Liberty, fearlessness and regular elections gives power in the hands of the people; (6) Independence of Judiciary protects the rights of the citizens; (7) The fundamental rights provide opportunity for the progress of the individual; (8) All decisions are taken through discussions in a peaceful way; (9) Decisions are taken after ascertaining public opinion; and (10) Constitution, legislature and judiciary check the abuse of power.

Defects of Democracy

(1) Many times people demand certain things which are beyond the ability of the government to fulfill and thus weaken the government; (2) A majority party can at times become dictatorial; (3) The competition among the political parties for power is another weakness; (4) Defections from political parties is another weakness and creates instability; (5) Muscle power, money, caste and other factors play their role during elections and cause damage to democracy; and (6) It is possible that anti-social elements manage to come to power.

Important Committees of the Constituent Assembly

- Union Powers Committee: Pt. Jawaharlal Nehru (Chairman) with 9 members.
- Committee on Fundamental Rights and Minorities: Sardar Vallabhai Patel (Chairman) with 54 members.
- Steering Committee: Dr. K.M. Munshi (Chairman), Gopalaswamy Ayyangar and Bishwanath Das.
- Provincial Constitution Committee: Sardar Vallabhai Patel (Chairman) with 25 members.
- Committee on Union Constitution: Pt. Jawaharlal Nehru (Chairman) with 15 members.

The Draft was prepared by Sir B. N. Rau, Advisor to the Constituent Assembly. A 7-member Committee chaired by Sir Krishnaswamy Iyer was set up to examine the draft. Dr. B. R. Ambedkar who was minister for Law from 15.08.1947 to 26.01.1950 piloted the Draft Constitution in the Assembly.

2

Fundamental Rights

As citizens of India, we are all assured some fundamental rights and duties. Fundamental Rights protects us from injustice and Fundamental Duties enables us to contribute to the welfare of the nation.

Rights: The privileges given to the citizens are their rights. Some are natural rights (like the right to live, right to self protection) and some others are legal rights (like right to equality, right to education). Rights are the bases of a democratic country.

Fundamental Rights: The Indian Constitution has given certain fundamental rights to all the citizens. These have been specified in the Constitution. They have also been guaranteed and supported by law. The FRs comes under the Part III of the Constitution of India. It is necessary for every individual to live a complete and satisfactory life. All citizens are assured six fundamental rights. They are as follows:

1. *Right to Equality:* Here, all are equal before the law and also nobody is above the law. All should get equal protection of the law. It states that all citizens should be treated as equals irrespective of religion, race, caste, gender, or birth of place. It means there is supremacy of law or Rule of Law. No citizen shall be subjected to any restrictions with regard to access to shops, public restaurants, hotels, places of public entertainment, worship places, on the use of wells, tanks, roads and other public places. All citizens enjoy equal opportunities to take up government employment. Under this right, Untouchability is an offence. Insulting the members of scheduled castes/scheduled tribes by calling them 'untouchables' is an offence.
2. *Right to Freedom:* The Constitution has listed six types of freedom:
   - Freedom of Speech and Expression
   - Freedom to Assemble Peacefully
   - Freedom to form Associations
   - Freedom to move freely throughout India
   - Freedom to reside and settle in any part of India
   - Freedom to practice any Profession, Occupation, Trade or Business

   The Constitution itself has specified certain circumstances under which individual freedoms may be restricted.
3. *Right against Exploitation:* The aim is to prevent exploitation of women, children and the weak. The Union and State governments have enacted several laws to prevent exploitation. For instance, both, giving and receiving dowry is punishable under the law; the system of bonded labor, and has been prohibited; employment of children in mining, manufacture of beedi and fire-works and such other dangerous occupations is prohibited. This is meant to protect members of the weaker sections. The governments has not only prohibited child labor, but has also made education compulsory up to the age of 14. All children, irrespective of gender, caste and religion, must now attend school.

4. *Right to Freedom of Religion:* Since India is a secular country, every citizen has a right to practice and propagate his/her religion. However, the State may impose restrictions in the interests of public order, morality and health.
5. *Cultural and Educational Rights:* This protects the interests of religious and linguistic minorities. They have the right to protect their language, script or culture. They may establish and administer their own educational institutions. For example, in Tamil Nadu, the Kannadigas (who are minority) have the right to establish Kannada medium schools. The Tamilians in Karnataka also have similar rights.
6. *Right to Constitutional Remedies:* The Constitution has not only given FRs to the citizens of India but also guaranteed them. When rights are violated, the citizens appeal to the court of law for their protection. The court of law is empowered to enforce the FRs. On any matter relating to a FR, a citizen may file a petition in the High Court/Supreme Court. Such petitions are known as Writ Petitions.

In brief, the FR forms the basis of our democratic system. However, the government is empowered to restrict them in the interests of the national security and socio-economic progress. The Indian Parliament may even curtail or suspend FRs under certain extraordinary circumstances. FR is from Article 12 to Article 35 in the Constitution of India. The Articles of FRs are as follows:

- Article 12: Definition
- Article 13: Laws inconsistent with or in derogation of the FR

Richt to Equality

- Article 14: Equality before law
- Article 15: Prohibition of discrimination on grounds of religion, race, caste, sex, or place of birth
- Article 16: Equality of opportunity in matters of public employment
- Article 17: Abolition of Untouchability
- Article 18: Abolition on Titles

Right to Freedom

- Article 19: Protection of certain rights regarding freedom of speech, etc
- Article 20: Protection in respect of conviction for offences
- Article 21: Protection of life and personal life
- Article 22: Protection against arrest and detention in certain cases

Right Against Exploitation

- Article 23: Prohibition of traffic in human beings and forced/bonded labor
- Article 24: Prohibition of employment of children in factories

Right to Freedom of Religion

- Article 25: Freedom of conscience and free profession, practice and propagation of religion
- Article 26: Freedom to manage religious affairs
- Article 27: Freedom as to payment of taxes for promotion of any particular religion
- Article 28: Freedom as to attendance at religious instructions or religious worship in certain educational institutions

Cultural and Educational Rights

➢ Article 29: Protection of interests of minorities
➢ Article 30: Right of minorities to establish and administer educational institutions
➢ Article 31A: Saving of laws providing for acquisition of estates
➢ Article 31B: Validation of certain Acts and Regulations
➢ Article 31C: Saving of laws giving effect to certain directive principles

Right to Constitutional Remedies

➢ Article 32: Remedies for enforcement of rights conferred by this Part
➢ Article 33: Power of Parliament to modify the rights conferred by this Part in their application to forces, etc.
➢ Article 34: Restriction on rights conferred by this Part while martial law is in force in any area
➢ Article 35: Legislation to give effect to the provisions of this Part
[**Note:** Articles 31, 31D and 32A has been repealed by Amendments]

The Article 32 (Clause 2) empowers the Supreme Court to issue directions, orders or writs which may be appropriate. The five writs enumerated are *Habeas Corpus, mandamus, prohibition, certiorari and quo warranto.*

1. *Habeas Corpus [H]:* (Writ requiring person to be brought before judges) It literally means 'have his body'. By this writ, the court can cause any person who has been detained or imprisoned to be physically brought before the court. The court then examines the reasons of his detention. If there is no legal justification, he is set free. The Supreme Court has laid down that production of the body of the prisoner before the court is not an essential feature of the writ. Disobedience of this writ is punishable as contempt of court. Hence, this kind of writ is very powerful.
2. *Mandamus [M]:* (Supreme Court's writ conveying command to lower courts) It literally means a command or order. It is a command directing a person, corporation, inferior court or government or any public authority to do the thing or perform the act specified in the writ. The thing or act must be in the nature of a public duty. This writ is a wakening call. It tells the sleeping authority which refuses to perform a public duty. It is a writ which demands activity. It sets the authority in motion.
3. *Prohibition [P]:* (Order that forbids something) This is the reverse of Mandamus. In case of Mandamus, the Supreme Court orders the Lower courts to be active whereas in case of Prohibition, it restricts or ask to be inactive. In other words, the object of the writ is to compel lower courts to keep themselves within the limits of the jurisdiction. It must be noted that prohibition lies only against judicial or quasi-judicial functions (courts and tribunals). It does not lie against the legislative or executive functions. It cannot be issued against private persons or associations.
4. *Certiorari [C]:* (Supreme Court issuing writ questioning decision of Lower court) It is used after the decision / action. The objective is to limit the role of a lower court to its jurisdiction. It can be issued only by a Superior Court. It is directed against the orders of an Inferior Court or Tribunal.
5. *Quo warranto [Q]:* (Writ regarding misuse of public offices) It is necessitated as some unlawful claimants seize by force (usurp) a public office. It literally is a question 'where is your warrant of appointment?' The Court by this writ examines the legality of the claim of a person to a public office or franchise. If he is not able to show his legal right, he may be ousted by the Court.

The above writs distinguished from each other

➢ M commands activity. P orders inactivity. C stops an authority in the middle of proceedings. It prevents usurpation of jurisdiction.
➢ M is generally addressed to administrative authorities. C and P generally control the courts and tribunals.
➢ C and P are instruments to control an inferior tribunal which has exceeded its jurisdiction or wrongly exercised its jurisdiction. M is issued against an inferior tribunal which has declined to exercise its jurisdiction.
➢ M may direct a tribunal to proceed according to law. C quashes the proceedings or removes the proceedings to itself on the ground of lack of jurisdiction or error apparent on the face of the record, etc.
➢ The grounds for issue of C and P are the same. P is issued at an earlier stage when the matter has not come to a close, to prevent the tribunal from going ahead. C lies where a tribunal after exercising jurisdiction where it had none or exceeding its jurisdiction where it had some, handed over a final decision.
➢ The object of P is prevention and C is prevention and cures both.
➢ M commands a person to perform a function which it is under a legal duty to perform. Q is an enquiry to ascertain whether a person holding an office has legal authority to do so. When he is not able to support his claim, he may be ordered to vacate.

Indian Citizenship

In order to link people to a government and to identify those who are members of a country, we have citizenship. There are five methods of acquiring the citizenship of India as per the Citizenship Act of 1955. These are as follows:

1. *Citizenship by Birth:* Every person born in India on or after 26th January 1950 shall be a citizen of India by birth. Those born before 1950, in the country are also entitled to Indian Citizenship.
2. *Citizenship by Descent:* A person born outside India on or after 26th January 1950, shall be a citizen of India by descent, if the father is a citizen of India at the time of the person's birth.
3. *Citizenship by Registration:* A provision is made under law that several classes of persons can acquire Indian citizenship by registering themselves before the President of India. For example, persons of Indian origin who have been residents in India for five years or persons who have married an Indian citizen can apply for Citizenship.
4. *Citizenship by Naturalization:* A foreigner can acquire Indian citizenship as per the Indian constitution. The citizenship so acquired is known as Citizenship by Naturalization.
5. *Citizenship by Incorporation of Territory:* If any new territory becomes a part of India, the people residing in that territory will acquire Indian Citizenship. For instance, in 1961 the rule of the Portuguese in Goa was overthrown. As a result, Goa became a part of India, and the residents of Goa became Indian citizens.

Loss of Indian Citizenship: The Citizenship Act of 1955 specifies three occasions when Indian citizenship is lost, namely,

1. *By Renunciation:* An Indian can voluntarily renounce the citizenship of India.
2. *By Termination:* When a citizen of India willingly acquires the citizenship of another country, the person loses his Indian citizenship.

3. *By Deprivation:* On certain occasions, a person can be deprived of his/her citizenship by an order of the Government of India. For example, if the Indian citizenship has been acquired by a person by fraud or the person has shown himself/herself to be disloyal towards the Constitution of India, that citizen can be deprived of Indian citizenship.

Rights of a Citizen: Anyone who is the citizen of India has certain rights. Such rights include

- Right to Vote: that is after the age of 18, every individual, irrespective of his/her social background and economic status, has the right to vote in all elections (till 1988, it was 21 years - Article 326).
- Right to hold Public Office: every adult is also entitled to stand for elections and to hold positions.
- Right to Property: every individual has the right to own property.

Duties of a Citizen: Accompanying these rights of the citizenship, the following are also some duties that a citizen should perform

- Obeying the Laws
- Being well-informed
- Casting votes during elections
- Understanding the problems of the country

Types of Persons

- *Citizens:* Persons who are full members of the State and who owe allegiance to it. They enjoy full civil and political rights.
- *Aliens:* Persons who are citizens of some other State. They are not entitled to all constitutional and other rights. Aliens may be friendly or enemy aliens. Enemy aliens are those whose country is at war with India.
- *Stateless Persons:* This category is very small and may not exist in some countries. They are persons who are not citizens of any country. They have only those rights which aliens have.

Human Rights by the Commission

- All are born free and have equal dignity/or rights.
- Everyone has the right to life, liberty and security of person.
- Everyone is entitled to all rights and freedom irrespective of race, religion, sex, language, or colour. No distinction shall be made on the basis of political or social origin, property or place of birth.
- No one shall be held in slavery or servitude; and slavery and slave trading is prohibited in all forms.
- All are equal before the law and all laws are applicable to all equally.
- No one shall be subjected to arbitrary arrest, detention or exile.
- Everyone has a right to protect him/herself against any criminal charges leveled against him/her.
- Everyone has the right to freedom of movement and residence within the borders of each state.
- Everyone has the right to nationality.
- Adult men and women have the right to start a family and enjoy all the family rights.
- Everyone has the right to have own property.
- Everyone has the right to freedom of thought, conscience and religion.
- Everyone has the right to take part in the government of his/her country.
- Everyone has the right to work to free choice of employment.
- No state or individual has a right to locate these rights which are Human Rights.

3

Directive Principles of State Policy

Our Constitution aims at the establishment of a Welfare State. To achieve this aim, the Constitution has framed certain principles and policies. It has also given certain directions to the state to serve as guidelines. Such guiding principles are known as Directive Principles of State Policy (DPSP). Also called the 'Instrument of Instructions'. These principles are for the good governance of the country and cannot be enforced in the courts.

The DP of State Policy is given under Part IV of the Constitution. This Part contains Articles from 36 to 51. These Articles deals with almost all the necessary duties and functions to be done by the state. These Articles deals with education, environment, village panchayats, equal justice & free legal aid, the wages for workers, etc.

The Provisions/Articles of DP of State Policy are as follows

1. Article 36: Defines the word 'State'
2. Article 37: Application of the Principles contained
3. Article 38: State to secure a social order for the promotion of welfare of the people
4. Article 39: Certain Principles of Policy to be followed by the state
5. Article 39A: Equal justice and free legal aid
6. Article 40: Organization of Village (Grama) Panchayats
7. Article 41: Right to work, to education and to public assistance in certain cases
8. Article 42: Provision for just and humane conditions of work and maternity relief
9. Article 43: Living wage and other welfare measures for the workers
10. Article 43A: Participation of workers in the management of industries
11. Article 44: Uniform Civil Code for the citizens
12. Article 45: Provision for free and compulsory education for children
13. Article 46: Promotion of educational and economic interests of Scheduled Castes, Scheduled Tribes and other Weaker sections
14. Article 47: Duty of the state to improve the level of nutrition, standard of living and to improve the public health
15. Article 48: Organization of agriculture and animal husbandry
16. Article 48A: Protection and improvement of environment and safeguarding of forests and wild life
17. Article 49: Protection of monuments and places and objects of national importance
18. Article 50: Separation of judiciary from executive
19. Article 51: Promotion of international peace and security

The DP may be grouped as follows

(*a*) Certain ideals
(*b*) Certain directions
(*c*) Certain rights of citizens

These rights are not FR and are not enforceable. The DP helps the State to implement some of the goals and ideals of the Constitution. The ideals, directions and rights of the citizens included under the DP of State Policy may be summarized as follows:

- Social justice: Assuring social, economic and political justice to the citizens for the purpose of promoting their welfare.
- Social justice to the weaker sections of the society: Providing adequate means of livelihood; preventing economic exploitation; giving facilities for their educational and economic development; and providing free legal aid.
- Women and child welfare: This includes equal pay for equal work; maternity relief to women; protecting children against exploitation, and providing opportunities for their healthy development; and giving free and compulsory primary education.
- Labor welfare: Promoting the welfare of workers and giving them opportunities to participate in the management of industries.
- Help to the needy: Public assistance to those who are unemployed, old and ill.
- Development of agriculture: Organizing agriculture and animal husbandry modern lines and developing cottage industries.
- Environment: Protecting and improving the environment, so that natural resources and the flora and fauna can be sustained.
- Protection and maintenance of places of historic interest: Historical monuments are part of our heritage and the state must protect and maintain them.
- Promotion of international peace and amity: The State must develop good relations with all neighboring states (countries).

Principles

The Directive Principles are the basic principles of a new social and economic order or of a welfare state. These may be grouped under three categories i.e., Socialistic Principles, Gandhian Principles and Liberal Principles.

Socialistic Principles

- To secure and protect a social order which stands for the welfare of the people (Art. 38).
- The state shall direct its policy towards securing: adequate means of livelihood to all citizens, a proper distribution of the material resources of the community for the common good, the prevention of concentration of wealth to the common detriment, equal pay for equal work for both men and women, the protection of the strength and health of workers and avoiding circumstances which force citizens to enter avocations unsuited to their age or strength, protection of childhood and youth against exploitation of moral and material abandonment (Art. 39).
- The state shall secure equal justice and free legal aid to the poor (Art. 39A).
- All people should get employment, education and public assistance in the case of unemployment (Art. 41).
- To secure just human conditions of work and maternity relief (Art. 42).
- Weaker sections of the society are given a proper care (Art. 46).

Gandhian Principles

- State shall organize village panchayats as units of self-government (Art. 40).
- To secure work, a living wage, a decent standard of life, leisure and social and cultural opportunities for people and in particular to promote cottage industries (Art. 43).
- To promote with special care, the educational and economic interest of the weaker sections of the people, especially the scheduled castes and tribes (Art. 46).
- To secure the improvement of the public health and the prohibition of intoxicating drinks and drugs (Art. 47).
- To organize agriculture and animal husbandry on scientific lines and preserve and improve the breeds and prohibit the slaughter of cows, calves and draught cattle (Art. 48).

Liberal Principles

- To secure a uniform civil code applicable to the entire country (Art. 44).
- To provide within ten years from the commencement of the Constitution, free and compulsory education to all children up to the age of 14 years (Art. 45).
- To protect all monuments of historical interest and national importance (Art. 49).
- To bring about the separation of the judiciary from the executive (Art. 50).
- To endeavor to secure, the promotion of international peace and security, the maintenance of just and honorable relations between nations, the settlement of international disputes by arbitration (Art. 51).

Difference between Fundamental Rights and Directive Principles

Though the objective of both FRs and DPs are identical, there are significant differences between the two:

- FRs are mostly political rights which tend to restrain the State. They are also called as *negative rights*. Articles 14 and 21 are negatively worded. DPs are social rights in the form of positive obligations of the State and pertain to the economic field.
- The scope of the FRs is limited but the DPs cover a vast area.
- FRs are justiciable. Courts protect them and compel the State to respect them. But Courts cannot direct the State to give effect to a DP. They are enforceable rights.
- FRs are legally enforceable because they are guaranteed rights.

4

Fundamental Duties

The Fundamental Rights (FRs) and Fundamental Duties (FDs) are like the two faces of a coin. The FDs are one's obligations towards the country. When citizens voluntarily perform them, the country is sure to make rapid progress. The FDs (Article 51A) did not form part of the Constitution as originally adopted. They were included on 11th December, 1976 by the 42nd Amendment. None of the major democracies like USA, Australia, Canada, France, Germany, etc. contain a table of FDs.

The Duties (10 + 01* = 11) of the citizens enumerated are as follows

1. To abide/respect by the Constitution and respect its ideals and institutions, the National Flag and the National Anthem
2. To cherish and follow the noble ideals which inspired our national struggle for freedom
3. To uphold and protect the sovereignty, unity and integrity of India
4. To defend the country/motherland and render national service when called upon to do so
5. To promote harmony and spirit of common brotherhood amongst all the people of India transcending religious, linguistic and regional or sectional diversities; to renounce practices derogatory to the dignity of women
6. To value and preserve the rich heritage of our composite culture
7. To protect and improve the natural environment including forests, lakes, rivers and wild life, and to have compassion for living creatures
8. To develop the scientific temper, humanism and the spirit of inquiry and reform
9. To safeguard the public property and to abjure violence
10. To strive towards excellence in all spheres of individual and collective activity so that the nation constantly rises to higher levels of endeavor and achievement
11. * Who is a parent or guardian to provide opportunities for education to his child or, as the case may be, ward between the age of 6 and 14 years

[* Inserted by the Constitution (86th Amendment) Act, 2002]

Comparison of Fundamental Duties (FD) with Directive Principles (DP)

Fundamental duties are comparable to the Directive Principles. The FDs are addressed to the citizens. The country expects them to perform certain FDs as citizens. They are not spectators but active participants in attainment of national goals. The DPs are goals setup by the Constitution for all governments. It is the duty of the state to apply these DPs in making laws (as per Article 37). But in case a State does not implement a DP, it cannot be penalized. There is no legal sanction. The only sanction is public opinion. Similarly, the FDs have no sanction attached. The citizen must introspect and endeavor to perform these duties. The sanction should be self-imposed. They can not be enforced by the court.

Our National Symbols

- *National Flag:* It has three colours-deep saffron (kesari) at the top, white in the middle and dark green at the bottom. In the center of the white band is a navy blue chakra (wheel). The chakra has 24 spokes. It is rectangular in shape (L:B=3:2). It should be either cotton or silk. The thread should prepared manually and the cloth hand-made. The saffron stands for sacrifice; white for truth, peace and purity; and green for the evergreen earth as well as agricultural and industrial prosperity. The design of chakra is taken from the capital of the Ashokan Pillar at Sarnath. This is called Dharma Chakra *i.e.*, Wheel of Law. It symbolizes constant movement.
- *National Anthem:* The song Jana-gana-mana was composed by Rabindranath Tagore in 1911 in the Bengali language. The playing time of full and short versions is approximately 52 and 20 seconds, respectively.
- *National Calendar:* Also called as Rashtriya Panchanga, prepared by Meghnad Saha.
- *National Animal:* Tiger
- *National Bird:* Peacock
- *National Flower:* Lotus
- *National Tree:* Banyan
- *National Fruit:* Mango.

5

Union Government

In India, there are 28 states and 6 centrally-administered territories and Delhi is under Capital Administration*. All these form the Union of India. The states have no power to recede from the Union. As indicated by the Constitution, there is a government at the Center and at the State level and they carry on administration according to the division of powers. Any act of government which goes against the Constitution is declared ultra vires (beyond powers) by the Supreme Court of India.

(*28 States: Andhra Pradesh, Assam, Bihar, Gujarat, Kerala, Madhya Pradesh, Tamil Nadu, Maharastra, Karnataka, Orissa, Punjab, Rajasthan, Uttar Pradesh, West Bengal, Jammu & Kashmir, Ngaland, Haryana, Himachal Pradesh, Manipur, Tripura, Meghalaya, Sikkim, Mizoram, Arunachal Pradesh, Goa, Uttaranchal, Chhattisgarh and Jharkhand

*07 Union Territories: Chandigarh, Delhi, Andaman & Nicobar Islands, Lakshadeep, Dadra & Nagar Haveli, Diu & Daman and Pondicherry)

Relationship between the Center and the States

Today, in a written Constitution, we find two kinds: one is unitary type, where there is only one government to the entire nation (Examples are England, France, etc.). The other one is federal type, where the powers of the nation are divided between the Center and States (Examples are India, USA, Switzerland, etc.). The Constitution has distributed the powers into three lists:

- *Central List:* There are 97 subjects like Defence, Foreign affairs, Finance, Railways, Civil Aviation, Meteorology, Monuments, Post & Telegraph, Telephone, Wireless, Prisons, Roads, etc. In these matters, the Center can make laws.
- *State List:* There are 66 subjects like Police, Forests, Land Revenue, Agriculture, Law Courts, Cattle and Health, Hospitals, Fisheries, Irrigation, Trade Unions, Labor Welfare, etc. Here, the state only can make the laws.
- *Concurrent List:* There are 47 subjects like Education, Electricity, Industries/Factories, Power, Joint Family, Marriage, Medical Service, Press, Religion, Monuments, etc. Here, the Center and State have the powers of making laws.

However, the administration of the centrally-administered territories is carried by the President. In 1993, Delhi was given the status as a state and the administration was assigned to the Legislature. It has a special status under central supervision. In case of emergency, the center suspends many rights and assumes many special powers. Taking into consideration of unity and security of the nation, the founding fathers of our Constitution have given more powers to the center. Hence, our Constitution is more unitary than federal in its nature. It is rightly termed as quasi-federal by some writers. The Indian Parliament has power to create new states and in the recent past three states of Chattisgarh, Uttaranchal and Jharkhand are created.

Ultra vires: It is the lack of power. It refers to incompetency. If a state legislated on a subject in the Union list, the resultant Act would be ultra vires and consequently void. Repugnancy refers to inconsistency. If the law made by a State belonging to the Concurrent List is inconsistent with a Union law then the question of repugnancy comes. The whole of the law is not void. It is void only to the extent of repugnancy.

The Union/Central Government

It has three organs. They are:

- Legislature: This organ makes the laws
- Executive: The laws made by the legislature are implemented by this organ
- Judiciary: This organ decides cases according to the laws

A. Union Legislature

It is also called as Parliament. The Parliament of India consists of the President of India and the two Houses, namely, Rajya Sabha (Upper House/House of States) and Lok Sabha (Lower House/House of People). The sessions of the Parliament are held in the Parliament House at New Delhi. Here, the Members of the Parliament make laws which are applicable to the whole of India. Though the President of the republic is not a Member of the Parliament, he is an indivisible part of the Parliament. Both the Houses of Parliament must meet at least twice a year. The Members of the RS and LS are called Members of the Parliament (MPs). They enjoy freedom of speech and expression in the Parliament and the opinions expressed by them cannot be questioned in a Court of Law.

Powers and Functions of the Parliament

- *Legislative:* The main function of the Parliament is to make laws. It can also amend or revoke (withdraw) existing laws.
- *Financial:* The Finance Bill must be presented and discussed first in the Lok Sabha. After being passed by the Lok Sabha, the Bill goes to the Rajya Sabha for approval. Thereafter, it is sent to the President of India for assent. Also, the Union Government cannot collect taxes and money without the approval of the Parliament. Hence, the Parliament has full control over the financial matters of the country.
- *Administrative:* The questions put by the members must be answered by the concerned ministers. The members are expected to keep a watch over the functioning of various departments. They can point out the lapses and misuse of powers on the part of the ministers.
- *Constitutional:* The Parliament has power to amend or change some Articles of the Constitution.
- *Other Powers:* The members of the Parliament and the members of the Legislative Assemblies of all states elect the President of India. However, the Vice-President of India is elected by the Members of the Parliament only.

Sessions of Parliament

Under Article 85, the President has the power to summon and prorogue either House of Parliament from time to time and to dissolve the Lok Sabha. The interval between the two sessions must not exceed six months. There are generally three sessions in a year.

- *The Budget Session:* It commences in the 3rd week of February. This being the first session of the year it commences with the address by the President on the first day to both the Houses assembled together. A few days later, the Railway Budget is presented. On the last day of the month, the General Budget is presented. The time for the presentation used to be 5 p.m. but from the year 2001, it has been changed to 11 a.m. After the presentation of the Budget, the Houses pass a motion of thank to the President for his/her address. After that the Railway Budget and then the demand for grants are taken. The Finance Bill which gives effect to the Budget proposals and the relevant Appropriation Bills are passed. As most of the time, an attention is devoted to the Budget; this session is called the Budget Session.

- *The Monsoon Session:* It begins usually in the 3rd week of July. It is the rainy season for us connected with the arrival of the monsoon, which gives the session its name. The session is mostly devoted to legislative business.
- *The Winter Session:* It starts in early November and ends in the 3rd week of December. Apart from the usual questions, calling attention and other motions, the major portion of time is set aside for legislative work.

Adjournment: It is the suspension of work in a sitting announced by the Presiding Officer. It may range from a few minutes to days together. When there is grave disorder, the Presiding Officer sometimes adjourns the House or suspends a sitting for a time to be named by him/her. In the course of the day he/she announces that the House adjourns for lunch to assemble again at the fixed hour. At the end of the day, the Presiding Officer adjourns the House to assemble on the next working day at fixed hour.

Adjournment sine die: Here, when the Presiding Officer adjourns the House without fixing and time or any date for the next meeting. Sine die means without setting a day for the next meeting. Usually on the last day of the session the House is adjourned sine die.

Prorogation: A House is prorogued by the President. He/she does so on the advice of the council of Ministers. It is generally done after the House is adjourned sine die but there is no bar to the President proroguing the House which is in session. Prorogation brings the session to an end.

Dissolution: It is in the power of the President who, save in exceptional circumstances, does so on the advice of the Council of Ministers. RS being a permanent chamber cannot be dissolved. Only the LS is subject to dissolution. It ends the life of LS. A new LS takes its place after the general elections are held.

Session: It is a period of time commencing on the day the first meeting of the House is held and ending on the day it is prorogued or dissolved.

Recess: It is the period spanning between the prorogation of a House and its assembly in a new session.

Meeting: it is generally divided into two sittings—from morning till lunch and post-lunch till adjournment. In each sitting, the time may be allotted for particular business. This is done on the advice of the Business Advisory Committee. In the morning when LS or RS assembles at 11.00 a.m., the first one hour is devoted to answering questions. This is called Question Hour. The next one hour is observed as Zero Hour where discussions, resolutions, government business, etc can be discussed without priority.

Rajya Sabha (RS)

The maximum number of seats/members in RS is 250. The members are not directly elected by the citizens of the country. The members of the State Assemblies elect 238 Members and the remaining 12 Members are nominated by the President of India (12 members are chosen from among the stalwarts in the field of Science, Arts, Commerce, etc. on the basis of merit of their service). It is a permanent body. Once in two years, one-third of its members retire and elections are conducted for these vacancies. The term of a membership is six years. To become a member, one should be a citizen of India and must not be less than 30 years of age.

The Vice-President of India is the Chairman and he/she conducts all the proceedings of the RS. Also, the members of the RS elect one among them as the Deputy Chairman.

Lok Sabha (LS)

The maximum number of seats/members in LS is 552. The members are directly elected by the citizens who are the above the age of eighteen. The duration of each LS is five years. However, under circumstances, it may be dissolved before the expiry of the full term by the President on the recommendation of the Prime Minister. Hence, LS is not a permanent body. Certain seats are reserved for the members of Scheduled Castes and Scheduled Tribes. The President of India can nominate two Anglo-Indian members to the LS. To become a member, one should be a citizen of India, and must not be less than 25 years of age. The Member must not hold any office of profit under the government; should not have been imprisoned; should not have been declared a person of unsound mind by a Court of Law; and should not be an insolvent. A member may contest for the election for any number of times.

The members elect from among themselves the Speaker and Deputy Speaker, who are the Presiding Officer(s) of the House. The Office of the Speaker is respectable. The powers and functions of the Speaker are:

- Conducting the proceedings of the LS as per the rules
- Deciding the matters to be discussed in the House
- Maintaining the decorum and dignity of the House

B. Union Executive

It is composed of the President, Prime Minister and Council of Ministers.

The Executive Head of the Indian Republic is called the **President**. The President is the Head of the State and is the first citizen of the country and represents the nation. The Official Residence of the President is known as Rashtrapati Bhavan. He/she does not belong to any political party. He/she is the custodian of the Constitution and symbol of unity of the nation. He/she is elected by an Electoral College consisting of Lok Sabha, Rajya Sabha and the members of the Legislative Assemblies of various states. No court of law can question his/her conduct. He/she may be removed for violation of the Constitution by a process known as Motion of Impeachment.

President—Qualifications and Terms

He/she must be a citizen of India; must have completed the age of 35 years; must be qualified for election as a member of the Lok Sabha; and term/tenure of the Office is five years and eligible for re-election (but according to custom, he/she can not contest for more than two terms).

President—Powers

- *Executive Powers:* He/she appoints the leader of the majority party or group in the LS as the Prime Minister. He/she also appoints the Ministers recommended by the Prime Minister. The Governors/Lieutenant Governors of the States/Territories; Ambassadors; High Commissioners; Consuls; Attorney-General; Comptroller and Auditor General; Finance Commission; The Chief Election Commissioner; Chairman and Members of Union Public Service Commission; and Special Officers for Scheduled Castes and Tribes and Linguistic Minorities are appointed by the President. He/she is the Commander-in-Chief of the Armed Forces (Army, Navy and Airforce). Wars, if any, are declared in the name of the President.
- *Legislative Powers:* He/she has the power to summon the Parliament. He/she may address a joint sitting of both the Houses. A Bill passed by both the Houses of Parliament becomes an Act only after it receives the assent of the President. He/she has a right to send back the Bills for reconsideration. When the Parliament is not in session, he/she has the power to legislate on the

recommendation of the Union Cabinet. Such legislation is known as an Ordinance. However, for an early dissolution, the advice of the Prime Minister is needed.

- *Judicial Powers:* The Judges of the Supreme Court and the High Courts are appointed by the President. He/she has a right to pardon and reduce the punishment given by various courts.
- *Financial Powers:* A Money Bill can be introduced in the LS only after obtaining the sanction of the President. The Budget also needs the consent of the President.
- *Emergency Powers:* To meet certain types of abnormal circumstances in the country, he/she has the power to declare National Emergency. This power is exercised by him/her on the advice of the Council of Ministers. There are three kinds of emergencies during which the President can declare emergency with the approval of the Parliament and they are: (a) when the constitutional machinery has failed in a state, he/she can declare emergency and can dissolve the legislature or suspend it, (b) when the country is threatened by external aggression; and (c) when the financial condition is in crisis, he/she can declare Financial Emergency.

(So far, emergency was declared three times in our country. Firstly, in October 1962 when China attacked India; secondly during Pakistani attack in August and September 1965 and December 1971; and thirdly during 1975 under the excuse of internal disturbances).

From past experience, it is felt that there is a need to make following changes in the Presidential election:

- He/she should not be a member of any political party in previous five years
- He/she should not have crossed the age of 65 years at the time of election
- Only one term to be fixed
- He/she not have faced any criminal cases anytime in his/her life
- He/she should have a minimum University degree

The mode of election of our President defers from that of the USA or France. He/she is elected by a body of electors constituting an Electoral College. It consists of:

- The elected members of the Lok Sabha and Rajya Sabha (nominated members of the LS and RS are not electors)
- The elected members of the Legislative Assembly of the states (nominated members are excluded)
- The members of the Legislative Assembly of the National Capital Territory of Delhi and of the Union Territory of Pondicherry (70th Amendment Act, 01st June, 1995)

(*Note:* Our first President, Dr. Rajendra Prasad is the only one to have been President for two consecutive terms)

Emoluments: By passing the President's Emoluments and Pension (Amendment) Act, 1998, Parliament has raised to Rs. 50000/- per mensem. The same Act provides for the payment of an annual pension of Rs. 300000/-to a person who held Office as President, on the expiration of his term or on resignation, provided he is not re-elected to the Office (Rs. 10000/- originally, raised to Rs. 20000/- in 1990 and to Rs. 50000/- in 1998 with effect from 01.01.1996).

Veto: It is the power of the executive to withhold or refuse assent to legislation. The purpose is to prevent ill-conceived legislation as well legislations, which may be ultra vires or unconstitutional.

Vetoes are classified into

- *Absolute Veto:* It is the power to say no to a Bill passed by both Houses of Parliament. Such a bill never becomes an Act. The power cannot be overridden by the legislature. The President has his/her power in relation to all Bills except Money Bills.

- *Qualified Veto:* It is that power to veto which can be overridden by the legislature by a special majority (in case of USA). In India, there is no requirement of special majority. If a Bill is adopted again by the Houses, the President cannot withhold assent. Hence, there is no qualified veto.
- *Suspensive Veto:* It is a veto that may be overridden by an ordinary or simple majority. Our President exercises this veto when he/she returns a Bill for reconsideration.
- *Pocket Veto:* When a Bill is presented to the President, he/she either gives his/her assent or refuse to give his/her assent. The Constitution does not prescribe any time limit within which the President has to declare his/her assent. The President may simply keep the Bill on his/her table indefinitely. Such action which is neither negative nor positive is called Pocket veto.

Pardon: It completely absolves the offender from all sentences, punishments and disqualifications. He/she comes to the same position as if he/she had never committed the crime.

Reprieve: It is temporary suspension of death sentence generally pending the proceedings for pardon or commutation.

Respite: It means awarding a lesser sentence in place of one originally awarded e.g., on the ground of pregnancy of a woman offender.

Remission: It reduces the length of sentence without affecting its character i.e., sentence of rigorous imprisonment for two years may be remitted to one year.

Commutation: It substitutes one form of punishment for another of a lighter character i.e., death sentence may be commuted to life imprisonment. Rigorous imprisonment can be commuted to simple imprisonment, which in turn may be commuted to fine.

Electoral College (Value of the Vote)

Article 55 has devised a way by which a value is attached to each vote of an MP and MLA. This is an attempt to emphasize the federal character of the Office of the President.

$$\text{The value of the vote of an MLA} = \frac{\text{Population of the state}}{\text{Total no. of MLAs}} \times \frac{1}{1000}$$

$$\text{The value of the vote of an MP} = \frac{\text{Value of votes of all MLAs of 28 states}}{\text{Total no. of MPs}}$$

The value of the vote of an MLA differs from one state to another. This method brings a measure of uniformity among the states and parity between the Union and the states as a whole.

Vice President—Qualifications, Terms and Powers

On the USA model, we have a Vice-president. But he/she is elected by both houses of the Parliament and not by the people as in the case of USA. He/she must be over the age of 35 years, a citizen of India, necessary qualification to be a MP and must have the qualifications which are required to become the President. The term of Office is five years. Whenever the Office of the President falls vacant due to death, resignation or ill health, etc., he/she will assume the Office of the President. However, within six months of time, a new President has to be elected. As in the case of USA, he/she cannot remain in the Office for the remaining period of five years term, when the President expires. He/she is the Chairman of the RS and conducts the proceedings of the House in accordance with the rules.

Prime Minister—Qualifications, Terms and Powers

As indicated by the Constitution, there shall be a Council of Ministers headed by a Prime Minister to aid and the advice the President in matters of administration. He/she is the Leader of the LS and it is his/her prerogative to choose ministers; allot portfolios; and decides the size of the Cabinet. He/she can also reshuffle the Cabinet. He/she can demand the resignation of any Minister. When the Prime Minister resigns, the Cabinet is also dissolved. He/she plays important role in the governance of the country. In the matter of national security, the responsibility is enormous. In external affairs, he/she plays a major role. He/she is a link between the President and the Cabinet. Generally, he/she meets the President in the Rasthrapati Bhavan once in a week.

Council of Ministers—Functions

- Ensuring the smooth functioning of the administration
- Framing the policies of the government and taking decisions accordingly
- Preparing the Union Budget
- Drafting the Bills to be introduced in the Parliament
- Formulating the foreign policy of the country
- Suggesting Amendments to the Constitution

The meeting of the Union Cabinet is held once in a week. The Prime Minister presides over it. The proceedings of the meeting are kept confidential. However, each Minister is responsible for his/her portfolio and jointly all the ministers are responsible collectively to the LS. The Ministry will remain in the Office only when they command the confidence of the LS. When it withdraws the confidence, the Ministry has to resign. The total number of ministers including the Prime Minister shall not exceed 15% of the total number members of LS (as per 91st Amendment Act, 2003). Ministers may be chosen form the LS or RS. A minister who is member of one House has the right to speak and to take part in the proceedings of the other House. A minister is allowed to vote only in the House of which he/she is a member. All the members of the Council of Ministers do not belong to the same rank. The Constitution does not classify Ministers into different ranks but in practice four ranks have come to be recognized:

- *Cabinet Ministers:* He/she has a right to be present and participate in every meeting of the Cabinet. For proclamation of an emergency under Article 352, the advice must come from the Prime Minister and other ministers of Cabinet rank.
- *Minister of State with Independent charge:* He/she is a minister of State who does not work under a Cabinet Minister. When any matter concerning his/her Department is on the agenda of the Cabinet, he/she is invited to attend the meeting.
- *Minister of State:* He/she is a minister who does not have independent charge of any Department and works under a Cabinet Minister. The work to such Minister is allotted by his/her Cabinet Minister.
- *Deputy Minister:* He/she is a minister who works under a Cabinet Minister or a Minister of State with independent charge. The work to him/her is allotted by the Minister under whom he is working.

A person who is not a member of either House may also be appointed as a Minister. He/she can continue as a Minister only for six months (Article 75-5). If he/she desires to continue as Minister he/she has to become a member of any one of the Houses of Parliament before the expiration of the period of six months.

C. Union Judiciary

In our country, we have a single system of judiciary. We do not have two types as in the case of USA; one for the Center and other for the States. Hence, the Supreme Court of our country is the highest Apex Court and its verdicts are final in the constitutional matters, customs and tradition and earlier decisions of the various courts. The judicial system of a country takes up disputes and gives judgment based on the laws. Both the judiciary and the laws play an important role in the society. The courts of law perform the important task of protecting the life, property, dignity and the rights of the citizens. They are not controlled by either the Legislature or the Executive. They are expected to function impartially and independently. Thus, in any country, judiciary plays the important role of interpreting and applying laws and adjudicating upon controversies between one citizen and another citizen/state—to maintain rule of law and to assure that the government runs according to law—in a country with a written Constitution. Judiciary is having additional function of safeguarding the supremacy of the Constitution by interpreting and applying its provisions and keeps all authorities within the constitutional framework.

Supreme Court

It consists of the Chief Justice of India and other 25 other Judges. It is created by an Act of Parliament (Article 124) and located in New Delhi. The Chief Justice and Judges of the Supreme Court are appointed by the President. He/she should be a citizen of India. He/she should have been a High Court Judge for at least five years or an Advocate of the High Court for at least ten years, or a distinguished Jurist. The age of retirement of Judge is 65. After his/her retirement, he/she cannot practice as an Advocate in any Court. If the judges are found guilty while discharging their duties, they can be removed from their Office by the President. The Acting Chief Justice can be appointed by the President, if the Office of the Chief Justice of India falls vacant or he/she is unable to perform his/her duties due to absence or otherwise.

(The Constitution as enacted in 1950 provided that the Court shall consist of the Chief Justice and not more than 7 other judges. The number of judges was increased to 10 in 1956, 13 in 1960, 17 in 1977 and 25 in 1986).

Functions

- Resolving the disputes between the Union and the States, and between the states
- Issuing writs to safeguard the fundamental rights of the citizens
- Interpreting the provisions of the Constitution
- Giving advice to the President of India

Powers

It has two types of cases to be tackled:

- Original Jurisdiction: Refers to direct cases that come to them from the parties of dispute
- Appellate Jurisdiction: Refer to those which on decided at lower courts and referred for review

Public Interest Litigation (PIL)

Sometimes, a Government or a Public Body violates the law, or indulges in suppressing or exploiting the citizens. Any citizen affected by such violations may directly complain to the Court. Such a letter of complaint is taken up as PIL by the Court. Without charging any Court fees, the court inquires into the complaint. The following are the possible areas where a PIL can be filed:

- Where a factory/industrial unit is causing air pollution and people nearly are getting affected
- Where, in an area/street, there are no street lights causing inconvenience to the commuters
- Where some 'Banquet Hall' plays a loud music, in nights causes noise pollution
- Where poor people are affected because of the State Government's decisions to impose heavy taxes

- For abolishing child labor, and bonded labor
- Where rights of working women are affected by sexual harassment
- For maintaining roads, sewages, etc. in good conditions
- For removal of big hoarding and signboards from the busy roads to avoid traffic problems.

Attorney-General of India: He is the first Law Officer of the Government of India. His duty shall be to give advice on such legal matters and to perform such other duties of a legal character as many, from to time, be referred or assigned to him by the President. There is no right to vote in the Parliament. He must have the same qualifications as are required to be a Judge of the Supreme Court.

Comptroller and Auditor-General of India: He is the person to control the entire financial system of the country (both Union & States). He is the guardian of the public purse and shall be the impartial head of the audit and accounts system of India. He must have the same qualifications as are required to be a Judge of the Supreme Court.

6

State Government

India is a Union of states. Today, there are 28 states. Other than these, there are six centrally-administered territories. Our Constitution provides for the Government of the Union as well as the Government of 27 states (total is 28). The State of Jammu & Kashmir (J&K) was allowed to frame its own Constitution. In J&K, the Parliamentary form of Government has been adopted and the Executive Head is the Governor. Part VI of the Constitution lays down a uniform structure for all the states. Generally, the state governments follow the model of the Central Government. There are minor variations. The Legislature in four States (Bihar, Maharashtra, Karnataka and Uttar Pradesh) is bicameral. All the remaining States have only one House called as unicameral. Andhra Pradesh, Tamil Nadu, West Bengal and Punjab have abolished the Legislative Council.

The three organs of the State Government are Legislature, Executive and Judiciary.

A. State Legislature

It is composed of the Governor and the two Houses (Vidhana Sabha-Legislative Assembly and Vidhana Parishad-Legislative Council). It makes the laws.

Legislative Assembly: It is the House of Representatives of the people. Its Members are elected by the people of all categories. In Karnataka Legislative Assembly, there are 224 seats.

Speaker (S), Deputy Speaker (DS) and Members of Legislative Assembly (MLAs): The MLAs elect among themselves one as the Speaker as Presiding Officer of the House. They are elected for a term of five years. However, the Assembly may be dissolved before the expiry of the full term. Hence, it is not a permanent body.

The qualifications required to become S, DS and MLA are as follows:

- Should be a citizen of India
- Should not be less than age of 25
- Should not hold any Office of profit under the Government
- Should possess other qualifications as decided by the Parliament.

Responsibilities of MLAs: They are the representatives of their respective constituencies. Their main responsibility is to keep in contact with the people and solve their problems. They must take special interest in the developmental activities and welfare programmes of their constituencies. Under the Constitution, the voters have no right to recall the MLAs who fail to discharge their duties.

The powers and functions of the Legislative Assembly are follows:

- It is the Legislature of a state. It has power to legislate on the subjects that come under the State List and Concurrent List

- In all financial matters (preparation of Budget), the decision of the Assembly is final
- It plays a role in the Amendment of the Constitution
- The members also play a role in the election of the President of India.

Legislative Council: The membership of the Legislative Council (MLC) is not more than one-third of the membership of the Legislative Assembly. The number of members in the Karnataka Legislative Council is 75. One-third of them are elected by the Legislative Assembly, one-third of them are elected from the local bodies, one-sixth each are elected by registered graduates and registered teachers, respectively. Some Members are nominated by the Governor, taking into consideration of the services rendered in the fields of social service, arts, or literature, etc. It is a permanent House and is not subject to dissolution. However, once in two years, one-third of its members retire. The term of each member is six years. The Chairman and the Deputy Chairman are elected by the members of the Council. The deliberations are carried by the Chairman.

Qualifications: To become a MLC, one has to possess the following:

- Should be a citizen of India
- Should not be less than 30 years of age
- Should possess other qualifications as decided by the Parliament

Although, the Council has limited powers in financial and administrative matters, there is a view that the Council is needed because,

- The members possess rich experience
- The members can delay the Legislation passed by the Assembly in a hurry and the Experts may be nominated by the Council

B. State Executive

It consists of the Governor, Chief Minister and the Council of Ministers. Generally, its composition and functions are similar to those of the Union Executive.

Governor: He/she is the Constitutional Head of the State Executive. But in actual practice, the Chief Minister is the Chief Executive Authority. The President of India nominates the Governor. His/her Office is five years. But, the President has the power to remove the Governor before the expiry of the term. In other words, the Governor may continue in the Office as long as he/she enjoys the confidence of the President.

Qualifications: The Governor

- Must be a citizen of India and must not be less than 35 years of age
- Must not be a member of either of Parliament or State Legislature

Powers: The Governor

- Appoints the Chief Minister and, on his/her advice, appoints the Council of Ministers
- Has right to know from the Chief Minister about the working of the administration
- May review and give assent or to express dissent over the Bills passed by the Legislature
- During President's Rule in the State, he/she is in charge of the administration of the State
- The Money Bills cannot be introduced or amended unless approved by the Governor
- He/she has power to pardon those who have been convicted (but has no power to pardon a death sentence)
- The Joint Session of the Assembly is called by him/her and has the right to address the Joint Session

- When the Assembly is not in session, he/she can issue Ordinances. Such Ordinances should obtain the consent of the Assembly within six months period. In case of non-approval, the Ordinance automatically lapses.
- The State Advocate General, the Chairman and the members of the Public Service Commission, the Vice Chancellors of the Universities, etc are appointed by the Governor.

Chief Minister: Just as the Prime Minister is the Head of the Union Government, the Chief Minister is the Head of the State Government. The Governor appoints the Leader of the majority party or group as the Chief Minister.

Powers and Functions of the Chief Minister

- The Governor appoints the ministers selected by the Chief Minister
- Allocates departments to the ministers and also changes their departments
- He/she has the power to remove the ministers. In other words, the ministers can continue as long they enjoy the confidence of the Chief Minister.
- Has the right to supervise all the departments.
- Plays important role in the appointment of some of the top officers of the State Administration.
- As the Leader of the ruling party, role in the Legislature is of great importance.
- Expected to maintain a good relationship with the Center.

Council of Ministers: The Governor of the State appoints the Council of Ministers on the advice of the Chief Minister. There are three kinds of ministers and they are Cabinet Ministers, Deputy Ministers and Ministers of State.

Functions

- To prepare the Budget and the various Bills and place them before the assembly for its approval
- To exercise control over the administration. To answer questions asked by the other members over the administration during the Question Hour
- Every minister is held responsible for the work of the department, which has been entrusted. However collectively all the Ministers are responsible to the legislature. When they lose the vote-of-confidence of the house, they have to resign
- Ministers are expected to tour the State to understand the various problems of the people and find solutions to them
- From time-to-time, the Cabinet is expected to meet and take necessary decisions about administration.

C. State Judiciary

The aim of the Judiciary is to provide justice to the people. Each State has High Court as per the Constitution. Some bigger states have High Court Benches in another city of their state. Smaller states are attached to near-by big State High Courts. The Chief Justice of High Court is appointed by the President of India in Consultation with the Governor of the State and the Chief Justice of India. Other judges of the High Court are appointed by consulting the High Court Chief Justice and the Governor. As on the year 2000, there are 21 High Courts in our country. Either English or regional language is used in the High Court. They are given salary and facilities like house, car and pension. He can also resign or can be removed from the Office by an order from the President.

High Court Judge—Qualification and Tenure

- Must be a citizen of India
- Must have served under the Indian Judiciary or an Advocate of the High Court for at least ten years.
- The age of retirement is 62 years.
- The President may appoint duly qualified persons as Additional Judges for a period not exceeding two years.
- Has to make and subscribe an oath or affirmation before the Governor or before his/her nominee.
- After retirement, he/she cannot plead or practice before any authority in India except before Supreme Court and other High Courts.
- The President can transfer a judge from one High Court to another.
- May be resigning from his/her Office by sending Resignation Letter to the President.

High Court—Powers/Functions

- To issue writs, to safeguard the Fundamental Rights and other legal rights of the citizens.
- Supervise the working of the Subordinate Courts and frames rules for their functioning.
- Interpret the Provisions of the Constitution.
- The court has territorial limitations of the State only. Only in few cases, additional responsibility of Union Territories is allotted.
- They are governed by the Civil and Criminal Procedures.

Subordinate/Lower Courts

Under the Indian Judiciary, there are several Subordinate Courts. The High Courts function under the Supreme Court. The Subordinate Courts, which function under the High Courts, include District and Sessions Judges Courts, City Courts, Taluk-level/Munisiff Courts, Judicial Magistrate, Metropolitan Magistrate, and Nyaya Panchayats.

The subordinate courts are of two types

- *Civil Court:* It takes up matters such as money transactions, property and contracts, and pass judgment.
- *Criminal Court:* It takes up matters such as murder, theft and robbery, and passes judgments.

The High Court has the power to admit appeals in civil and criminal cases from the Subordinate Courts. Hence, appeals may be made to the High court against the judgments given by the Lower Courts. Similarly, appeals may be made to the Supreme Court against the judgments given by the High Courts.

Lok Adalat

Under our present judicial system, the legal procedure is complicated, expensive and time-consuming. As an alternative, the government has set up other forms of legal institutions that function faster and are less expensive. One of them is the Lok Adalat.

The state and district-level officers organize Lok Adalats, from time to time, at places convenient to the people. They take up cases from the parties which can be settled amicably. The judgment is as good as the judgment given by the Civil Courts. It is worth noting that the judgment is not only final but also binding on both the parties. No appeal can be made against such judgment in any higher court. This saves time and money.

7

Constitutional Provisions

Provisions for Scheduled Castes (SC) and Scheduled Tribes (ST)

The President of India has the power (Article 341) to declare with respect to any State or Union Territory the castes, races, or tribes or parts of or groups within the castes, etc. as SCs in relation to a State or Union Territory. Similarly, under article 342, the President has the power to specify the tribes or tribal communities or groups within them as STs in relation to State or Union Territory. In case of a State, the President must consult to the Governor of the State.

Article 330 ordains that seats shall be reserved in the LS for SCs/STs. Similar reservation is made in case of Legislative Assembly. The number of seats reserved shall be in proportion to their population in the State or Union Territory. Until 2001, there were one hundred nineteen seats reserved in the house of the people for these communities. Seventy-nine seats were reserved for the SCs and forty seats for the STs. Such reservation was originally to continue till 1960 but by successive Amendments it has now been extended till 2010.

Both the Central and State Governments have taken up special provisions and plans for the socio-economic development of these classes. Every five-year plan has the budgetary allocation for the development and improvement of the standard of living of these classes. In 1978, the Minority Commission was set up by the Government of India to look up continuously, the problems of minorities and suggesting remedial measures.

Article 338 provided for appointment for a National Commission for SCs and STs. By the 87th Amendment Act, 2003, a new Article has been inserted (Article 338 A). Henceforth, here will be two Commissions, i.e., National Commission for SCs and National Commission for STs. These Commissions will consist of a Chairperson, Vice-Chairperson and three other members. These commissions have been assigned the following duties:

- To investigate and monitor all matters relating to the safeguards provided under the Constitution or by any other law or any order of the Government
- To inquire into specific complaints with respect to deprivation of the rights
- To participate and advise on the planning process of socio-economic development of the SCs and STs
- To present to the President an Annual Report on the working of the safeguards
- To make such recommendations in the report as to the measures that should be taken by the Union or any State for the effective implementation of the safeguards
- To discharge such other functions as the President may specify

The condition of certain castes in India like SCs and STs, was pitiable. Great thinkers and reformers like Buddha, Basaveshwara, Dayananda Saraswathi, Gandhiji and Dr. Ambedkar fought against this evil.

Fully bearing this background in mind, the makers of our Constitution have provided many provisions to assure equality, liberty and social justice. They have embedded these ideas in the Preamble of the Constitution with following provisions, which are as follows:

- Some seats are reserved in the State Assemblies and LS
- Some constituencies are declared reserved from these to contest
- Certain percentage of jobs in the Government and educational institutions are reserved (15% for SCs and 7.5% for STs)
- Special and Mobile Courts have been setup to safeguard the rights and also disposal of cases relating to the practice of untouchability

In the field of education, care is taken to provide all facilities like supply of free books by opening Book Banks. Free boarding and lodging facilities are provided by opening hostels. The Government is giving Scholarships to these students. Employment Exchange Offices have been opened for the disabled, SCs/STs. Also, elaborate measures have been taken up to improve their standard of life in the field of agriculture, horticulture, animal husbandry and small-scale industries. Now, these people have occupied key positions in administration, education, law and order, etc., this is a good sign.

Provisions for Women

Our Constitution has granted the Right to Equality to all citizens, including women. However, in many ways, women are denied this right and they are discriminated against. For example, there are more non-literate women than men. More boys get to complete high school than girls, girls do more domestic work than boys, and taking the population as a whole there are more men than women. Why these differences are?

During the last two centuries, various measures are taken to improve the status of women in India. Social reformers like Raja Ram Mohan Roy, Swamy Dayananda Saraswathi, Rabindranath Tagore, Annie Besant, Eswarchandra Vidyasagar, Gandhiji, Sarojini Naidu, etc. have rendered yeomen service for the cause of women's upliftment. Women's education, abolition of child marriage, abolition of sati and legal provision for widow marriage are the various steps taken to improve the conditions of women.

According to the Marriage Act of 1954, the age is fixed at 21 years for men and 18 years for women. Intercaste marriages are encouraged. Under Article 23, prohibiting traffic of in human beings and forced labour like beggary and similar forms shall be an offence punishable in accordance with law. Dowry Prevention Act of 1961, abolishes dowry system. Under Child Marriage Restriant Act, child marriage is illegal and steps are taken to prevent it. There is a provision for 33% reservation of seats for women in all the local bodies. Under the Indira Women Welfare Programme, many schemes have been developed for the welfare of the women. In 1998, Shtree Shakthi scheme was enforced for the development of rural women. Balika Samruddi Yojana was enforced to protect women from sexual harassment and the Rastreeya Mahila Vimochana was introduced. The year 2001 was declared as the 'Year of the Women Empowerment' to the promotion of the development of women.

After independence, various measures have been taken by the government to improve the status of women. Some of them are:

- In matters of public employment, equal opportunities are provided for both men and women by the Constitution (Articles 14 & 15)
- The education of girls stressed by creating various facilities by the government
- Adult Education Centers for women have been opened
- A Commission is constituted for the welfare of women and children

- Polygamy is discouraged by law
- Child marriage is abolished
- A law is passed to give equal share in ancestral property
- Widow marriage is encouraged
- Dowry system is banned legally
- Provide shelter to such of the women who are in trouble, arrangements are made for their temporary shelter (since1969)
- In all the walks of life, women are given equal opportunities together with men

Provisions for Children

All those who are below the age of 14 are identified as *children*. Pandit Jawaharlal Nehru said that children are the wealth of the country and that a 'Child of today is the citizen of tomorrow'. Although the Constitution guarantees certain rights to children, many children in our country are without proper care, nourishment and education. Some of the specific problems faced by children are:

- Child Abuse: When children are subjected to physical punishment and or mental torture, this is known as Child Abuse. Some examples are severely beating; being indifferent towards them; employing them in dangerous jobs and behaving badly with them.
- Exploitation of Girl Child: She is forced to do difficult and tedious domestic chores. For example, girls of a family are expected to carry water and or firewood over long distances, while the boys of the family do not do such work. It is common for families those are having economic problems to send their daughters to work as domestic servants to houses of rich people as bonded labourers until their parents repay the loans.
- Problems of Child Labour: Children are employed not only in fields and in homes, but also in hotels, garages and in factories like match-box, crackers, textiles, etc.
- School Dropouts: Children are pulled out by their parents so that they can contribute in their fields or contribute to family's income. Dropping out of school is against interests of child. Currently, there are many schemes which try to retain children in school.

The General Assembly of UNO adopted a Universal Charter in November 1989 for the welfare of the children. The Rights of the Child under the Charter have follows:

• Right to Life	• Right to Education
• Right to Health	• Right for obtaining Nutritious Food
• Right to Leisure	• Right to Play
• Right to get Good Standard of Life	• Right of Protection against Exploitation & Negligence
• Right for Protection from Abuse & Immoral Traffic	• Right against subjecting to Drugs & Intoxicants
• Right against Forced Employment	• Right against Violence

Irrespective of caste, race, religion, language, sex, society, the rights are to be strictly adhered to by all the nations and for no reason these rights could be denied. Since 1974, the government has undertaken various projects and programmes for the all round development of children which include the nutrition, inoculation, health checking, pre-school education, etc. The Government of India has opened 'Balavikas Kendras' under the aegis of the Indian Council for Child Welfare for the development of the children. In 1955, National Children's Board was established to promote the cause of the child welfare. Both Central and State Governments have taken various measures to protect the rights of the children and steps have been taken for the eradication of child labor.

Provisions for Other Backward Classes (OBC)

Seats are reserved in the Legislatures for SCs and STs. The state is free to make special provisions for the advancement of socially and educationally backward classes and for women and children.

Not intended with making special provisions for the SCs, who a specific category of socially depressed people (generally identifiable with the Gandhian term 'harijan'), the Constitution has made separate provisions for the amelioration and advancement of all 'backward classes'. Of course, the Constitution does not define OBCs. The SCs and STs are no doubt backward classes, but the fact that the SCs and STs are mentioned together with the expression 'backward classes' in the foregoing provisions shows that there may be OBCs of people besides the SCs and STs. The Constitution provides for the appointment of a 'Commission to investigate the conditions of backward classes (Article 340). Such a Commission was appointed in 1953 (Kaka Saheb Kalelkar as Chairman), with the following terms of appointment:

- To determine the tests by which any particular class or group of people can be called backward
- To determine a list of such backward communities for the whole of India
- To examine the difficulties of backward classes and to recommend steps to be taken for their amelioration

This Commission submitted its Report to the Central Government in 1955, the tests recommended by the Commission appeared to the Government to be too vague and to be of much practical value; hence, the State Governments have been authorized to give assistance to the backward classes according to the lists prepared by the State Governments themselves.

The Second Backward Classes Commissioner, B. P. Mandal, submitted his Report in 1980. In August, 1990, the Government declared reservation of 27% seats in government service on the basis of this report. This was challenged as unconstitutional. A nine-Judge Bench has decided this case in November, 1992, rejecting that challenge. The Court has not itself enumerated the 'backward classes' but has directed the Government to set up a Commission to specify the backward classes, in the light of the principles laid down by the Court. Following the recommendations of the Commission, the Central Government has reserved 27% seats in all recruitments to be made from 09th September, 1993.

8

Emergency Provisions

Emergency Provisions of our constitution enable the federal government to acquire the strength of a unitary system whenever the exigencies of the situation so demand. The Constitution provides for three different types of abnormal situations which call for departure from the normal governmental machinery (Refer 44th Amendment Act, 1978):

1. *National Emergency:* Article 352 empowers the President to make a Proclamation of Emergency if he/she is satisfied that the security of India or of any part of the territory of India is threatened by war, external aggression, or armed rebellion.
   - First Proclamation—26th October, 1962 when Chinese aggression and revoked on 10th January 1968
   - Second Proclamation—03rd December 1971 was made on the ground of undeclared war by Pakistan
   - Third Proclamation—25th June 1975 was made on the ground of internal disturbance given by Smt. Indira Gandhi

   Note: The 2nd and 3rd proclamations were revoked on 21st March 1977
2. *State Emergency:* It is a situation arising out of failure of Constitutional Machinery in a State (Article 356). The Constitution does not employ the word emergency for this situation.
3. *Financial Emergency:* It is a situation in which the financial stability of India is threatened (Article 360).

Effects of Proclamation of Emergency (PoE)

It has wide range ranging effects on the polity. It brings about a change in the distribution of powers between the Union and the States. Powers of the Union increase considerably. The fundamental rights suffer an eclipse and the executive acquires unprecedented powers.

The effects of a PoE may be discussed under five heads. They are the following:

- *Extension of Executive Power:* While the PoE is in operation, the Executive Power of the State extends to giving of directions to any state as to the manner in which the executive power of the state is to be exercised. If the proclamation is confined to a specified area the power to give directions shall not be limited to the states in that area. Directions may be given to the other states. Thus, the state governments are brought under the control of the Center.
- *Extension of Legislative Power:* While a PoE is in operation, the Parliament gains the power to make laws with respect to many matters in the State List. The limitations imposed by state list are removed. The state continues to possess Legislative Powers but the powers become subject to

the overriding powers of the Parliament. Parliament may act immediately in the interest of the nation without waiting for a state to take necessary steps. In a way the Constitution becomes Unitary.

- *Effect on Distribution of Finances:* While a PoE is in operation, the President is vested with the power to alter and modify the Provisions of the Constitution relating to the distribution of the revenues between the Union and the States. Such modification shall continue till the end of the financial year in which the proclamation ceases to operate. The changes are effected by the President by issuing an order. Every order is to be laid before each House of Parliament.
- *Effect on the Fundamental Rights (FRs):* Articles 358 and 359 describe the effect of the PoE on the FRs. Article 358 removes all fetters put on the State by Article 19. The State may make a law abridging any of the freedoms conferred by Article 19.
- *Miscellaneous Effects:* While PoE is in operation, the Parliament may by law extend the duration of LS for a period not exceeding one year at a time. But the period shall not exceed beyond six months after the proclamation has ceased to operate. During the Emergency imposed by Smt. Indira Gandhi, the life of the LS was extended by one year (Amendment Act 109 of 1976).

Effects of National Emergency

At the time of national emergency, the country almost loses its federal structure and becomes unitary in form as the Parliament vests maximum powers with it.

- Parliament can make laws for the whole of the country or any part of the country which has been kept under emergency with respect to any matter in the State List.
- If a law passed by the Parliament is in conflict with the state law, then the central law prevails.
- The President is entitled to issue an ordinance regarding a state subject even if the Parliament is not in session.
- The Parliament is authorized to make the laws, delegate powers and impose duties on Government of India and its Officers, as to carry out the laws made by it.
- The union Government can issue directions or give instructions to any state government in exercising its executive powers.
- Changes can be made in the allotment and distribution of revenues between the union and the State by the President.
- The FRs can be suspended and their enforcement by the Supreme Court and other Courts of Law stand suspended. Thus, making the people restrict the enjoyment of the FRs.

Effects of State Emergency

- The President is empowered with all the functions of the State Government or he may confer the authority and powers to the Governor of the state and Administrator in the case of union territories to conduct the administration.
- The Parliament has authority to make the law on the items in the State List.
- Parliament is also empowered to authorize the President to issue an order to sanction expenditure from the Consolidated Fund of the State, subject to the approval of the Parliament later.
- The President delegates special powers to the Union or State servants for the smooth running of the administration of the state.
- The powers and jurisdiction of the High Court does not come under Article 356.

Note: The President's Rule has been imposed more than 108 times under this Article 356 to dismiss unwanted state governments: The conditions are

- On the ground of political instability.
- Breakdown of the law and order.
- Due to corruption and maladministration.
- To control and stop opposition and unwanted parties from forming governments both before and after elections.
- While creating new states.

Effects of Financial Emergency

- During the financial emergency, "the executive authority of the Union shall extend to the giving of directions to any state to observe such canons of financial property as may be specified in the direction" which the President may think necessary for the purpose.
- The President may direct to make necessary cut or reduction in the salaries and allowances of all government servants which include the salaries of Judges of Supreme Court and High Courts.
- The President can veto the Money Bills of the states which means the Money Bill or Financial Bills passed by the State Legislatures are reserved for the consideration of the President.

(**Note:** However, the financial emergency has not been proclaimed so far, by the President)

9

Electoral Process

The Preamble to the Constitution declares that India is a DEMOCRATIC REPUBLIC. This implies that all citizens who are eligible to vote will have the right to participate in the elections. We have a Parliamentary form of Government so the party securing a major share of the votes of the citizens or a coalition of parties who are able to obtain support of a majority of Legislators in the Popular House (Lok Sabha or Legislative Assembly, as the case may be) form the Government. The vote in an election is the cherished right of every citizen in a democracy. Right of voting is the essence of democracy. Irrespective of caste, creed, race, religion, language and sex, all those who have completed the age of 18 years are extended the voting right in India and we call it as "Universal Adult Franchise" system (reduced the age from 21 to 18 years in the 61st Amendment, 1989).

Every citizen has the right to vote. When the number of candidates contests for the elections, selecting a good candidate is not an easy task. In such cases, the citizen should be very careful and use his/her discretion to select a proper person. It is a challenging task to the voter because he/she has to choose a good person who is loyal and service-minded and devoted to the public cause. The voter has to identify a party which is good for the progress of the nation and vote for its candidate. Voters should not come under the influence of money, muscle power, caste, race, religion, etc. The winning candidates should devote themselves towards the progress of their electorate. The candidates, after elections, should not change their party as it would destabilize the government. The elected candidates should be a model of selfless service, honesty and cooperation.

India has Representative form of Government. The representatives are elected. There is an Election Commission (EC) in India, to conduct elections from time to time. Till 1989, it consisted of one Chief Election Commissioner. In 1989, one more Commissioner was added. On 01.10.1993, provision was made to appoint two Commissioners. Thus, the EC at the Center has one Chief Election Commissioner (CEC) and two Election Commissioners. They are appointed by the President. The EC has conducted the regular and by-elections to the Parliament and State Legislatures. The Commissioners has an appointment for a term of 6 years or till the age of 65 years, whichever is earlier.

The EC performs the following functions:

- *Elections to the Parliament:* Elections to the Office of President and Vice President; and Elections to State Legislatures (including Union Territories)
- *Preparation of Electoral rolls:* Conduct of the elections; Counting of votes and Declaration of results
- Advice the President in regard to the question whether a MP (Article 103) or MLA has become subject to any disqualification (Article 192)
- Advice the President in the appointment of Regional Commissioners at State level

Elections are conducted by secret ballot. The contesting candidates are assigned different symbols so that even an illiterate voter can vote by identifying the symbol. Recently, electronic voting machines are introduced. According to the Peoples Representatives Act, all matters of dispute arising in the elections are settled by a High Court or the Supreme Court of India. The elections are conducted according to the calendar of events prepared and published by the EC.

Process of Election

1. *Submission of Nominations:* President in case of Lok Sabha and the Governor in the case of Legislatures, issue the Notification of Election. The contesting candidates are expected to submit their nominations to the Returning Officer, before the prescribed date. Every nomination should be accompanied by a deposit as prescribed. Deposit money is forfeited in case the candidate does not get the minimum number of votes prescribed.
2. *Scrutiny of Nominations:* The contesting candidates should properly fill up the nomination forms and satisfy the various conditions prescribed by the EC. During the process of scrutiny, all such issues are examined. After such scrutiny alone, the names of the eligible candidates to the election are announced.
3. *Withdrawal of Nomination:* The contesting candidates are given a chance to withdraw their nominations. A date is fixed for this purpose.
4. *Election Propaganda:* After the declaration of the names of the contesting candidates, propaganda/ canvass work starts to woo the electorate. The independent candidates belonging no political parties also contest in elections. Meetings, rallies, processions, pamphlets and other means of communication used for the purpose of wooing the voters. All such election campaigns must come to end before 36 hours of commencing polling. However, one is allowed to go from house to house and carry on the propaganda work.
5. *Election Day:* For the sake of the voters, the EC has created a number of election booths. On the day of election, the voters can go to their nearest prescribed booth and exercise their vote. To carry out the election work, a number of Officers are appointed. Security arrangements are also made. A voters' list is prepared. With the help of the list, Officers are able to identify the voters. The list contains the name, sex, age and address of the voters. Recently, the EC has insisted on providing Identification Cards to the voters. The agents of various political parties are present in the booth during elections and their job is to identify the voters and check malpractices. Voters cast their votes through ballot paper or voting machines as the case may be. The ballot paper consists the names and symbols of the candidates, which helps the voter. The sealed ballot boxes/voting machines are given tight security till the day of counting.
6. *Counting of Votes:* A number of counting centers are created and in the presence of the candidates or their agents, the sealed boxes/machines are opened for counting. One who gets the majority is declared as Winner. There is scope for recounting under special circumstances. The election disputes can be settled through courts.

(**Note:** After elections and after the announcement of the results, the Chief Election Commission issues the notification that 'New Lok Sabha' has been duly constituted. Similarly, State Chief Electoral Officer of the State issues a notification that 'New Assembly' has been duly constituted).

Adult Suffrage

It shall be the rule for elections. In other words, if a citizen is 18 years of age on the date fixed by the legislature and disqualified by any law, he/she is not entitled to be registered as a voter. The common disqualifications are based on unsoundness of mind, conviction for crime, corrupt practice at an election, etc. They are contained in the Representation of People Act. It means that barring exceptions every citizen who is an adult possesses the right to vote. A person may be registered as a voter in only one constituency. He must also be ordinarily resident in the constituency in which he desires to be registered. Seats have been reserved for SCs and STs. There is a provision for nomination of not more than two members of the Anglo-Indian community in the Lok Sabha and one member in a State Assembly. Apart from these, there is no reservation for any religion or community.

10

Basics of Engineering Ethics

Ethics: It is basically a philosophy and a body of knowledge dealing with human behavior and science of morality (Greek word ethos, means customs). It refers only to professional behavior. Morality (Latin word mores) refers to any aspect of human action. Thus, it concerns the goodness of voluntary human conduct that affects the self or other living things.

Applied Ethics: It deals with specific prescriptions of behavior, values and beliefs in a given context.

Ethical Standards: They can be compiled, published and prescribed for practice for all professions engaged in service to the society/humanity such as Education, Engineering, Medical, Business, Finance, Science, Research, Governance, Politics, etc.

Profession: It is used as a synonym for 'job' or 'occupation'. Also, it is referred to a free act of commitment to a way of life. Professions are occupations requiring sophisticated knowledge, group commitment to some public good, and a significant degree of self-regulation.

Professional: A person who is 'duly qualified' in some field by virtue of special knowledge usually gained by specific and accredited education and possessing skills acquired through learning and experience. It means merely to earn one's living through the profession. e.g., Engineer, Doctor, Lawyer, etc.

We speak of professional football and tennis players, as opposed to amateurs who do not draw an income from these sports. We also speak of professional sanitation workers, taxicab drivers, bartendes, and even mercenaries and killers.

Ethics

- At the time of graduation, we all take oath that we abide by Code of Ethics (CoE) in the respective professions.
- Ability to distinguish right and the wrong and having the conviction to do right things all the times.
- Most of the times our conscience will tell us what is right or wrong.
- Lack of moral values and conviction, greed, hunger for power and other situational compulsions drive people to commit unethical acts.

There are five aims in studying ethics

- Stimulating our moral imagination
- Helping us recognize moral issues
- Helping us analyze key ethical concepts
- Engaging our sense of responsibility
- Helping us address unclarity, uncertainty and disagreement about moral issues

Practice in preventive ethics involves stimulating the moral imagination, developing the ability to recognize ethical issues when they arise, developing analytical skills in dealing with ethical problems, eliciting in engineers a sense of responsibility for their actions, and helping engineers to tolerate and also to resist disagreement and ambiguity.

Why Study EE?

- To increase the ability of concerned engineers, managers, citizens and others to responsibly confront moral issues raised by technological activity.
- The moral problems those must be resolved involve vagueness, conflicting reasons, and disagreements over the principles those apply. Moral dilemma arises when two or more moral obligations conflict with one another and not all of them can be fully respected.
- The study of EE helps to develop skills in dealing with moral dilemmas. The direct aim should be to empower individuals to reason more clearly and carefully concerning moral questions. To help the individual acquire moral autonomy, i.e., the skill and habit of thinking rationally about ethical issues on the basis of moral concern.

Professional Ethics (PE)

Professional Ethics is the set of standards adopted by professionals insofar as they see themselves acting as professionals. Personal Ethics is the set of one's own ethical commitments, usually given in early home or religious training and often modified by later reflection. Common morality is the set of moral ideals shared by most members of a culture or a society.

The following examples illustrate some of the possible relationships among the above three

- An engineer refuses to design military hardware because he/she believes war is immoral. This refusal is based on personal moral convictions, not on professional or common morality.
- A civil engineer refuses to design a project he/she believes will be contrary to the principles of sustainable development.
- An engineer insists on complete honesty in the reporting of technical information to his/her client or employer. This insistence could be based on personal, professional, or common morality.

Engineering Ethics (EE)

- It is the study of the moral issues and decisions confronting individuals and organizations engaged in engineering
- It is the study of related questions about the moral ideals, characters, policies and relationships of people and corporations involved in technological activity
- It refers to the set of specifically moral problems and issues related to engineering
- It is the activity and discipline aimed at understanding the moral values that ought to guide engineering practice, resolving moral issues in engineering, and justifying moral judgments concerning engineering

Aims of Engineering Ethics

- *Exciting the moral imagination:* In general, imagination is helpful in predicting the problems and the consequences also to arrive at the alternative solution thereby choosing the best possible solution when ethical problems are encountered. Thus, abundant imagination is a powerful tool for an engineer.

- *Recognition of ethical issues:* Engineers are required to take professional decisions such that it will not lead to ethical crises.
- *Developing analytical skills:* Generally engineering students are good in technical and analytical skills. However, they must be cautious in analyzing the moral issues. In this process, they must have clear thinking about concepts of utility, justice, rights, duties and respect for the persons.
- *Sense of responsibility:* Professional can become moral agents by having a sense of responsibility. Though the significance is given to codes by the professionals, cannot be relied upon uncritically. In this connection, many codes also distinguish between ethical standards and ethical ideals. Ethical Standards or requirements are basic obligations and duties. The ethical ideals go beyond basic obligations and engineers are required to aspire to meet the ideals that make one as moral agent.
- *Tolerating disagreement and ambiguity:* While sorting out the difficult understanding of ethical concepts, it reveals a certain amount of vagueness, ambiguity and disagreements. Lack of consensus may prove frustrating to arrive at technical solutions to problems. Some may try to authoritatively resolve by bringing the matters under the shade of codes, but it is pointed out that the codes do not provide ready solutions to all moral problems. No Code of Ethics is self-interpreting. Its principles and rules are enunciated in general terms and need to be applied with judicious thinking to particular circumstances.

EE is a type of PE and as such must be distinguished from personal ethics and from the ethical obligations that one may have as an occupant of other social roles. EE is concerned with the question of what the standards in EE should be and how to apply these standards to particular situations. One of the values of studying EE is that it can serve the function of helping to promote responsible engineering practice. Part of responsible engineering practice is the exercise of preventive ethics: the practice of sound ethical decision-making to avoid more serious problems later.

Why Codes of Ethics?

As with law, medicine, etc., engineering is a learned profession. As a profession, engineering constantly involves the exercise of expert judgment and discretion in the performance of services. Engineers are expected to use their education, training and experience in a manner that comforts with the public health and safety. But where do engineers look for guidance in determining the most appropriate course of action to follow in the earlier cited cases? One possible source is law. Statutes, regulations, court decisions, etc. certainly provide a basis to make certain decisions concerning conduct and behavior. However, the law does not address many issues concerning appropriate professionals conduct. Another possible resource might be colleagues, family members or friends.

Sometimes these sources might be extremely valuable as a sounding board, but in some other cases, they might lack the necessary education and training to provide useful feedback or the feedback might be biased or prejudiced by some fact or circumstance. For that reason, professional organizations, such as the National Society of Professional Engineers (NSPE), Virginia, develop CoE to assist engineers in making decisions in their everyday practice and employment. Professional CoE reflects basic 'norms' of conduct that exist within a particular profession and provide general guidance relating to a variety of issues. They do provide guideposts those can be helpful in assisting engineers in evaluating the circumstances they encounter and provide possible approaches those may be taken in addressing the ethical issues involved.

Clearly, EE is an issue that goes to the heart of engineering practice. It reflects the customs, habits, and values of engineering as a profession and reflects the time-tested experience, seasoning and training of practicing engineers. In some senses, a CoE is a "timeline" for the profession because it mirrors the conventions, routines and patterns of the profession but shifts as those conventions, routines and patterns change.

As the profession of engineering grows in stature within our society, engineering and engineers will be increasingly examined and scrutinized by the public, the media, the government, and the profession itself on moral and ethical questions. Having a thoroughly developed CoE of this magnitude, along with members those adhere to the code, will be vitally useful in the process.

Types of Inquiry

EE combines inquiries into values, meaning, and facts. The following are the types

- Normative inquiries, which are most central, seek to identify the values those should guide individuals and groups. Normative questions are about ought to be and what is good (bearing in mind that here our concern is with moral values). Examples are how far does the obligation of engineers to protect public safety extend in given situation?; Whose values ought to be primary in making judgments about acceptable risks in a design for a public transport system?; Which particular laws and organizational procedures affecting the engineering practice are morally warranted?; What moral rights should engineers be recognized as having in order to help them fulfill their professional obligations?
- Conceptual inquiries seek to clarify important concepts or principles or ideas, whether the ideas are expressed by single words or by statements and questions. For example, what does safety mean, and how is it related to the idea of risk? What does it mean when Code of Engineers say engineers should protect the safety, health and welfare of the public? What is a bribe? What is a profession, and what defines professionals?
- Factual or Descriptive inquiries seek to provide facts needed for understanding and resolving value issues using proven scientific techniques. They provide important information about the business realities of contemporary engineering practice, the history of the engineering profession, the effectiveness of professional societies in fostering moral conduct, the procedures used in making risk assessments, and psychological profiles of engineers. Determining the facts in these areas provides an understanding of the background conditions that generate moral problems. It also enables us to deal realistically with alternative ways of resolving those problems.

Philosophy

Much of EE can be viewed as a part of applied (or practical) philosophical ethics, as are medical ethics, legal ethics, and business ethics. Business ethics is the closest cousin of EE. Since most engineers are salaried employees, and since engineering decisions are usually tied to business decisions, it is not surprising that moral problems in engineering and business often overlap. The question, for example, of what is wrong with offering and accepting more than nominal gifts when negotiating contracts for engineering services are at once an issue in EE and business ethics.

11

Responsibility of Engineers

A professional is always to understand and act appropriately on his/her responsibilities. An engineer may be service provider to clients through independent consultancy or by being member of consulting firms. Engineers have basic job responsibilities, whether they work for clients or corporate employers. NSPE Code of Ethics expects that 'Engineers shall have concern about professional matters for clients as faithful agents. The responsibility of practicing engineers will have harms and benefit to the society'.

There are set of rules of conduct those have been established by the engineering community outlining the obligations of professional (registered) engineers to the society, to employers and clients, and to fellow engineers. These rules are established in our attempt to safeguard life, health and property, to promote the public welfare, and to maintain a high standard of integrity. As the rules are binding on all registered engineers, it is the responsibility of each engineer to be familiar with the rules. In addition to the rules, each registered engineer must meet standards of high moral and ethical conduct when practicing the engineering profession. Each professional body maintains the right and obligation to enforce such rules of conduct by assessing penalties when such rules are broken.

Engineering Registration is a privilege and not a right. It is a privilege to practice engineering in the area (s) of competence in which certification has been granted. This privilege demands that engineers responsibly represent themselves before the public in a truthful and objective manner. Engineers must compete fairly with others and avoid all conflicts of interest while faithfully serving the legitimate needs and interests of their employers and clients.

Thus, responsibility of engineer is defined as the application of engineering education, training and experience to provide excellent sustainable engineering solutions for the benefit of our employers and clients towards the improvement of the quality of work life of everyone in the community. Legal and moral responsibility are distinct, but they are related to each other. Responsibility is attributed to persons in both law and morality. However in the law corporations and the institutions can be given legal standings as persons, whereas in morality it is high debatable whether corporations and institutions can be persons. These two areas aside, notions of legal and moral responsibility have much in common.

For example, in regard to responsibility for causing harm, in both law and morality, we distinguish

- Intentionally causing harm (knowingly and deliberately causing harm)
- Negligently causing harm (not knowingly causing harm but failing to exercise 'due care')
- Recklessly causing harm (not aiming to cause harm but acting in conscious awareness that harm is likely to result)

Views of Responsibility

There are three views of responsibility

- *The Minimalist View of Responsibility:* The engineers are to discharge their duties/hold responsibilities confirming to the standard, operating procedures thus fulfilling the job terms of their employment. They are accountable for any harm/damage/loss. This works well in many occasions, however standard procedures lead to be minimal, sticking on to minimum acceptable standards. Standard procedures are based on the past experience and the expected results of present practice and leads to difficulty in exercising the procedures in the event of unexpected/ surprising problems. The responsibility of individual is exclusively defined and is linked with the idea of individual fault or blame. Everyone wants to be safe thereby putting blame on others or stating their responsibility. Avoiding blame or being safe becomes the prime concern in the minimalist view.

It holds that engineers have a duty to conform to the standard operating procedures of their profession and to fulfill the basic duties of their job as defined by the terms of their employment. They are accountable for harms caused by their failure to fulfill these responsibilities. Although this approach works well in many instances, standard operating procedures tend to be minimalist, stipulating only minimally acceptable standards. Furthermore, although these standards are based on past experience and the expected outcomes of present practice, unexpected problems can arise that standard operating procedures are not well equipped to handle. It also emphasizes a negative approach to responsibility. It tends to define responsibility in terms of a kind of exclusivity: "It's my job, not his", or "It's his job, not mine". Responsibility is linked with the idea of individual fault, or blame; and it is interpreted in narrow, legalistic terms. Avoidance of blame, or "staying out of trouble", tends to be the dominant concern.

- *Reasonable Care View of Responsibility:* The reasonable care view extends beyond the minimalist views concern of being safe. In minimalist view, the concern is about what will happen to those who cause harm and who will be held liable either legally or morally. Whereas with reasonable care view, the concern is to give attention to those who are at risk of being harmed and to prevent the progress/adverse effect of harm. This view will be expected and accepted by a common prudent non-professional citizen.

It moves beyond the Minimalist view's concern to "stay out of trouble". We might say that the Minimalist view is most directly concerned with what will happen to those who cause harm (those who will be held liable either legally or morally). Here, we must take reasonable care to ensure that mistakes are prevented and the public welfare is protected. However, this is more directly concerned with the perspective of those who are at risk of being harmed and trying to prevent that harm. This appeal to "a standard of reasonableness as seen by a normal, prudent non-professional".

- *Good Works (Excellence) View of Responsibility:* Good work is the concept of responsibility beyond the legal and moral responsibility and the call of duty. Here engineers have a positive attitude with their excellent professional competence. For an engineer to do good work the reason, people, place, money, etc. becomes irrelevant. Engineers shall do good work without any extra motive of profit in any way. It should not be taken as a saintly or heroic act, but it is an admirable one.

This is captured in the expression "above and beyond the call of duty". A simple example outside the engineering context illustrates what we mean by the concept of good works. Raju wakes up at his usual time and prepares to go to work. When he looks out the window, he is shocked to see his long driveway drifted over with snow; this was not in last night's weather forecast. He has only a snow shovel, not a plow. He realizes he will be very late to work—and very tired. As he bundles up to go out and shovel, Raju is surprised to see his driveway being cleared by a neighbour with a snowplow. Although they are neighbours, they have never met before. No doubt, Raju appreciates what his neighbour is doing. What would he think if his neighbour had done nothing to help? Would he fault him, think he had failed to do his duty, or think his neighbour had some sort of moral deficiency? These responses are unlikely. His neighbour has gone "above and beyond the call of duty". His is not a saintly or heroic act, but it is an admirable one.

Impediments to Responsibility

- *Self-Interest:* It is essential for engineers to realize their responsibility and employ it in the practice. However, certain hurdles are to be overcome in implementing it in practice. Engineering CoE, like the codes of other professions, articulate standards of conduct for engineers as engineers. However, engineers are not simply engineers. They are people with personal hopes and ambitions not restricted to professional ideals. Sometimes, concern for our own interests tempts us to act contrary to the interests of others, perhaps even contrary to what others expect from us as professionals. Sometimes concern for self-interest blocks us from seeing or fully understanding our professional responsibilities. Taken to an extreme, this is a form of egoism—an exclusive concern to satisfy one's own interests, even at the possible expense of others. This is popularly characterized as "looking out for number one".
- *Fear:* It is difficult for few engineers to act responsibly due to fear. Even when we are not tempted to take advantage of others for personal gain, we may be moved by various fears—fear of acknowledging our mistakes, fear of losing one's job, or fear of some sort of punishment or other bad consequences. Fears of these sorts can make it very difficult for us to act responsibly.
- *Self-Deception:* One way of resisting the temptations of self-interest is to confront ourselves honestly and ask if we would approve of others treating us in the same way we are contemplating treating them. This is Golden Rule reasoning; and it can have a powerful psychological effect on us. However, for it to work, we must recognize what we are contemplating doing for what it is. Rationalization often gets in the way of this recognition. Some rationalizations show grater self-awareness than others, particularly those that exhibit self-defensiveness or excuse-making ("I am not really doing this just for myself" or "Everyone takes shortcuts once in a while—it's the only way one can survive"). Other rationalizations seem to betray a willful lack of self-understanding. This is called self-deception, an intentional avoidance of truths we would find it painful to confront self-consciously.
- *Ignorance:* An obvious barrier to responsible action of ignorance of vital information. For example, if an engineer does not realize that a design poses a safety problem, he will not be in a position to do anything about it. Sometimes, such a lack of awareness is willful avoidance—a turning away from information to avoid having to deal with the challenges it may pose. But often it is due to the lack of imagination, not looking in the right places for necessary information, a failure to persist, or the pressure of deadlines. Although there are limits to what engineers can be expected to know, these examples suggest that ignorance is not always a good excuse.
- *Egocentric Tendencies:* A common feature of human experience is that we intend to interpret situations from very limited perspectives and this takes very special efforts to acquire a more objective viewpoint. This is what psychologists call egocentricity. It is especially prevalent in us as young children, and it never completely leaves us. Although egocentric thinking is sometimes egoistic (self-interested), it need not be. It is actually a special form of ignorance.

- *Microscopic or Confined Vision:* Like egocentric thinking, it embraces a limited perspective. However, whereas egocentric thinking tends to be inaccurate (failing to understand the perspective of others), it may be very accurate and precise. When we look into a microscope, we see things that we could not see before—but only in the narrow field of resolution on which the microscope focuses. We gain accuracy and detailed knowledge—at a microscopic level. At the same time, we cease to see things at the more ordinary level. This is the price of seeing things microscopically. Only when we lift our eyes from the microscope will we see what is obvious at the everyday level.
  Responsibility of Engineers.
- *Uncritical Acceptance of Authority:* Engineering CoE emphasize the importance of engineers exercising independent, objective judgment in performing their functions. This is sometimes called *professional autonomy*. At the same time, the CoE insist that engineers have a duty of fidelity to their employers and clients. Independent consulting engineers may have an easier time maintaining professional autonomy than the vast majority of engineers, who work in large, hierarchical organizations. Most engineers are not their own bosses, and they are expected to defer to authority in their organizations.
- *Groupthink:* A noteworthy feature of the organizational settings within which engineers work is that individuals tend to work and deliberate in groups. This means that an engineer will often participate in group decision making, rather than function as an individual decision maker. Although this may contribute to better decisions ("two heads are better than one"), it also creates well-known, but commonly overlooked tendencies to engage in what Irving Janis calls groupthink—a situation in which groups come to agreement at the expense of critical thinking. Concentrating on groups that are characterized by high cohesiveness, solidarity, and loyalty (all of which are prized in organizations), Janis identifies eight symptoms of groupthink:
  - An illusion of invulnerability of the group to failure
  - A strong "we feeling" that views outsiders as adversaries or enemies and encourages shared stereotypes of others
  - Rationalizations that tend to shift responsibility to others
  - An illusion of morality that assumes the inherent morality of the group and thereby discourages careful examination of the moral implications of what the group is doing
  - A tendency of individual members toward self-censorship, resulting from a desire not to "rock the boat"
  - An illusion of unanimity, construing silence of a group member as consent
  - An application of direct pressure on those who show signs of disagreement, often exercised by the group leader who intervenes in an effort to keep the group unified
  - Mind guarding, protecting the group from dissenting views by preventing their introduction (by, for example, outsiders who want to present their views to the group)

Concepts of Responsibility

There are two concepts of responsibility that should not be confused with moral responsibility.

- Causal responsibility consists simply in being a cause of some event. In this sense, we speak of lightning as being responsible for a house's catching fire. People can be casually responsible for an event without necessarily being morally responsible for it. For example, a 2-year-old child may cause a fire while playing with matches, but it is the parents who left the matches within the child's reach who are morally responsible for the fire.

- Legal responsibility should also be distinguished from moral responsibility. An engineer or engineering firm can be held legally responsible for harm that was so unlikely and unforeseeable that little or no moral responsibility is involved.

Main Levels of Moral Development: Laurence Kohlberg (1927 - 1987)

- *Pre-conventional level:* A conduct is regarded as whatever directly benefits oneself, by the desire to avoid punishment or to satisfy own needs.
- *Conventional level:* The norms of one's family, group, or society are uncritically accepted as the final standard of morality.
- *Post-conventional level:* The individual comes to regard the standard of right and wrong as a set of principles—concerning rights and the general good that are not reducible to self-interest or social conventions. He calls these as individual autonomous.

12

Honesty, Integrity and Reliability

The concern with truth telling extends far beyond the boundaries of the engineering profession. Religious and secular literature contains many injunctions to tell the truth. If we consider the engineering profession to be like a building, honesty is its foundation. Without honesty, the value of engineering services is undermined. Unreliable engineering judgment is worse than none at all.

Engineers can misuse the truth in different ways. These can include failing to communicate the truth (item 1-5 below), communicating the truth when they should not (item 6), and allowing their judgment with regard to the truth to be corrupted (item 7).

1. **Lying:** when we think of dishonesty, we usually think of lying. One of the reasons for the difficulty is that not very falsehood is a lie. If an engineer mistakenly conveys some test results on soil samples, he is not lying, even though he may not be telling the truth. To lie, a person must intentionally or at least knowingly convey false or misleading information. But even here complications arise. A person may give information that he believes to be false, even though it is actually true. In this case, we may be perplexed as to whether we should describe his/her action as lying. His/her intention is to lie, but what he says is actually true.
2. **Deliberate deception:** If an engineer discusses technical matter in a manner implying knowledge that he in fact does not have to impress an employer or potential customer he is certainly engaging in deliberate deception, even if he is not lying. In addition to misrepresenting one's own expertise, one can misrepresent the value of certain products or designs by praising their advantages inordinately. Such deception can sometimes have more disastrous consequences than outright lying.
3. **Withholding information:** Omitting or withholding information is another type of deceptive behavior. If a person deliberately fails to bring up some of the negative aspects of a project he is promoting to his superior, he engages in serious deception, even though he is not lying. Failing to report that you own stock in a company whose product you are recommending is a form of dishonesty.
4. **Failing to adequately promote the dissemination of information:** The paramount ethical obligation of engineers is to protect the health and safety of the public. This may require engineers not only to disclose information but to do what they can to see to it that this information is properly disseminated. Those affected must receive the information, especially if the information can avoid a disaster.
5. **Failure to seek out the Truth:** Reliable judgment may include more than avoiding dishonesty in its various forms. An honest engineer is one who is committed to finding the truth, not simply avoiding dishonesty. Suppose an engineer suspects that some of the data he has received from the test lab are inaccurate. In using the results as they are, he is not lying, nor is he concealing the

truth. But he may be irresponsible in using the results without inquiring further into their accuracy. Honesty in this positive sense is part of what is involved in being a responsible engineer.

6. **Revealing Confidential or Proprietary Information:** One can misuse the truth not only by lying or otherwise distorting or withholding it but also by disclosing it in inappropriate circumstances. Engineers in private practice might be tempted to disclose confidential information without the consent of the client. Information may be confidential if it is either (*a*) given to the engineer by the client or (*b*) discovered by the engineer in the process of work done for the client.
7. **Allowing One's judgment to be corrupted:** An important part of any professional service is professional judgment. Allowing this to be corrupted or unduly influenced by conflicts of interest or other extraneous considerations can lead to another type of misusing the truth.

Types of Dishonesty

- *Trimming:* It is the smoothing of irregularities to make the datalook extremely accurate and precise. This is a temptation to which not only engineering students but engineering researchers as well are susceptible. As one person guilty of this form of dishonesty put it, "I smoothed out the data. I took the curves and smoothed them out".
- *Cooking:* It is retaining only those results that fit the theory and discarding others. In a famous case of alleged cooking, Physicist Robert A Millikan, who later received the Nobel Prize, was accused of selecting the data he reported in his famous paper on the electronic charge. The paper was based on a series of experiments on liquid droplets. It contained an explicit statement that his findings were based on "a selected group of drops" but not "all the drops experimented upon during 60 consecutive days". Evidently, he had enough data to make a sound case without selecting the data, but he was accused of misrepresenting the data anyhow.
- *Forging:* It is inventing some or all of the research data those are reported and even reporting experiments to obtain those data those were never performed. John Darsee was a medical student doing research. He published papers based on his research there that were subsequently withdrawn due to falsified data. His research was in medicine. The disastrous effects that inaccurate data could have had on medical practice are frightening. Equally disastrous effects could occur in engineering. Imagine the consequence of using a published theory on a new lightweight bridge design that was based on falsified data.
- *Plagiarism:* It is the use of intellectual property of others without proper permission or credit. It is really a type of theft. The example is when the extended passages involving the exact words or the data of another are used without proper permission or attribution.

Intellectual Property Rights (IPR)

It is property that results from mental labor. It can be protected in several ways:

- *Trade Secrets:* These are formulas, patterns, devices, or compilations of information, which are used in business to gain an advantage over competitors who do not possess the trade secret. The formula for Coca-Cola is an example of a trade secret. Trade secrets must not be in public domain and the secrecy must be protected by the firm, because trade secrets are not protected by patents.
- *Patents:* They are the documents issued by the government those allow the owner of the patent to exclude others from making use of the patented information for 20 years from the date of filling. To obtain a patent, the invention must be new, useful, and non-obvious. As an example, the puncture-proof tire is patented.

- *Trademarks:* They are words, phrase, designs, sounds, or symbols associated with goods or services. "Coca-Cola" is a registered trademark.
- *Copyrights:* They are rights to creative products such as books, pictures, graphics, sculpture, music, movies, and computer programs. The author retains the copyright for 50 years after his/her death. It protects the expression of the ideas, but not the ideas themselves. The script of Star Wars is copyrighted.

Engineer's Moral Rights

1. Human Rights—possessed by virtue of being people or moral agents
   Examples
   - Fundamental Right to pursue legitimate personal interests
   - Right to make a living
2. Professional Rights—possessed by virtue of being professionals having special moral responsibilities
   Examples
   - Basic right of professional conscience (the right to exercise professional judgment in pursuing professional obligations)
   - Right to refuse to engage in unethical activity
   - Right to express one's professional judgment, including the right to dissent
   - Right to warn the public of dangers
   - Right to fair recognition and remuneration for professional services
3. Employee Rights—rights those apply or refer to the status of employees
   - Contractual—arising solely out of an employee contract

   Example
   - Right to receive a salary of a certain amount
   - Noncontractual—existing even if not formally recognized in a contract or company policy

   Examples
   - Right to choose outside activities
   - Right to privacy and employer confidentiality
   - Right to due process from the employer
   - Right to non-discrimination and absence of sexual harassment at the workplace

Whistle-blowing

- It occurs when an employee or former employee conveys information about a significant moral problem outside approved organizational channels (or against strong pressure) to someone in a position to take action on the problem.

Types

- In external whistle-blowing, the information is passed outside the organization
- In internal whistle-blowing, the information is conveyed to someone within the organization

Integrity

- Moral integrity is the unity of character on the basis of moral concern, and especially on the basis of honesty. The unity is consistency among our attitudes, emotions, and conduct in relation to justified moral values.

- Integrity is a bridge between responsibility in private and professional life. Morality requires that our lives be unified where fundamental values are at stake, not compartmentalized.
- Maintaining integrity is made complicated by the fact that few (if any) jobs allow a perfect mesh between one's personal ideals and one's work activities. Most professionals testify that some compromise is an inescapable, and even desirable, aspect of their careers within corporations where team-play and sharing responsibility with others are essential aspects of their work.
- Compromise can mean two things. In a negative sense it means to undermine integrity by violating one's fundamental moral principles. In a positive sense, it means to settle differences by mutual concessions or to reconcile conflicts through adjustments in attitude and conduct.

Honesty

- It has two aspects: truthfulness (meeting responsibilities concerning truth-telling) and trustworthiness (meeting responsibilities concerning trust). These two aspects of honesty are interwoven: being truthful is essential to being worthy of trust, and vice versa.
- Here is a list of even more specific virtues that truthfulness and trustworthiness imply:
  - ➢ Honesty in Acts includes not stealing, not padding expense sheets, not engaging in bribes and kickbacks. More positively, it implies respect for the property of others.
  - ➢ Honesty in Speech means not deceiving, that is, not intentionally misleading others, whether by pretending, manipulating someone's attention, lying, or withholding information that someone has a right to know.
  - ➢ Honesty in beliefs (intellectual property) means forming one's beliefs without self-deception or other forms of evading unpleasant truths and accentuating evidence favorable to one's self-esteem and biases.
  - ➢ Discretion is sensitivity to the legitimate areas of privacy of the employer or client, especially with regard to confidential information.

Reliability of Engineers

- They should disseminate information
- They should take cases only when they are properly prepared
- They should do good to society and try to enrich the profession
- They should not misuse confidence of clients
- They should not reveal confidential information
- They should not allow their judgment be corrupted
- They should not withhold truth
- They should not testify cases in which they are not competent and cannot do justice

13

Risk, Safety and Liability in Engineering

Engineering necessarily involves risk. Even if engineers did not innovate, but rather designed things in the same way year after year, the chance of producing harm would exist. New hazards could be found in products, processes, and chemicals those were once thought to be safe. But the element of risk is greatly increased because engineers are constantly involved in innovation. A bridge or building is constructed with new materials or with a new design. New machines are created and new compounds synthesized, always without full knowledge of their long-term effects on humans or the environment.

Virtually all engineering codes give a prominent place to safety, stating that engineers must hold paramount the safety, health, and welfare of the public. The relationship of risk to safety is very close. If products, structures, processes, and substances are unsafe, they subject humanbeings and the environment to undue risk. Therefore, the statements in the codes having to do with safety are relevant to the topic of risk.

For different disciplines of engineering, there are different codes of ethics for the engineers like Accreditation Board for Engineering and Technology (ABET), New York; Engineers' Council for Professional Development (ECPD), New York; National Society of Professional Engineers (NSPE), Virginia; and Institute of Electrical and Electronic Engineers (IEEE), The Institution of Engineers (India); Potarians CoE, etc.

The development of new technology is intimately connected with risk. The obligation of engineers is to be ethically responsible with regard to risk. The first step in the process of becoming ethically responsible about risk is to be aware of the fact that risk is often difficult to estimate and can be increased in ways that may be subtle and treacherous. The second step is to be aware that there are different approaches to the determination of acceptable risk. In particular, engineers have a strong bias toward quantification in their approach to risk, which may make them insufficiently sensitive to the concerns of the lay public and even the government regulator. The third step is to be aware of the legal liabilities regarding risk.

In assessing and managing risk with regard to technology, the engineer should be aware that there are at least three different approaches to risk. One such approach is that of the risk expert. Experts define risk as the product of the probability and the magnitude of harm. They define an acceptable risk in broadly utilitarian terms, where the risk must at least equal the benefit.

Engineers' responsibility to protect the health and safety of the public requires them to reduce risk when this can be done as a result of technological innovation. As new risk-reducing technology becomes available. The responsibility of engineers is to reduce risk changes. Engineers should also be aware of the ethical and professional issues regarding risk those are raised in the law. One of the issues is that the standards of proof in tort law are different from the standards of proof in science. The standard of proof in tort law is the preponderance of evidence, meaning that there is more and better evidence in favor of the plaintiff than the defendant. This is a much lower standard of proof than would be demanded in science.

Sociologist Charles Perrow confirms some of the problems by arguing that there are two characteristics of high-risk technologies those make them especially susceptible to accidents, so that we can speak of "normal accidents". These two characteristics are the "tight coupling" and the "complex interactions" of the parts of a technological system. These two factors not only make accidents likely but also difficult to predict and control. This, in turn, makes risk difficult to estimate.

Processes are tightly coupled if they are connected in such a way that one process is known to affect another and will usually do so within a short time. In tight coupling, there is usually little time to correct a failure and little likelihood of confining a failure to one part of the system, so that the whole system is damaged. A chemical plant is tightly coupled, because a failure in one part of the plant can quickly affect other parts of the plant. By contrast, a university is loosely coupled, because if one department ceases to function, the operation of the whole university is usually not threatened.

Processes can also be complexly interactive, in that the parts of the system can interact in unanticipated ways. No one dreamed that when 'A' failed, it would affect 'B'. Chemical plants are also complexly interactive, in that parts affect one another in feedback patterns those cannot always be anticipated. A post office, by contrast, is not so complexly interactive. The parts of the system are related to one another for the most part in a linear way and do not usually interact in unanticipated ways to cause the post office to cease functioning. If a post office ceases to function, it is usually because of well-understood failure.

Examples of both technical systems include not only chemical plants but also nuclear power plants, space missions, and nuclear weapon systems. Being both, they can have unanticipated failures, and there is little time to correct the problems or keep them from affecting the entire system. This makes the accidents difficult to predict and disasters difficult to avoid, once a malfunction appears.

Unfortunately, it is difficult to change both systems to make accidents less likely. To reduce complexity, decentralization is required, enabling operators to have the ability to react independently and creatively to unanticipated events. To deal with tight coupling, however, centralization is required, in which operators follow orders quickly and without question to avoid a failure or limit its effects. It may not be possible to make a system both loosely coupled and non-complex. According to Perrow, accidents in complex, tightly coupled systems are inevitable and "normal". Engineers know that, to some extent, one can include localized and autonomous automatic controls to protect against complexity failures, coupled with manual overrides to protect against tight coupling failures.

Keys to a Successful Engineering Practice

- Write a Business Plan and update it quarterly.
- Do not leap into setting up your own firm just because you have been laid off, especially if you never thought about self-employment.
- Do extensive research before starting a new business or making major decisions about the direction of your existing business.
- Be persistent and tenacious. Stick it out when the going gets tough.
- Spend sometime each day, 20%, on marketing your business.
- Learn to delegate business tasks to employees and personal tasks to spouse and children.
- Come out of dinosaur age and computerize your records, book-keeping and client files.
- Take care of yourself. Eat properly, exercise regularly. Take vacations.
- Identify 'A' clients, those people who account for your profitability. Then pamper them.
- Involve employees in solving company problems and suggesting new ways of doing tasks, getting clients, meeting deadlines, etc.

- Continually improve communication skills with employees, clients, and suppliers. Nothing can kill your business faster than misunderstandings.
- Emphasize benefits, not features, to clients when selling. Always tell them what is in it for them.
- Do not wait for a financial crisis to develop a good relationship with your banker. Develop a package of financial and professional information about the company to give it to bankers. Then update your banker quarterly about your progress and plans.
- Review your business insurance coverage annually and adjust coverage to match changing needs. To cut costs, be willing to accept a higher deductible or go with a preferred-provider organization.
- Learn networking techniques and use them everyday everywhere. This decade is known as the "Networking 2000s" because people do business with people they know.
- Survey your clients on an ongoing basis to find out how well you are satisfying their needs, representing the company, and correcting problems. Ask former clients why they left; they will shine the light on needed changes.
- Treat employees the way you want to be treated. Give them tools to do their best work. Stay out of their way. Remain flexible to their needs and reward good work.
- Do not try to be all things to all people. Small firms cannot compete with the giants by duplicating everything they do. Find the niche that you can do better than the big guys and home that advantage.
- Control costs for everything from paper clips to workers compensation insurance.
- Learn to understand your financial reports and study them. Watch for telltale signs of embezzlement. Learn to identify your most profitable services, not merely the big revenue generators.
- Add value to your services. Always give more than expected.
- Get several quotes for major purchases. It will keep existing suppliers on their toes and may turn up significant cost savings top your firm.
- Develop professional relationships, also called strategic partnerships, with other firms. You can be team members on bigger projects, refer business to each other and help each other in emergencies or when the workload gets too heavy.
- Seek professional help. Attorneys, Consultants, Professional organizations and Government Agencies are just a few sources of meaningful help.
- Be sure to laugh each day!!!

Protecting Engineers from Liability

- They have to practice their profession have a risk of failure of their design and are liable to be penalized.
- They have to use proper factor of safety to avoid risks. This may sometimes be oversafe.
- They have to quantify their risk, from the view point of layman, expert and government.

The Hippocratic Oath for Scientists, Engineers and Executives

✓ I will strive to apply my skills only with the utmost respect for the well-being of humanity, the earth and all its species;

✓ I vow to practice my profession with conscience and dignity;

✓ I will not permit considerations of nationality, politics, prejudice or material advancement to intervene between my work and this duty to present and future generations; and

✓ I take this oath solemnly, freely and upon my honour.

Note: Hippocrates, Greek Physician, Circa 400 BC

Annexure

"Multiple-Choice Questions"

(Note: All 'a's are answers)

Chapter 1: Preamble and Evolution of Indian Constitution

1. Who is the person fondly known as the Chief Architect of the Indian Constitution?
   (*a*) Dr. B.R. Ambedkar (*b*) Dr. Rajendra Prasad
   (*c*) Pandit Jawaharlal Nehru (*d*) Sri Mahatma Gandhi
2. First attempt in world to constitute a Constituent Assembly to frame a Constitution was made by
   (*a*) America (*b*) France
   (*c*) Britain (*d*) Russia
3. The first attempt by Indian to write a Constitution to India was done by a Committee headed by Motilal Nehru, which is known as:
   (*a*) Nehru Report (*b*) Swaraj Report
   (*c*) The White Paper (*d*) Independence Report
4. The idea of the Constitution of India was flashed for the first time by
   (*a*) M.K. Gandhi (*b*) M.N. Roy
   (*c*) B.R. Ambedkar (*d*) Rajendra Prasad
5. The plan of setting up of a Constituent Assembly to draw up the future Constitution for India was given by
   (*a*) The Cabinet Mission Plan (*b*) Independence Act, 1947
   (*c*) Wavell Plan (*d*) Government Committee
6. The members of the Constituent Assembly were
   (*a*) Elected by Provincial Assemblies (*b*) Elected directly by the people
   (*c*) Nominated by the government (*d*) Represented by the Princely States
7. Which of the following word was added into the Preamble of the Constitution by the 42nd Amendment Act, 1976?
   (*a*) Socialist (*b*) Sovereign
   (*c*) Federal (*d*) Republic
8. From which Constitution was a concept of a 5-year plan borrowed into our Constitution?
   (*a*) USSR (*b*) USA
   (*c*) UK (*d*) Ireland
9. The procedure of Amendment to the Constitution is borrowed from the Constitution of
   (*a*) South Africa (*b*) USA
   (*c*) Australia (*d*) Britain

10. Which countries are the best example for the Federal and Unitary Governments?
    (*a*) America and Britain (*b*) Britain and America
    (*c*) India and Russia (*d*) Canada and Australia
11. Which of the following is not a Democratic Institution of the Rig Vedic era?
    (*a*) Grama (*b*) Samithi
    (*c*) Vidatha (*d*) Sabha
12. During Medieval India, which kings first established 'Local Self Government'?
    (*a*) Cholas (*b*) Pallavas
    (*c*) Rayas of Vijayanagara (*d*) Nolambas
13. The East India Company was established in the year
    (*a*) 1600 (*b*) 1857
    (*c*) 1755 (*d*) 1873
14. Which Charter empowered the British Governors of Presidencies to make Bye-Laws, Rules, Regulations in conformity with the British laws?
    (*a*) Charter of 1726 (*b*) Charter of 1683
    (*c*) Charter of 1677 (*d*) Charter of 1600
15. Who started Dual Government in Bengal?
    (*a*) Robert Clive (*b*) Warren Hastings
    (*c*) Lord Cornwallis (*d*) Lord Dalhousie
16. Who is the first Governor General of Bengal?
    (*a*) Warren Hastings (*b*) Lord Cornwallis
    (*c*) Lord Hastings (*d*) Lord Cubbon
17. Which is the first written document in the Constitutional History of India?
    (*a*) The Regulating Act, 1773 (*b*) The Pitts India Act, 1784
    (*c*) The Charter Act of 1793 (*d*) The Charter Act of 1813
18. Which Act created for the first time in India 'Government of India'?
    (*a*) Charter Act of 1833 (*b*) Charter Act of 1813
    (*c*) Charter Act of 1793 (*d*) The Act of 1786
19. Which Act created for the first 'The Supreme Court'?
    (*a*) The Regulating Act, 1773 (*b*) The Pitts India Act, 1784
    (*c*) The Amending Act, 1781 (*d*) The Act of 1786
20. The first Law Commission was appointed in India for codification of laws under Chairmanship of
    (*a*) Lord Maculey (*b*) Lord Hastings
    (*c*) Lord Sinha (*d*) Lord Wellesly
21. Which Act made the beginning of a Parliamentary System in India?
    (*a*) Charter Act of 1853 (*b*) Charter Act of 1833
    (*c*) Charter Act of 1813 (*d*) The Act of 1786
22. Under which of the following Act, the Crown of England took the affairs of the Government of India into its own hands?
    (*a*) Government of India Act, 1858 (*b*) Government of India Act, 1935
    (*c*) Indian Councils Act, 1861 (*d*) Indian Councils Act, 1909
23. The Governor General of India was also the representative of British Crown to Princely States in India and hence was known as the
    (*a*) Viceroy of India (*b*) Secretary of State of India
    (*c*) Commander of India (*d*) Director of India

24. Which Act for the first time gave an opportunity for Indians to enter into the sphere of Legislature?
    (*a*) Indian Councils Act, 1861 (*b*) Councils Act, 1892
    (*c*) Government of India Act, 1858 (*d*) Charter Act, 1813
25. Which Act made the beginning of Electoral System in India?
    (*a*) Indian Councils Act, 1892 (*b*) Indian Councils Act, 1861
    (*c*) Government of India Act, 1858 (*d*) Charter Act, 1813
26. Which of the following Act made the Indian Legislature bicameral for the first time?
    (*a*) Government of India Act, 1919 (*b*) Government of India Act, 1935
    (*c*) Indian Councils Act, 1909 (*d*) Indian Independence Act, 1947
27. The famous Dandi March done by Gandhiji was against
    (*a*) Salt Tax (*b*) British Rule
    (*c*) Untouchability (*d*) Sati system
28. Which proposal was referred as 'Post-Dated Cheque'?
    (*a*) The Cripps Proposal (*b*) The August Offer
    (*c*) The Cabinet Proposal (*d*) Governor's Offer
29. Indian National Congress started 'Quit India Movement' after the failure of
    (*a*) Cripps Mission (b) August Offer
    (*c*) Wavell Plan (*d*) Sepoy Mutiny
30. Gandhiji gave a call to all Indians 'Do or Die', which is popularly known as
    (*a*) Quit India Movement (*b*) Independence Movement
    (*c*) Garibi Hatoah (*d*) Salt Satyagraha
31. Which Plan rejected the demand for the independent Pakistan?
    (*a*) Cabinet Mission Plan (*b*) Cripps Proposal
    (*c*) Wavell Plan (*d*) Hastings Proposal
32. Partition of British India into two independent nations India and Pakistan was done according to
    (*a*) Mountbatten Plan (*b*) Wavell Plan
    (*c*) Cabinet Mission Plan (*d*) Hastings Plan
33. The Federal features of the Indian Government was introduced by the
    (*a*) Government of India Act, 1935 (*b*) Government of India Act, 1919
    (*c*) Indian Councils Act, 1909 (*d*) Indian Independence Act, 1947
34. Which feature was borrowed by the Indian Constitution from the British Constitution?
    (*a*) All (*b*) Parliamentary System of Government
    (*c*) Rule of law (*d*) Law making procedure
35. The Constitution supports
    (*a*) Rule of Law (*b* Rule of Men
    (*c*) Rule of Individuals (*d*) Rule of Women
36. In Britain, Parliament is supreme; accordingly which among the following is supreme in India?
    (*a*) Constitution (*b*) Legislature
    (*c*) Executive (*d*) Judiciary
37. The Government of India Act 1935 provided for
    (*a*) All (*b*) Dyarchy at center
    (*c*) Provincial autonomy (*d*) Establishment of Federal Court
38. The Act of 1935 abolished
    (*a*) Dyarchy in the Provinces (*b*) Provincial autonomy
    (*c*) Dyarchy at Center (*d*) Union Territory Act

39. The Constitution of India was enacted by a Constituent Assembly set up
    (*a*) Under the Cabinet Mission Plan, 1946 (*b*) Under the Indian Independence Act, 1947
    (*c*) Through a resolution of Provisional Government (*d*) By Indian National Congress
40. The Constituent Assembly of India was created as per the proposal of
    (*a*) Cabinet Mission (*b*) Cripps Mission
    (*c*) Simon Mission (*d*) Indian National Congress
41. In which year did the Cripps Mission come to India?
    (*a*) 1942 (*b*) 1949
    (*c*) 1945 (*d*) 1935
42. The Constituent Assembly set up under the Cabinet Mission Plan had a strength of
    (a) 389 (*b*) 411
    (*c*) 298 (*d*) 487
43. The strength of the Constituent Assembly, after withdrawal of Muslim League, was reduced to
    (*a*) 299 (*b*) 329
    (*c*) 331 (*d*) 359
44. How many committees were set up by the Constituent Assembly for framing the Constitution?
    (*a*) 13 (*b*) 9
    (*c*) 17 (*d*) 7
45. Who of the following acted as the Constitutional Advisor to the Constituent Assembly?
    (*a*) B.N. Rau (*b*) B.R. Ambedkar
    (*c*) Rajendra Prasad (*d*) Sachidananda Sinha
46. Demand for a Constitution, framed by a Constituent Assembly was made by
    (*a*) Gandhiji (*b*) Nehru
    (*c*) Ambedkar (*d*) Rajendra Prasad
47. The idea of a Constituent Assembly to frame a Constitution for India was first mooted by
    (*a*) Swaraj Party in 1928 (*b*) Indian National Congress in 1936
    (*c*) Muslim League in 1942 (*d*) All Parties Conference in 1946
48. Who started with presentation of the 'Objective Resolution' on 22.01.1947?
    (*a*) Jawaharlal Nehru (*b*) Ambedkar
    (*c*) Rajendra Prasad (*d*) Gandhiji
49. When was the 'Objective Resolution' moved and adopted?
    (*a*) 13.12.1946 and 22.01.1947 (*b*) 13.12.1946 and 29.08.1947
    (*c*) 13.12.1946 and 26.11.1949 (*d*) 13.12.1946 and 22.02.1947
50. The members of the Constituent Assembly were
    (*a*) Elected by Provincial Assemblies (*b*) Nominated by the rulers of the Indian States
    (*c*) Directly elected by the people (*d*) Nominated by the Indian National Congress
51. The Constituent Assembly of India held its first meeting on
    (*a*) 09.12.1946 (*b*) 16.08.1947
    (*c*) 26.11.1947 (*d*) 26.01.1948
52. Who acted as the Provisional President of the Constituent Assembly?
    (*a*) Sachidananda Sinha (*b*) Rajagopalachari
    (*c*) Rajendra Prasad (*d*) Jawaharlal Nehru
53. The Constituent Assembly elected on 11.12.1946 as its Permanent Chairman
    (*a*) Rajendra Prasad (*b*) Jawaharlal Nehru
    (*c*) B.R. Ambedkar (*d*) K.M. Munshi

54. Who elected the Chairman of the Drafting Committee of the Constituent Assembly?
(*a*) B.R. Ambedkar (*b*) Jawaharlal Nehru
(*c*) Rajendra Prasad (*d*) Rajagopalachari
55. The Chairman of the Drafting Committee to prepare a Draft Constitution of India was
(*a*) Jawaharlal Nehru (*b*) B.R. Ambedkar
(*c*) Rajendra Prasad (*d*) Radhakrishnan. S
56. The name of Dr. B. R. Ambedkar is associated with which of the following?
(*a*) Chairman-Drafting Committee (*b*) Chairman-Constituent Assembly
(*c*) Lahore Session (*d*) Indian National Congress
57. Who among the following was not a member of the Drafting Committee?
(*a*) Rajendra Prasad (*b*) Gopalachari Ayyangar
(*c*) B.R. Ambedkar (*d*) Alladi Krishnaswami
58. Many Provisions in our Constitution have been borrowed from Government of India Act
(*a*) 1919 (*b*) 1935
(*c*) 1940 (*d*) 1947
59. The Government of India Act 1919 introduced a system of dyarchy in the provinces. 'Dyarchy' means a system of
(*a*) Double government (*b*) Bureaucratic government
(*c*) Responsible government (*d*) Nominating Government
60. When was the Constituent Assembly established to form the Constitution?
(*a*) 06.12.1946 (*b*) 26.12.1946
(*c*) 10.06.1946 (*d*) 26.11.1949
61. The Constitution of India was adopted on
(*a*) 26.11.1949 (*b*) 26.01.1950
(*c*) 26.01.1949 (*d*) 31.12.1949
62. The Constitution of India came into force on
(*a*) 26.01.1950 (*b*) 26.01.1952
(*c*) 16.08.1948 (*d*) 26.11.1949
63. The Constitution of India contains (Articles, Parts, Schedules, Amendments)
(*a*) 445, 26, 12, 92 (*b*) 395, 22, 12, 42
(*c*) 345, 20, 10, 24 (*d*) 400, 10, 8, 12
64. How much time did the Constituent Assembly took to prepare the Constitution of India?
(*a*) 02Y, 11M, 18D (*b*) 05Y, 11M, 19D
(*c*) 03Y, 10M, 07D (*d*) 04Y, 11M, 17D
65. Who had given the idea of a Constitution for India of all?
(*a*) M.N. Roy (*b*) Jawaharlal Nehru
(*c*) Gandhiji (*d*) Subhash Chandra Bose
66. The Constitution of India is
(*a*) Written and bulky document (*b*) An evolved constitution
(*c*) Based on conventions (*d*) Unwritten Document
67. The Constitution framed by a Committee consisting of the people representatives is called as
(*a*) Written Constitution (*b*) Unwritten Constitution
(*c*) Evolved Constitution (*d*) Unitary Constitution
68. Constitution which provides for a series of semi-autonomous states joined together as a nation is
(*a*) Federal Constitution (*b*) Unitary Constitution
(*c*) Rigid Constitution (*d*) Complex Constitution

69. Centralization of power is an important feature in
(*a*) Federal Constitution (*b*) Unitary Constitution
(*c*) Flexible Constitution (*d*) Rigid Constitution
70. The Constitution which can be amended by simple act of the legislature is known as
(*a*) Flexible Constitution (*b*) Unitary Constitution
(*c*) Rigid Constitution (*d*) Federal Constitution
71. Which one of the following provisions of the Constitution came into force soon after its adoption on 26.11.1949?
(*a*) All of these (*b*) Provisions relating to Citizenship
(*c*) Elections (*d*) Provisional Parliament
72. India has been described under Article 1 of the Constitution as a
(*a*) Union of States (*b*) Confederation
(*c*) Federation (*d*) Federation with strong unitary bias
73. The Constitution of India is
(*a*) Partly rigid and partly flexible (*b*) Rigid
(*c*) Very rigid (*d*) Flexible
74. The Constitution of India describes India as
(*a*) A Union of States (*b*) Unitary State
(*c*) Quasi-federal (*d*) Union Territories
75. The Indian Constitution is recognized as
(a) Federal in form and unitary in spirit (*b*) Parliamentary
(*c*) Federal (*d*) Unitary
76. The feature common of both Indian and American Federation is
(*a*) Supreme Court to interpret Constitution (*b*) Single Citizenship
(*c*) Presidential system (d) Seventh Schedule
77. The Indian Constitution came into force on 26.01.1950, hence this day is celebrated as
(*a*) Republic Day (*b*) Independence Day
(*c*) Gandhi Jayanthi (*d*) Nehru Jayanthi
78. January 26th was selected as the date for the inauguration of the Constitution because
(*a*) Congress had observed it as the Independence Day in 1930
(*b*) It was considered to be an auspicious day
(*c*) On that day the 'Quit India Movement'
(*d*) Salt Satyagraha day was started in 1942
79. 26th November, 1949 is a significant day in our constitutional history because
(*a*) The Constitution was adopted on this day
(*b*) India took a pledge of complete independence on this day
(*c*) India became Republic on this day
(*d*) The first Amendment to the Constitution was passed on this day
80. Which one of the following exercised the most profound influence on the Indian Constitution?
(*a*) The GoI Act, 1935 (*b*) The US Constitution
(*c*) British Constitution (*d*) The UN Charter
81. The Parliamentary system of Government in India is based on the pattern of
(*a*) Great Britain (*b*) France
(*c*) USA (*d*) Canada

82. To whom does the People of India gave the Constitution to
(*a*) Themselves (*b*) British
(*c*) All persons (*d*) Members of Constituent Assembly
83. The beginning word 'WE' in the Preamble refers to the
(*a*) Citizens of India (*b*) British Rulers
(*c*) Members of Constituent Assembly (*d*) All the above
84. The important test to identify the basic features of the Indian Constitution is
(*a*) Preamble (*b*) Directive Principles of State Policy
(*c*) Fundamental Rights (*d*) Fundamental Duties
85. The Preamble to the Constitution does not contain
(*a*) Adult Franchise (*b*) Democratic
(*c*) Sovereignty (*d*) Fraternity
86. India is a Sovereign Socialist Secular Democratic Republic. In the Indian Constitution, this expression occurs in
(*a*) Preamble (*b*) Fundamental Rights
(*c*) Citizenship (*d*) Directive Principles
87. The Preamble to the Constitution declares India as
(*a*) Sovereign Socialist Secular Democratic Republic
(*b*) Sovereign Democratic Republic
(*c*) Sovereign Secular Socialist Democratic Republic
(*d*) Independent Country
88. The Preamble of Indian Constitution has been amended so far
(*a*) Once (*b*) Twice
(*c*) Thrice (*d*) Four
89. The Preamble was amended by the
(*a*) 42nd Amendment (*b*) 24th Amendment
(*c*) 44th Amendment (*d*) 22nd Amendment
90. 'Fraternity' means
(*a*) Spirit of brotherhood (*b*) Fatherly treatment
(*c*) Unity and integrity of the nation (*d*) Elimination of economic injustice
91. The words "Socialist Secular" in the preamble were
(*a*) Added by 42nd Amendment (*b*) Added by the 44th Amendment
(*c*) Added by the 24th Amendment (*d*) Part of the original Preamble
92. 'Liberty' in our Preamble does not include Freedom of
(*a*) Action (*b*) Belief
(*c*) Religion (*d*) Thought
93. Which among the following is an aid to the Statutory Interpretation?
(*a*) Preamble (*b*) Fundamental Rights
(*c*) Directive Principles (*d*) Fundamental Duties
94. Which is the key to open the minds of the makers of the Constitution?
(*a*) Preamble (*b*) Fundamental Rights
(*c*) Directive Principles (*d*) Fundamental Duties
95. If the Head of the State is an elected functionary for a fixed term, it is known as ____ State.
(*a*) Republic (*b*) Federal
(*c*) Unitary (*d*) Democratic

96. The Preamble to the Indian Constitution is borrowed from the
(*a*) Objective Resolution (*b*) Britain Constitution
(*c*) Canada Constitution (*d*) Australia Constitution
97. Objective Resolution was silent as to the concept of ____ which was inserted into the Preamble by the Constituent Assembly.
(*a*) Democratic (b) Sovereignty
(c) Republic (d) Justice
98. Universal Adult Franchise shows that India is a _______ country.
(*a*) Democratic (*b*) Secular
(*c*) Sovereignty (*d*) Socialist
99. Who proposed Preamble before the Drafting Committee of the Constitution?
(*a*) Jawaharlal Nehru (*b*) Mahatma Gandhi
(*c*) B.N. Rau (*d*) B.R. Ambedkar
100. The Preamble of our Constitution reads
(*a*) We, the people of India in our Constituent Assembly adopt, enact and give to ourselves this Constitution
(*b*) We, the citizens of India in our Constituent Assembly adopt, enact and give to ourselve this Constitution
(*c*) We, the people of Constituent Assembly adopt, enact and give to ourselves this Constitution
(*d*) We, the people of Bharat in our constituent assembly adopt, enact and give to ourselves this constitution
101. India is called a 'Republic' because
(*a*) The Head of the State in India (President) is an elected head for a fixed period
(*b*) The people of India are sovereign
(c) The Ministers are responsible to Parliament
(*d*) Ministers hold Office during the pleasure of the President
102. 'Sovereignty' in a democracy rests with the
(*a*) People (*b*) Prime Minister
(*c*) President (*d*) Central Government
103. The Preamble secures Justice, Liberty, Equality and Fraternity to
(*a*) All citizens (*b*) All persons
(*c*) Residents of India (*d*) Non-residents of India
104. The Preamble of the Constitution indicates
(*a*) The source of the Indian Constitution
(*b*) The extent of governments power to make law
(*c*) The facilities to be given to backward class people
(*d*) The circumstances under which the Constitution can be amended
105. It is not the objective enshrined in the Preamble to
(*a*) secure shelter and proper livelihood to all
(*b*) equality of status
(*c*) liberty of thought and expression
(*d*) social, economic and political justice
106. The idea of social, economic and political justice has been taken from _____ Revolution.
(*a*) French (*b*) Russian
(*c*) American (*d*) Greek

107. The concept of equality and fraternity has been taken from _____ Revolution.
(*a*) Russian (*b*) Greek
(*c*) American (*d*) French

108. Which of the following is described as the 'Soul of the Constitution'?
(*a*) Preamble (*b*) Fundamental Rights
(*c*) Fundamental Duties (*d*) Directive Principles

109. Which one of the following is not treated as part of the Constitution?
(*a*) Fundamental Duties (*b*) Preamble
(*c*) Fundamental Rights (*d*) Directive Principles

110. Democracy in India rests on the fact that
(*a*) People have the right to choose and change the government
(*b*) The Constitution is written
(*c*) There are fundamental rights (*d*) There are Directive Principles of State Policy

111. The word 'Democracy' is derived from the Greek words
(*a*) Demos and Kratos (*b*) Demos and Cartos
(*c*) Democratos (*d*) Democritic

112. India opted for a Federal form of government because of
(*a*) Linguistic and regional diversity (*b*) Vast territory
(*c*) Cultural Integration (*d*) Diversified Country

113. What is the chief (ultimate) source of political power (authority) in India?
(*a*) People (*b*) Constitution
(*c*) Parliament (*d*) Supreme Court

114. A Flexible Constitution
(*a*) Can be amended easily
(*b*) Cannot be amended easily
(*c*) Can be amended only after undergoing a special procedure
(*d*) Does not allow frequent changes

115. The Judiciary acts as an guardian of the Constitution in a
(*a*) Federal government (*b*) Unitary government
(*c*) Flexible constitution (*d*) Evolved constitution

116. India is a Secular state because
(*a*) It is described so in the preamble of the constitution
(*b*) It is an anti-religion
(*c*) It gives facilities to those who do not believe in any religion
(*d*) It is dominated by believers in a particular religion

117. Our Constitution has laid emphasis on securing social, economic and political justice to all the citizens of the country. These objectives are aimed at securing a
(*a*) Welfare State (*b*) Secular State
(*c*) Democratic government (*d*) Happy and Prosperous State

118. Modern States are generally considered as
(*a*) Welfare States (*b*) Police States
(*c*) Dictatorial States (*d*) Indepndent States

119. A State which does not promote or interfere in the affairs of religion is referred to as
(*a*) Secular (*b*) Socialist
(*c*) Democratic (*d*) Sovereign

120. The Constitution is a
   (*a*) Dynamic Law (*b*) Fixed Law
   (*c*) Rigid Law (*d*) Static Law
121. The Constitution of India provides
   (*a*) Single citizenship (*b*) Double citizenship
   (*c*) Multiple citizenship (*d*) No citizenship
122. The Constitution provides
   (*a*) All of these (*b*) Responsibilities
   (*c*) Limitations (*d*) Powers
123. The fundamental organs of the State are established by
   (*a*) Constitution (*b*) Parliament
   (*c*) Government (*d*) President
124. Detailed provisions regarding acquisition and termination of Indian citizenship are contained in
   (*a*) Act passed by the Parliament in 1955 (*b*) The Indian Independence Act, 1947
   (*c*) Part VII of the Constitution (*d*) Parliamentary Ordinance
125. Which of the following is not a condition for becoming a Indian citizen? [Citizenship by]
   (*a*) Acquiring property (*b*) Birth
   (*c*) Descent (*d*) Naturalization
126. A person can lose citizenship through
   (*a*) All of these (*b*) Termination
   (*c*) Renunciation (*d*) Deprivation
127. The aims and objectives of the Constitution have been enshrined in
   (*a*) The Preamble (*b*) Chapter of Fundamental Rights
   (*c*) Chapter on Fundamental Duties (*d*) The Chapter on Directive Principles of State Policy
128. The Office of the Governor General of India was for the first time created under
   (*a*) Regulating Act, 1773 (*b*) Indian Councils Act, 1861
   (*c*) Dundas Bill, 1783 (*d*) State Councils Act, 1890
129. According to the Act of 1858, the territory was divided into
   (*a*) Provinces (*b*) States
   (*c*) Zones (*d*) Districts
130. When did the British Crown assume sovereignty over India from East India Company?
   (*a*) 1858 (*b*) 1885
   (*c*) 1853 (*d*) 1847
131. Morley-Minto Reforms were implemented by the Indian Councils Act in
   (*a*) 1909 (*b*) 1892
   (*c*) 1861 (*d*) 1900
132. Which of the following is also known as the Act of 1919?
   (*a*) Montague-Chelmsford Reform Act (*b*) Regulating Act
   (*c*) Montague-Morley Act (*d*) Land Revenue Act
133. Under which of the following Act was Provincial Autonomy introduced in India?
   (*a*) Government of India Act, 1935 (*b*) Indian Councils Act, 1909
   (*c*) Indian Councils Act, 1882 (*d*) Indian Councils Act, 1861
134. Who made the Constitution of India?
   (*a*) The Constituent Assembly (*b*) The Indian Parliament
   (*c*) The British Parliament (*d*) All State Assemblies

135. A Constituent Assembly is convened to
(*a*) Frame the Constitution of the country (*b*) Pass the budget of the country
(*c*) Change ordinary law (*d*) To make ordinary law policy

136. The Constituent Assembly was set up to under the
(*a*) Cabinet Mission Plan of 1946 (*b*) Government of India Act of 1919
(*c*) Government of India Act of 1935 (*d*) Indian Independence Act of 1947

137. Which party was not associated with the Constituent Assembly of India?
(*a*) The Communist Party (*b*) Hindu Mahasabha
(*c*) Schedule Castes Federation (*d*) All of these

138. The Republic of India established by the Constitution is not
(*a*) Unitary (*b*) Sovereign
(*c*) Socialist (*d*) Secular

139. The mind and ideals of the framers of the Constitution are reflected in the
(*a*) Preamble (*b*) Directive Principles of State Policy
(*c*) Fundamental Rights (*d*) All of these

140. In our Constitution, what justice is not given to the citizens?
(*a*) Technical (*b*) Social
(*c*) Economic (*d*) Political

141. The present Five-year Plan (2002-2007) is
(*a*) 10th (*b*) 9th
(*c*) 11th (*d*) 12th

142. 'Amend' means
(*a*) Remove the difficulties (*b*) Make the meaning more clear
(*c*) Make the object of the act more clear (*d*) Omit

143. 'Enact' means
(*a*) Pass a law (*b*) Single action
(*c*) Single chapter (*d*) Rectify the mistakes in the law

144. Who advocated 'Grama Swarajya' for the growth of the villages?
(*a*) Gandhiji (*b*) Nehru
(*c*) Ambedkar (*d*) Shastri

145. 'Poornaswarajya' was declared as the goal of the Congress in December 1929 in the
(*a*) Lahore Session (*b*) Bombay Session
(*c*) Fazipur Session (*d*) Bangalore Session

146. Our Constitution prohibits _____
(*a*) Untouchability (*b*) Liquor
(*c*) Politics (*d*) Freedom

147. The Constitution declared India as a Republic on _______.
(*a*) 26.01.1950 (*b*) 26.11.1949
(*c*) 15.08.1947 (*d*) 02.10.1950

148. Who has given the following statement: "Democracy means a Government of the people, by the people and for the people"?
(*a*) Abraham Lincoln (*b*) Jawaharlal Nehru
(*c*) M.K. Gandhiji (*d*) Gopalakrishna Gokhale

149. Which one of the following features was borrowed by the framers of the Constitution from the US Constitution?
(*a*) All of these (*b*) Judicial Review
(*c*) Fundamental Rights (*d*) Removal of Judges of the Supreme Court
150. The ideals of liberty, equality and fraternity enshrined in the Preamble of the Constitution were adopted under inspiration from
(*a*) The French Revolution (*b*) The Russian Revolution
(*c*) The American Declaration of Independence
(*d*) The UN Charter
151. What is the chief force of political power in India?
(*a*) The People (*b*) The Constitution
(*c*) The Parliament (*d*) The Parliament and State Legislatures
152. The Constitution describes the Indian Union as
(*a*) India i.e., Bharat (*b*) India i.e., Bharatvarsha
(*c*) India i.e., Hindustan (*d*) Bharat i.e., India
153. The Constitution of India describes India as
(*a*) Union of States (*b*) Federation
(*c*) Quasi-federal (*d*) Group of Union Territories
154. The two persons who played a vital role in the integration of princely states were
(*a*) Sardar Patel and V. P. Menon (*b*) Sardar Patel and Nehru
(*c*) Sardar Patel and Rajendra Prasad (*d*) Sardar Patel and K. M. Munshi
155. The States were reorganized on linguistic basis in
(*a*) 1956 (*b*) 1951
(*c*) 1947 (*d*) 1949
156. Which State enjoys the distinction of being the first linguistic state of India?
(*a*) Andhra Pradesh (*b*) West Bengal
(*c*) Tamil Nadu (*d*) Punjab
157. The Indian Federal system is modeled on the Federal system of
(*a*) Canada (*b*) USA
(*c*) Australia (*d*) New Zealand
158. India is known as Parliamentary Democracy because
(*a*) Executive is responsible to the Parliament
(*b*) MPs are directly elected by the people
(*c*) President is not MP
(*d*) Powers have been clearly distributed between Center and States
159. The Indian State is regarded as federal because the Indian Constitution provides for
(*a*) Sharing of power between Center and States
(*b*) Written Constitution
(*c*) Rigid Constitution (*d*) Dual Judiciary
160. In which Case did Supreme Court hold that the Preamble was a part of the Constitution?
(*a*) Keshavananda Bharti Case (*b*) Golaknath Case
(*c*) Berubari Case (*d*) Manipal Case
161. In which case did Supreme Court hold that Preamble was not a part of the Constitution?
(*a*) Berubari Case (*b*) Keshavananda Bharti Case
(*c*) Golaknath Case (*d*) Maneka Gandhi Case

162. The Ninth Schedule
   (*a*) Was added to the Constitution by the 1st Amendment
   (*b*) Formed part of the original Constitution
   (*c*) Was added to the Constitution by the 24th Amendment
   (*d*) Was added to the Constitution by the 42nd Amendment
163. Which Schedule details the boundaries of the states and the union territories?
   (*a*) I (*b*) VI
   (*c*) VII (*d*) VIII
164. The details of salaries, allowances, etc of the President, Vice-President, Speaker, judges of Supreme Court, etc. are provided in Schedule
   (*a*) II (*b*) III
   (*c*) IV (*d*) VI
165. Which Schedule gives details regarding the subjects included in the three lists—Central, State and Concurrent Lists?
   (*a*) VII (*b*) VIII
   (*c*) IX (*d*) X
166. In the Indian Constitution
   (*a*) There are three lists: the union list, the state list and the concurrent list
   (*b*) The powers of the union and the state governments are defined in the two separate lists
   (*c*) The powers of the union government are defined while the residuary powers belong to the state
   (*d*) The powers of the state are defined while residuary are defined while the residuary powers belong to the state
167. Which of the following statements is correct?
   (*a*) Rule of Law is a basic feature of the Constitution which cannot be amended under Article 368 of the Constitution
   (*b*) Rule of Law is one of the Indian Constitution which can be amended under Article 368 of the Constitution
   (*c*) Rule of Law is only an implied feature of the Indian Constitution
   (*d*) All of these
168. As per Article 262 of Indian Constitution, disputes relating to waters shall be solved by
   (*a*) Parliament (*b*) Supreme Court
   (*c*) States involved in dispute (*d*) President
169. Which one of the following declares India as a Secular State?
   (*a*) Preamble of the Constitution (*b*) DPSP
   (*c*) FRs (*d*) 9th Schedule
170. By which of the following a new state is formed?
   (*a*) Constitutional Amendment (*b*) LS
   (*c*) People's Referendum (*d*) President
171. The final interpreter to Indian Constitution is
   (*a*) Supreme Court (*b*) Parliament
   (*c*) President (*d*) Speaker of LS
172. Every Amendment of Indian Constitution has to be approved by the
   (*a*) Parliament (*b*) States
   (*c*) People (*d*) Union Territories

173. Which one of the following states has a separate Constitution?
    (*a*) Jammu & Kashmir (*b*) Nagaland
    (*c*) West Bengal (*d*) Sikkim
174. Apart from the Jammu & Kashmir, which other State has been provided special protection in certain matters?
    (*a*) Nagaland (*b*) Meghalaya
    (*c*) Himachal Pradesh (*d*) Tripura
175. Article 356 of the Constitution of India deals with
    (*a*) Proclamation of President's Rule in a State
    (*b*) Autonomy of States
    (*c*) Removal of the Chief Minister (*d*) Appointment of the Governor
176. The State of Jammu & Kashmir was accorded special status under
    (*a*) Article 370 (*b*) Article 356
    (*c*) Article 268 (*d*) Article 365
177. The Constitution of Jammu & Kashmir was framed by
    (*a*) A special Constituent Assembly setup by the state
    (*b*) A special Constituent Assembly setup by Parliament
    (*c*) The same Constituent Assembl which framed Indian Constitution
    (*d*) King of Kashmir
178. The Constitution of Jammu & Kashmir came into force on
    (*a*) 26.01.1957 (*b*) 15.08.1952
    (*c*) 26.01.1952 (*d*) 26.01.1950
179. The special status of Jammu & Kashmir implies that the State has separate
    (*a*) Constitution (*b*) Defence force
    (*c*) Judiciary (*d*) Revenue Rules
180. In case of Jammu & Kashmir, an Amendment to the Constitution become applicable
    (*a*) Only after the President issued the necessary orders under the Article 370
    (*b*) Only after it is ratified by the State Assembly by two-third majority
    (*c*) Only after it is ratified by the State Legislature
    (*d*) Automatically
181. Under the Parliamentary system of the Government,
    (*a*) The Cabinet as a whole is responsible to the Legislature
    (*b*) The members of the Cabinet are not from the Legislature
    (*c*) The Legislature cannot be dissolved earlier
    (*d*) The Prime Minister is the Head of the State
182. Who is authorized to initiate a Bill for Constitutional Amendment?
    (*a*) Either House of Parliament (*b*) Both Parliament and State Legislatures
    (*c*) Lok Sabha only (*d*) Rajya Sabha only
183. The power of Parliament to amend the Constitution
    (*a*) Includes power to amend by way of addition, variation or repeal
    (*b*) Is not procedurally limited and restricted
    (*c*) Is unrestricted by any inherent and implied limitations
    (*d*) Is extra-constitutional authority
184. Which Article empowers the Parliament to amend the Indian Constitution?
    (*a*) 368 (*b*) 311
    (*c*) 13 (*d*) 245

185. Ninth Schedule to the Constitution is added by way of ____ Constitutional Amendment.
(*a*) 1st (*b*) 7th
(*c*) 24th (*d*) 42nd

186. What is contained in the Tenth Schedule of the Indian Constitution?
(*a*) Provisions regarding disqualification on grounds of defection
(*b*) Languages recognized by the Constitution
(*c*) Laws those can be challenged in any Court of Law
(*d*) Forms of oath or affirmation

Chapter 2: Fundamental Rights (FRs)

1. India is referred as ____ under the Indian Constitution.
(*a*) Bharat (*b*) Hindustan
(*c*) Country (*d*) Indus

2. Who is empowered to admit a new State to the Union of India?
(*a*) Parliament (*b*) Prime Minister
(*c*) President (*d*) Supreme Court

3. Which important Human Right is protected in Article 21 of our Constitution?
(*a*) Right to Life and Liberty (*b*) Right to Equality
(*c*) Right to Freedom of Speech and Expression (*d*) Right to Freedom of Religion

4. The Constitution confers a special authority for the enforcement of FRs on the
(*a*) Supreme Court (*b*) Parliament
(*c*) President (*d*) State Legislature

5. The FRs of the Indian Citizen in our Constitution are contained in (OR) FRs are guaranteed under ____ of the Indian Constitution.
(*a*) Part III (*b*) Part IV
(*c*) Part V (*d*) Part VI

6. Under Article 368, Parliament has no power to repeal FRs because they are
(*a*) Basic Structure of Constitution (*b*) Human Rights
(*c*) Enshrined under Part III (*d*) All of these

7. FRs can be claimed against the
(*a*) State (*b*) Judiciary
(*c*) Individuals (*d*) All of these

8. The FRs, which cannot be suspended even during the emergency, are Articles ____.
(*a*) 20 & 21 (*b*) 14 & 15
(*c*) 23 & 24 (*d*) 29 & 30

9. Clause (1) of Article 13 is applicable only to
(*a*) Pre-constitutional laws (*b*) Post-constitutional laws
(*c*) Personal laws (*d*) Corporate laws

10. Original Constitution classified FRs into seven categories but now there are
(*a*) Six (*b*) Five
(*c*) Eight (*d*) Regrouped into social, economic and political

11. India's desire for civil liberties started from the struggle for independence against the
(*a*) British Rule (*b*) Portuguese Rule
(*c*) Spanish Rule (*d*) Dutch Rule

12. India borrowed the idea of incorporating FRs in the Constitution from
    (*a*) USA (*b*) France
    (*c*) China (*d*) Great Britain
13. The concept of Single Citizenship is borrowed from the Constitution of
    (*a*) Britain (*b*) Australia
    (*c*) Canada (*d*) America
14. The concept of Dual Citizenship in the Union of India was recommended by _____ Committee.
    (*a*) L.M. Singhvi (*b*) Ashok Mehta
    (*c*) Raj-Mannar (*d*) Balwantrai Mehta
15. Under which Article of the Indian Constitution, citizenship of a person can be determined at the commencement of the Constitution?
    (*a*) 5 (*b*) 6
    (*c*) 8 (*d*) 9
16. Which Article describes the persons voluntarily acquiring Citizenship of a foreign state not to be an Indian Citizen?
    (*a*) 9 (*b*) 10
    (*c*) 11 (*d*) 12
17. Who is authorized to lay down qualifications to acquire the citizenship?
    (*a*) President (*b*) Parliament
    (*c*) Prime Minister (*d*) Speaker
18. Which of the following is a qualification to acquire citizenship by naturalization?
    (*a*) A person is in service of Government of India from 12 months
    (*b*) A person engaged in trade with the Indian citizen
    (*c*) A person born in India
    (*d*) A person who has completed his graduation within the territory of India
19. FRs are not applicable to
    (*a*) Armed Forces (*b*) Prime Minister
    (*c*) President (*d*) No such discrimination
20. Which Article of the Constitution empowers the Parliament to enact the provisions for acquisition and termination of citizenship?
    (*a*) 11 (*b*) 10
    (*c*) 6 (*d*) 5
21. By which FR other FRs is protected?
    (*a*) Right to Constitutional Remedies (*b*) Right to Equality
    (*c*) Right to Freedom (*d*) None
22. Right to Property is a legal right under the Article ____.
    (*a*) 300A (*b*) 300
    (*c*) 301 (*d*) 31
23. Which of the following is not a FR? [Right to]
    (*a*) Property (*b*) Assemble peacefully
    (*c*) Move freely (*d*) Constitutional remedies
24. Which of the following has ceased to be a FR in the Indian Constitution? [Right to}
    (*a*) Property (*b*) Freedom of speech
    (*c*) Form educational institutions (*d*) None of these

25. Which among the following is not a FR? [Right to]
(*a*) Strike (*b*) Against exploitation
(*c*) Equality (*d*) Freedom of religion
26. Which FR has been a subject of maximum controversy and litigation? [Right to]
(*a*) Property (*b*) Freedom of Speech
(*c*) Constitutional remedies (*d*) Religion
27. The Right to private property was dropped from the list of FRs by the (OR) Right to property took the shape of legal right by way of
(*a*) 44th Amendment (*b*) 42nd Amendment
(*c*) 40th Amendment (*d*) 24th Amendment
28. The Right to equality guaranteed by the Indian Constitution does not include
(*a*) Economic equality (*b*) Equality before Law
(*c*) Equal Protection of Law (*d*) Social equality
29. 'Equality before the Law' implies
(*a*) Absence of any privilege in favor of any person
(*b*) Equal opportunity in social and economic matters to all citizens
(*c*) That the law should be same both in case of men and women
(*d*) That all the religions should be treated equally
30. Which Resolution for the first time expressed the concept of equality before the law?
(*a*) Swaraj Bill (*b*) Simon Commission
(*c*) Cabinet Mission (*d*) Minto Commission
31. The FRs of the Indian Citizen were
(*a*) Enshrined in Original Constitution (*b*) Outlined in Act passed by Parliament in 1952
(*c*) Incorporated in the Constitution by 42nd Amendment
(*d*) Added by 44th Amendment
32. Which one of the FRs was described by Dr. B.R. Ambedkar as the Heart and Soul of the Constitution? [Right to]
(*a*) Constitutional Remedies (*b*) Property
(*c*) Religion (*d*) Freedom and Speech
33. Which of the following confers upon the citizens the right to approach a court of law for the protection and restoration of FRs? (Right)
(*a*) Constitutional remedies (*b*) Right against exploitation
(*c*) Equality (*d*) Liberty
34. The Right to Constitutional Remedies are
(*a*) Fundamental Rights (*b*) Natural Rights
(*c*) Legal Rights (*d*) Constitutional Rights
35. The Constitutional remedies under the Article 32 can be suspended by the
(*a*) Parliament (*b*) President
(*c*) Prime Minister (*d*) Supreme Court
36. Writs can be issued for the enforcement of FRs by the
(*a*) Supreme Court (*b*) Parliament
(*c*) President (*d*) Prime Minister
37. Which one of the following FRs is restrained by the Preventive Detention Act? [Right to]
(*a*) Freedom (*b*) Religion
(*c*) Equality (*d*) Constitutional Remedies

38. Who enjoys the right to impose reasonable restrictions on the FRs of Indian citizen? (OR) Who has the power to empower the Courts other than the Supreme and High Courts to issue writs and order for the enforcement of the FRs?
    (*a*) Parliament (*b*) Supreme Court
    (*c*) President (*d*) Prime Minister
    (*e*) Chief Justice of India
39. Who can abridge any FR without damaging or destroying the basic features of the Constitution?
    (*a*) Parliament (*b*) President
    (*c*) Prime Minister (*d*) Council of Ministers
40. Which one of the following Courts is responsible for the enforcement of FRs?
    (*a*) Supreme Court (*b*) High Courts
    (*c*) District and Sessions Courts (*d*) None of these
41. Which of the following is the guardian of the FRs of the citizens? (OR) Who is the Protector and Guarantor of the FRs?
    (*a*) Supreme Court (*b*) President
    (*c*) Parliament (*d*) Lok Sabha
42. Any violation of FRs can be presented to
    (*a*) Both Supreme and High Court (*b*) High Court only
    (*c*) Supreme Court only (*d*) Any Court within of India
43. Who is authorized to impose restrictions on FRs?
    (*a*) Legislature (*b*) Judiciary
    (*c*) Executive (*d*) All of these
44. The FRs of the Indian citizen
    (*a*) Can be suspended by the President during national emergency
    (*b*) Can be suspended by the President during all types of emergencies
    (*c*) Can be suspended by the President with the prior approval of Supreme Court conditions
    (*d*) Can be suspended by the President under any conditions
45. FRs
    (*a*) Those basic conditions of social life without which a citizen cannot be at his/her best self
    (*b*) The Rights of the Police
    (*c*) The Rights of the rulers (*d*) The Rights of Peticians
46. The FRs ensure the protection of
    (*a*) Citizens against arbitrary rule (*b*) People against exploitation by traders
    (*c*) The pride of citizens (*d*) Law & Order in the country
47. Our Constitution grants to the citizens ______ FRs
    (*a*) Six (*b*) Five
    (*c*) Ten (*d*) Seven
48. Ultra vires means
    (*a*) Without authority (*b*) Procedural error
    (*c*) Error in fact finding (*d*) Error of law
49. Who are not entitled to form Union?
    (*u*) Police (*b*) Students
    (*c*) Teachers (*d*) Entrepreneurs
50. By the Citizenship Act of 1955, when he/she will be loosing the Citizenship?
    (*a*) All of these (*b*) Deprivation
    (*c*) Termination (*d*) Renunciation

51. Who quoted 'Child of today is the Citizen of tomorrow'?
(*a*) Jawaharlal Nehru (*b*) Vallabhai Patel
(*c*) Gandhiji (*d*) B.R. Ambedkar

52. Generally, the census is conducted for _____ year(s)
(*a*) 10 (*b*) 9
(*c*) 5 (*d*) 1

53. Who quoted 'Freedom is my Birth Right'? (*b*) The Rights of the Police
(*a*) Lokamanya Tilak (*b*) Sardar Patel
(*c*) Jawaharlal Nehru (*d*) Mahatma Gandhiji

54. What is the minimum age in years for casting vote?
(*a*) 18 (*b*) 19
(*c*) 20 (*d*) 21

55. Which Article and Amendment changes the right to vote from 21 to 18 years?
(*a*) 326 & 61st (*b*) 365 & 61st
(*c*) 320 & 16th (*d*) 228 & 16th

56. 'Creamy Layer' means
(*a*) Persons having higher incomes (*b*) Highly-cultured persons
(*c*) Persons holding high posts (*d*) Highly-educated persons

57. 'Backward class (BC)' can be classified into
(*a*) Most BC (*b*) Highly BC
(*c*) More BC (*d*) Moderately BC

58. Mandal Commission deals with
(*a*) Reservation for backward class people (*b*) Rights of the minority
(*c*) Laws relating to sexual harassment (*d*) Laws relating to child labour

59. This is one of the grounds for classification
(*a*) Annual income (*b*) Taxation
(*c*) Social status (*d*) Religion

60. 'Equal Protection of Law' means
(*a*) The same law shall apply to all who are similarly situated
(*b*) The same law shall apply to all, irrespective of religion, race, caste
(*c*) There should not be any discrimination while protecting men and women
(*d*) Laws applicable to backward class and minority people

61. Seats in Educational Institutions can be reserved for
(*a*) Socially and educationally backward class people
(*b*) Socially backward class people
(*c*) Educationally backward class people (*d*) Muslims

62. Minimum percentage of reservation in a educational institution is
(*a*) 50% (*b*) 60%
(*c*) 70% (*d*) 75%

63. Minority may be
(*a*) Linguistic or religious (*b*) Regional or national
(*c*) Racial or regional (*d*) National or racial

64. This is not the ground to impose restriction on Right of freedom of speech and expression
(*a*) Public nuisance (*b*) Friendly relations with foreign states
(*c*) Defamation (*d*) Incitement to an offence

65. Which of the following courts is responsible for the enforcement of FRs?
(*a*) Supreme Court (*b*) High Court
(*c*) District and Sessions Court (*d*) Any Court
66. Which of the following statements is correct?
(*a*) FRs are superior to the DPSP (*b*) DPSP are superior to FRs
(*c*) There is no relationship between FRs and DPSP
(*d*) None of these
67. In which case did the Supreme Court restrict the authority of Parliament to amend FRs and declared these rights to be absolute, permanent and unalterable?
(*a*) Golak Nath Case (*b*) Keshavananda Bharti Case
(*c*) Minerva Mills Case (*d*) None
68. In the famous Keshavananda Bharti vs. State of Kerala Case, the Supreme Court asserts the power of the parliament to amend the Constitution under Article 368 subject to
(*a*) Certain implied and inherent limitation of not amending the Basic Structure of the Constitution
(*b*) No limitation whatsoever
(*c*) Can amend even the Basic Structure (*d*) None of these
69. 'Rule of Law which permeates the entire fabric of the Indian Constitution excludes arbitrariness'. This principle is laid down in
(*a*) Maneka Gandhi vs. Union Government Case
(*b*) Keshavananda Bharti Case
(*c*) Sunil Batra vs. Delhi Administration Case
(*d*) Vishaka vs. State of Rajasthan Case
70. The protection guaranteed under Article 21 is available even to convicts in jails. The convicts are not by mere reasons of their conviction deprived of the entire FRs which they otherwise possess. This is the principle laid down in
(*a*) Sunil Batra vs. Delhi Administration Case
(*b*) Vishaka vs. State of Rajasthan Case
(*c*) Maneka Gandhi vs. Union Government Case
(*d*) Keshavananda Bharti vs. State of Kerala Case
71. Gender equality includes protection from sexual harassment and right to work with dignity, which is universally recognized as basic Human Right. This principle is laid down in
(*a*) Vishaka vs. State of Rajasthan Case (*b*) Maneka Gandhi vs. Union Government Case
(*c*) Indra Sawhaney vs. Union of India (*d*) MC Mehta vs. Union of India
72. The Supreme Court held that the nuisance caused by the pollution of the river Ganga is a public nuisance which is wide spread and affecting the lives of large number of persons and therefore any particular person can take proceedings to stop it. This PIL is
(*a*) MC Mehta vs. Union of India (1988) (*b*) MC Mehta vs. Union of India (1987)
(*c*) DS Nakara vs. Union of India of India
(*d*) Peoples Union for Democratic Rights vs. Union
73. Charging capitation fees for admission to educational institutions is illegal and amounted to denial of citizen's right to education. This principle is laid down in
(*a*) Mohin Jain vs. State of Karnataka Case
(*b*) MC Mehta vs. Union of India Case
(*c*) Minerva Mills vs. Union of India Case
(*d*) DS Nakara vs. Union of India Case

74. The right to establish an educational institution and imparting education is not a commercial activity. This principle is laid down in
    (*a*) Unnikrishnan vs. State of Andhra Pradesh Case
    (*b*) Mohin Jain vs. State of Karnataka Case
    (*c*) Minerva Mills vs. Union of India Case
    (*d*) DS Nakara vs. Union of India Case
75. The principle of Judicial review of President's Rule in State under the Article 356 is laid down in
    (*a*) SR Bommai vs. Union of India
    (*b*) Minerva Mills vs. Union of India
    (*c*) Maneka Gandhi vs. Union Government
    (*d*) Keshavananda Bharti vs. State of Kerala
76. Who among the following has voting rights?
    (*a*) An adult resident citizen of a State (*b*) A citizen of a State
    (*c*) Any inhabitant of a State (*d*) An adult literate citizen of a State
77. The right to strike is
    (*a*) None of these (*b*) Directive Principles of State Policy
    (*c*) Fundamental Rights (*d*) Fundamental Duties
78. Which one is not a FR?
    (*a*) The right to strike (*b*) The right against exploitation
    (*c*) The right to equality (*d*) The right to freedom of religion
79. Which one of the following FRs has been subject of maximum litigation since the inauguration of the Constitution? (Right to)
    (*a*) Property (*b*) Freedom of speech
    (*c*) Constitutional remedies (*d*) Right against exploitation
80. The rule of Equality before law is not applicable to
    (*a*) Governor of State (*b*) Union Law Minister
    (*c*) Chief Justice of India (*d*) Prime Minister
81. Right to Equality is guaranteed under the Article
    (*a*) 14 (*b*) 13
    (*c*) 16 (*d*) 15
82. Article 14 guarantees equality before the law to
    (*a*) All persons (*b*) Citizens of India
    (*c*) All persons residing in the territory of India
    (*d*) Persons of Indian origin
83. 'Right to Equality' means
    (*a*) Permits the state to make special provisions for women, children and backward classes
    (*b*) Permits the state to make discrimination on ground of residence
    (*c*) Prevents the state from making special provisions for women, children and backward classes
    (*d*) Permits the state to nationalize all means of production and distribution
84. Equal opportunity in matters of public employment is guaranteed under the Article
    (*a*) 16 (*b*) 17
    (*c*) 14 (*d*) 15
85. Which among the following FRs abolishes discrimination?
    (*a*) Equality (*b*) Freedom of religion
    (*c*) Against exploitation (*d*) Cultural and Educational

86. Indian Constitution says 'untoucability' is abolished and its practice in any form is prohibited. This is provided under (Right to)
(*a*) Equality (*b*) Liberty
(*c*) Right against exploitation (*d*) Constitutional remedies
87. Untouchability is associated with _______ inequality.
(*a*) Social (*b*) Political
(*c*) Economic (*d*) Religious
88. 'Right to Freedom' can be restricted in the interest of
(*a*) All of these (*b*) Security of the state
(*c*) Friendly relations with foreign states (*d*) Public order
89. This is not the ground to impose restriction on the right of freedom of speech and expression.
(*a*) Law and order (*b*) National security
(*c*) Contempt of court (*d*) Morality or decency
90. Which one of the following right conferred by the Constitution is also available to non-citizens?
(*a*) Right to constitutional remedies
(*b*) Freedom to acquire property or to carry on any occupation, trade or business
(*c*) Freedom to move, reside and settle in any part of India
(*d*) Freedom of speech, assembly and association
91. The Sikhs in India are permitted to carry Kirpans. Under which FR are they permitted to do so?
(*a*) Right to freedom of religion (*b*) Right to freedom
(*c*) Right to life and liberty (*d*) Personal Rights
92. Freedom of Speech under the Indian Constitution is subject to reasonable restrictions on the grounds of protection of
(*a*) Sovereignty and integrity of the country (*b*) Dignity of the Office of the Prime Minister
(*c*) Dignity of the Council of Ministers (*d*) All the above
93. Which one of the following is considered as Bulwark of Democracy? (Right to)
(*a*) Speech (*b*) Form Association
(*c*) Move freely (*d*) Reside in any place
94. One of the restrictions of freedom of speech and expression is
(*a*) Contempt of Court (*b*) Degrading the Office of the President
(*c*) Spreading discontent among the citizens
(*d*) Holding unlawful assembly
95. At present, the Right to Property is a
(*a*) Human Right (*b*) Legal Right
(*c*) Fundamental Right (*d*) Natural Right
96. Which one of the following is not a FR? (Right to)
(*a*) Property (*b*) Freedom
(*c*) Equality (*d*) Cultural and Education
97. The main objective of the Cultural and Educational Rights granted to the citizens is to
(*a*) Help the minorities to conserve their culture
(*b*) Evolve a single integrated Indian culture
(*c*) Preserve the rich cultural heritage of India
(*d*) All of these
98. A person can move to Supreme Court directly in vent of violation of FRs under Article
(*a*) 32 (*b*) 34
(*c*) 19 (*d*) 20

99. A citizen's FRs are protected
(*a*) When the citizen approaches the court for remedy
(*b*) Automatically by the Supreme Court
(*c*) By Parliament when the issue is brought before it by the executive
(*d*) By the executive when the citizen brings the issue before it

100. The FRs of a citizen can be suspended by the
(*a*) President during a National Emergency
(*b*) Parliament through a law enacted by two-third majority
(*c*) Supreme Court (*d*) President during Natural Calamity

101. For the enforcement of the FRs, the courts can issue
(*a*) A Writ (*b*) A Decree
(*c*) An Ordinance (*d*) A Notification

102. Which FR granted by the Constitution prohibits traffic in human beings?
(*a*) Right against Exploitation (*b*) Right to Freedom
(*c*) Right to Equality (*d*) Right to Speech

103. 'Traffic in Human beings' means
(*a*) Selling or purchasing men and women (*b*) Transporting human beings
(*c*) Traffic in places having dense population
(*d*) Illegal sale of human organs

104. Right against exploitation prohibits
(*a*) Traffic in human being (*b*) Women working at nights in factories
(*c*) Giving in marriage minor girls (*d*) Lending money at high interest

105. Right to practice and propagate any religion is the subject to
(*a*) Public order (*b*) Public interest
(*c*) Public convenience (*d*) Public consent

106. Right to property was eliminated from the list of FRs during the tenure of
(*a*) Morarji Desai (*b*) Rajiv Gandhi
(*c*) Indira Gandhi (*d*) Charan Singh

107. Legal equality under the Indian Constitution implies that
(*a*) There should be equality amongst equals and inequality among unequals
(*b*) The state cannot enact different laws for different groups of people
(*c*) Everybody is equal before the law
(*d*) There should be no special law for any category of people

108. Who of the following can amend the FRs granted by the Constitution?
(*a*) Parliament (*b*) Supreme Court
(*c*) President (*d*) High Court

109. A citizen can directly move the Supreme Court for any violation of FR under the Article ____.
(*a*) 34 (*b*) 33
(*c*) 32 (*d*) 31

110. The main objective of the FRs is to
(*a*) Ensure individual liberty (*b*) Promote a socialistic pattern of the society
(*c*) Ensure independence of judiciary (*d*) Ensure all of them

111. Under the Indian Constitution, a citizen
(*a*) Can be deprived of life and liberty only in accordance with the procedure established by the law
(*b*) Can be deprived of life and liberty by the President during Emergency
(*c*) Cannot be deprived of life and liberty under any conditions
(*d*) None of these

112. Constitution grants Right against exploitation to "Children / Women / Tribals / Dalits"
(*a*) C and W (*b*) C and T
(*c*) C, W and T (*d*) W, T and D

113. Which of the Provision authorizes Parliament to discriminate in favor of women against men?
(*a*) Article 15 (3) (*b*) Article 15 (1)
(*c*) Article 16 (1) (*d*) All of these

114. Article 15 (3) confers a special provisions to
(*a*) Women and Children (*b*) Women
(*c*) Children (*d*) SCs and STs

115. Article 15 (4) confers a special provisions for the advancement of
(*a*) SCs and STs (*b*) Women and Children
(*c*) Women (*d*) Children

116. The prohibition imposed by the Article 20 is applicable to
(*a*) Criminal cases (*b*) Civil cases
(*c*) Constitutional cases (*d*) Cases of all types

117. The principle "No person shall be prosecuted and punished for same offence more than once" is
(*a*) Double jeopardy (*b*) Testimonial compulsion
(*c*) Ex-post facto law (*d*) Single jeopardy

118. If an Act is not an offence on the date of its commission, a law enacted in future cannot make it so, is the principle of
(*a*) Ex-post facto law (*b*) Double jeopardy
(*c*) Testimonial compulsion (*d*) Single jeopardy

119. 'Ex-post-facto-law' means
(*a*) Passing criminal law with retrospective effect
(*b*) A law applicable only during emergency
(*c*) An invalid law (*d*) An outdated law

120. An arrested person should be allowed
(*a*) To consult his Lawyer (*b*) To contact nearest Magistrate
(*c*) To contact his Relatives (*d*) To contact higher Police Officer

121. Every person who has been arrested has the right to be produced before the
(*a*) Magistrate (*b*) State Governor
(*c*) Supreme Court Judge (*d*) High Court Judge

122. A person arrested has to be produced before the Magistrate within
(*a*) 24 hours (*b*) 48 hours
(*c*) One week (*d*) 72 hours

123. The right of the accused to be informed about his ground of arrest is
(*a*) Mandatory (*b*) Directory
(*c*) Discretion of the Executive (*d*) Indirectory

124. No person who is arrested shall be detained in custody without being informed
(*a*) On the grounds for such arrest (*b*) Of the orders of the court
(*c*) Of the time when he will be produced before the Magistrate
(*d*) None

125. The provisions enshrined under the Article 22 are
(*a*) Mandatory (*b*) Directory
(*c*) Discretion of the Judge (*d*) Depends upon the nature of offence

126. Article 21A was inserted under the Indian Constitution by way of ____ Constitutional Amendment.
(*a*) 86th (*b*) 73rd
(*c*) 44th (*d*) 42nd

127. Earlier to 86th Amendment, Article 21A is in the form of
(*a*) Directive Principles of State Policy (*b*) Fundamental Duties
(*c*) Fundamental Rights (*d*) Rule of Law

128. What is the object of Article 21A of the Constitution?
(*a*) Primary Education (*b*) Secondary Education
(*c*) Higher Education (*d*) Post Graduation

129. Right to education guaranteed under the Article 21A shall be between the age group of
(*a*) 6 to 14 (*b*) 7 to 15
(*c*) 5 to 14 (*d*) 1 to 14

130. Right to Primary Education guaranteed under the Article 21A was inserted into the Constitution by ____ Constitutional Amendment.
(*a*) 86th (*b*) 74th
(*c*) 97th (*d*) 61st

131. Which of the following has been included in the list of FRs to Indian citizen?
(*a*) Education to all children between 6-14 years of age
(*b*) Social security to every elder person
(*c*) Equal opportunities to every woman wishing to join Indian Defence Services
(*d*) Job to each and every single woman

132. Right to Education is a part of
(*a*) Right to life (*b*) Right to social equality
(*c*) Right to freedom of expression (*d*) Right to freedom of profession

133. Right to Life includes Right to
(*a*) Get education (*b*) Make a will
(*c*) Contest for election (*d*) Die

134. Education has became the joint responsibility of the Center and State Governments through a Constitutional Amendment in
(*a*) 1976 (*b*) 1975
(*c*) 1977 (*d*) 1978

135. The Constitution does not protect the right of the minority with regard to
(*a*) Cult (*b*) Culture
(*c*) Script (*d*) Language

136. Which among the following Articles guarantees the right of minorities to establish and administer the educational institutions?
(*a*) 30 (*b*) 31
(*c*) 29 (*d*) 28

137. The right to establish educational institutional under Article 30 is applicable to
(*a*) Linguistic Minority (*b*) Religious Minority
(*c*) Citizens (*d*) All persons
138. Right to decent environment includes
(*a*) Right to life (*b*) Right to religion
(*c*) Freedom to reside in any part of the country
(*d*) Right to equal protection of law
139. A person is detained under Preventive Detention Law when
(*a*) He is likely to cause harm to the public (*b*) He has committed offences against the public
(*c*) He is about to escape from India
(*d*) He has violated law made by the Central Government
140. The forced labour does not include service rendered under
(*a*) Compulsion of economic circumstances (*b*) Physical force
(*c*) Moral force (*d*) Mental force
141. This is one of the basis for classification of areas
(*a*) Geographical (*b*) Economic
(*c*) Intelligibie differentia (*d*) Social and economic backward
142. Sexual harassment of working women is violation of
(*a*) Fundamental Rights (*b*) Fundamental Duties
(*c*) Directive Principles of State Policy (*d*) Rule of Law
143. The popular name for a Nine-Judge Bench of the Supreme Court as in 'Indra Sawhney vs. Union of India Case' is
(*a*) Mandal Commission Case (*b*) Golak Nath vs. State of Punjab
(c) Keshavananda vs. State of Kerala (*d*) Minerva Mills vs. Union of India
144. The Freedom of speech and expression does not include
(*a*) Calling for 'Bundh' (*b*) Commercial advertisements
(*c*) The right to express ones own conviction
(*d*) The right to propagate the views of other persons
145. Freedom of press is included in Right to
(*a*) Freedom of speech and expression (*b*) Education
(*c*) Personal liberty (*d*) Carry any profession
146. Freedom of press is protected under the Article
(*a*) 19(1)(a) (*b*) 19(1)(b)
(*c*) 19(1)(c) (*d*) 19(1)(d)
147. 'Right to Privacy' includes Right to
(*a*) Personal liberty (*b*) Practice any profession
(*c*) Reside in any part of India (*d*) Move freely in India
148. A citizen of India may be debarred from the Right to vote on the ground of
(*a*) All (*b*) Crime or corrupt or illegal practice
(*c*) Non-resident (*d*) Unsoundness of mind
149. Freedoms guaranteed under the Article 19 are suspended during emergency on the ground of
(*a*) War or external aggression (*b*) Internal disturbance
(*c*) Failure of constitutional machinery (*d*) Financial crisis
150. Right to Freedom guaranteed under Article 19 ____ during emergency.
(*a*) Can be suspended (*b*) Can be restrained
(*c*) Cannot be suspended (*d*) Cannot be restrained

151. Article 19(2) under the Indian Constitution speaks about
(*a*) Reasonable restrictions (*b*) Absolute restrictions
(*c*) Legal rights (*d*) None of these
152. India has recognized
(*a*) No religion as National Religion (*b*) Only one religion as National Religion
(*c*) Three religions as National Religion (*d*) Five religions as National Religion
153. Freedom of religion guaranteed under the Article 25 is applicable to
(*a*) All persons (*b*) Persons residing within India
(*c*) Persons of Indian Origin (*d*) Citizens only
154. The secular provisions under the Indian Constitution are guaranteed under Article____.
(*a*) 25 (*b*) 24
(*c*) 23 (*d*) 22
155. Article 25 guarantees freedom of religion, but it is subject to
(*a*) All (*b*) Morality
(*c*) Health (*d*) Public order
156. 'Contempt of Court' places restriction on which of the following FR? (Right)
(*a*) Freedom (*b*) Equality
(*c*) Against exploitation (*d*) Constitutional remedies
157. Right to life and personal liberty guaranteed under Article 21 implies
(*a*) Right of every human being to live with dignity (*b*) Mere animal existence
(*c*) Right to survive (*d*) Right to live full life
158. Any law depriving personal liberty guaranteed under the Article 21 had to confirm with
(*a*) Both Articles 20 and 22 (*b*) Article 20
(*c*) Article 22 (*d*) Article 19
159. Any law laid down by the Parliament to deprive the personal liberty should be
(*a*) All (*b*) Reasonable
(*c*) Just (*d*) Fair
160. This is not a Writ
(*a*) Writ of Prevention (*b*) Writ of Habeas Corpus
(*c*) Writ of Mandamus (*d*) Writ of Certiorari
161. How many types of writs are there?
(*a*) 5 (*b*) 6
(*c*) 7 (*d*) 8
162. Writ can be directly filed in the
(*a*) Supreme Court (*b*) District and Sessions Court
(*c*) Court of Civil Judge (*d*) Magistrate Court
163. The writ of Habeas Corpus is issued
(*a*) In the form of an order calling upon a person who has detained another person to bring that person before court and show authority for such detention
(*b*) By a superior court to the lower court directing it to transfer the record of proceedings in case for its review
(*c*) By a superior court to a subordinate court to do something in the nature of its allotted duty
(*d*) In the form of an order to stop proceedings in a certain case

164. The writ of Quo Warranto is an order from a superior court
   (*a*) Whereby it can call upon a person to show under what authority he is holding the office
   (*b*) Directing to produce a person detained by an official before the nearest court within 24 hours
   (*c*) To an inferior court to stop proceedings in a particular case
   (*d*) To the lower court to transfer a case pending before it to the superior court for trial
165. The writ of Mandamus is issued by a superior court to
   (*a*) To command a person or public authority to do something in the nature of the public duty
   (*b*) To produce an illegally detained person before a court within 24 hours
   (*c*) To command a person or public authority to stop proceedings in case in national interest
166. The writ of Certiorari is issued by a superior court
   (*a*) To an inferior court to transfer the record of proceedings in a case for review
   (*b*) To an inferior court to stop further proceedings in a particular case
   (*c*) To an officer to show his right to hold a particular office
   (*d*) To a public authority to produce a person detained by it before the court within 24 hours
167. The writ of Prohibition is issued by a superior court
   (*a*) To prevent an inferior court or tribunal from exceeding its jurisdiction or acting contrary to the rules of natural justice
   (*b*) To an inferior court or body exercising judicial or quasi-judicial functions to transfer the record of proceedings in a case for its review
   (*c*) Whereby it can call upon a person to show under what authority he is holding the office
   (*d*) To an authority to produce an illegally detained person before the court for trial
168. Writ of Prohibition
   (*a*) Prohibits lower court exceeding its jurisdiction
   (*b*) Prohibits judicial and quasi-judicial authority from taking an action
   (*c*) Prohibits a person to continue in a public post
   (*d*) Prohibits police from interfering in one's private affairs
169. The writ issued by the superior court directing any constitutional, statutory or non-statutory agency from not continuing their proceedings is known as
   (*a*) Prohibition (*b*) Certiorari
   (*c*) Mandamus (*d*) Quo-warranto
   (*e*) Habeas Corpus
170. Writ of Certiorari is issued when a
   (*a*) Judicial authority acts in excess of jurisdiction
   (*b*) Search warrant is issued against a person
   (*c*) Person is illegally detained (*d*) Person is illegally arrested
171. The writ in the form of order which removes a suit from an inferior court to superior court to prevent an excess of jurisdiction is known as
   (*a*) Certiorari (*b*) Mandamus
   (*c*) Quo-warranto (*d*) Habeas Corpus
172. Exploitation of any sort is prohibited under the Article
   (*a*) 23 (*b*) 22
   (*c*) 20 (*d*) 19
173. A laborer is entitled to get at least minimum wages, otherwise ____ Article is violated.
   (*a*) 23 (*b*) 24
   (*c*) 19 (*d*) 14

174. Child labor is prohibited under the Article
(*a*) 24 (*b*) 23
(*c*) 15(4) (*d*) 16(4)
175. Conflict of interest may be
(*a*) Potential (*b*) False
(*c*) Created (*d*) Imaginary
176. A person is detained under the Special Law when
(*a*) There is likelihood of committing offence against public
(*b*) There are chances of escaping from India
(*c*) He has committed civil wrong (*d*) He has committed criminal offence
177. When a person is detained under a Special Law
(*a*) An Advisory Board must be constituted within three months
(*b*) A chargesheet must be filed within three months in the proper court
(*c*) He should be produced within three months before the Magistrate
(*d*) He should be released within three months
178. Writ of Mandamus can be issued on the ground of
(*a*) Non-performance of public duties (*b*) Unlawful detention
(*c*) Unlawful occupation of public office (*d*) All of these
179. Writ of Quo-warranto can be issued on the ground of
(*a*) Unlawful occupation of public office (*b*) Unlawful detention
(*c*) To quash the order of the lower court (*d*) All of these
180. Which of the following writ is issued by the Supreme Court if it sends an order to restrain a person from acting in an office to which he/she is not entitled?
(*a*) Quo Warranto (*b*) Mandamus
(*c*) Habeas Corpus (*d*) Certiorari
181. Writ of Habeas Corpus means
(*a*) Produce the person before the court (*b*) We command
(*c*) Natural right (*d*) Quashing order
182. Which one of the following is a bulwark of personal freedom?
(*a*) Habeas Corpus (*b*) Mandamus
(*c*) Certiorari (*d*) Quo Warranto
183. Which one of the following writs literally means 'you may have the body'?
(*a*) Habeas Corpus (*b*) Mandamus
(*c*) Quo Warranto (*d*) Certiorari

Chapter 3: Directive Principles of State Policy (DPSP)

1. The framers of our Constitution borrowed the concept of DPSP from the Constitution of (OR) The idea of DPSP is borrowed from the Constitution of
(*a*) Ireland (*b*) USSR
(*c*) Switzerland (*d*) France
2. DPSP are contained in (OR) Welfare provisions under Indian Constitution are guaranteed under
(*a*) Part IV (*b*) Part III
(*c*) Part II (*d*) Part I
3. Who described the DPSP as the 'Novel Feature of the Indian Constitution'?
(*a*) Ambedkar (*b*) Motilal Nehru
(*c*) Madhava Rao. N (*d*) L.M. Singhivi

4. The DPSP aim at
   (*a*) Providing a social and economic base for a genuine democracy in the country
   (*b*) Ensuring strengthening of the country's independence
   (*c*) Ensuring individual liberty (*d*) None of these
5. DPSP are
   (*a*) Positive instructions to government to work for the attainment of set objectives
   (*b*) Negative injections to govt. to refrain from encroaching on freedom of people
   (*c*) Directives to the State to enhance the international prestige of the country
   (*d*) Directives to the government to pursue a policy of government
6. DPSP are in the nature of
   (*a*) Guidelines to State (*b*) Obligations to State
   (*c*) Limitations of State (*d*) None of these
7. The Constitution assures economic justice to the Indian citizens through
   (*a*) DPSP (*b*) FRs
   (*c*) FDs (*d*) All of these
8. The DPSP are included in our Constitution from Articles
   (*a*) 36 to 51 (*b*) 37 to 52
   (*c*) 38 to 43 (*d*) 39 to 54
9. All of the following Articles deals with DPSP except
   (*a*) 32 (*b*) 37
   (*c*) 43 (*d*) 50
10. The DPSP are
    (*a*) Social Rights (*b*) Political Rights
    (*c*) Constitutional Rights (*d*) Legal Rights
11. The DPSP are
    (*a*) Non-justiceable (*b*) Sometimes justiceable
    (*c*) Always justiceable (*d*) Justiceable
12. By whom the DPSP be amended?
    (*a*) Parliament, supported by more than 50% of States
    (*b*) MPs of LS and RS
    (*c*) MPs of RS (*d*) MPs of LS
13. Planning in India derives its objectives from the
    (*a*) DPSP (*b*) Preamble
    (*c*) FRs as well as DPSP (*d*) FDs
14. The aim of the DPSP is to establish
    (*a*) Welfare State in the country (*b*) Communist State in our country
    (*c*) Capitalist State in our country (*d*) None of these
15. The enforcement of the DPSP depends on
    (*a*) Resources available with the government
    (*b*) The Judiciary
    (*c*) The will of the Government in the power
    (*d*) All of these
16. The DPSP may be classified into
    (*a*) Socialist, Gandhians and Liberals (*b*) Gandhians, Liberals and Communists
    (*c*) Liberals and Communists (*d*) Socialists and Communists

17. This Act was not passed to implement DPSP
(*a*) Arms Act (*b*) Forest Act
(*c*) Water Pollution Act (*d*) Maternity Benefit Act
18. Which one of the following is a DPSP?
(*a*) Raising the standards of living of the people
(*b*) Giving equal Rights to all people
(*c*) Giving freedom to all people (*d*) Giving political rights to all people
19. Under which Article has the State been directed to secure for the citizens a Uniform Civil Code throughout the territory of India?
(*a*) 44 (*b*) 45
(*c*) 46 (*d*) 47
20. 'Common (Uniform) Civil Code' means
(*a*) Common Civil law applicable to all
(*b*) Civil law applicable to Hindus, Muslims and Christians in certain matters
(*c*) Common Civil Procedure Code (*d*) Common Civil law applicable to Common man
21. 'Uniform Civil Code' means
(*a*) A codified law applicable to all persons of India irrespective of their religion
(*b*) A code related to individual's public life
(*c*) A code meant for Hindus only (*d*) None of these
22. Which among the following DPSP that has not been implemented so far
(*a*) Uniform Civil Code (*b*) Promotion of International Peace and Security
(*c*) Separation of Judiciary from the Executive
(*d*) Organization of panchayats
23. Article 51 mandates India's Foreign Policy to
(*a*) All of these
(*b*) Encourage settlement of international disputes by arbitration
(*c*) Maintain just and good relations between nations
(*d*) Promote International Peace and Security
24. The phrase 'Economic Justice' is found in
(*a*) Preamble and DPSP (*b*) Preamble and FRs
(*c*) FRs and FDs (*d*) DPSP and FDs
25. The Right to adequate means of livelihood is to be provided by the State under the Article
(*a*) 39 (*b*) 38
(*c*) 40 (*d*) 37
26. Article 45 mandates the State to provide for
(*a*) Early childhood care and education for all children until they complete the age of 6 years
(*b*) Free and compulsory education for all children
(*c*) Free and compulsory education for children up to 14 years of age
(*d*) Free and compulsory education for children up to 18 years of age
27. It is the obligation of the State to protect every monument or place or object of artistic or historic interest and of national importance under the Article
(*a*) 49 (*b*) 50
(*c*) 48 (*d*) 48A

28. The DPSP seek
    (*a*) To make the Constitution an instrument of social change
    (*b*) Strengthen Judiciary
    (*c*) To curb the Authoritarian Rule (*d*) To establish Supremacy of the Constitution
29. In which part of the Constitution does the concept of welfare finds elaboration?
    (*a*) DPSP (*b*) FDs
    (*c*) FRs (*d*) Preamble
30. If India has to provide socio-economic welfare to its citizens , it should give enforceability to
    (*a*) DPSP (*b*) FDs
    (*c*) FRs (*d*) None of these
31. Certain socio-economic provisions are guaranteed under the
    (*a*) DPSP (*b*) FRs
    (*c*) FDs (*d*) Preamble
32. The State imposing tax on capital and wealth according to taxation laws is protected under Article
    (*a*) 39 (*b*) 40
    (*c*) 45 (*d*) 50
33. According to the interpretation of the Supreme Court, the word 'Material Resources' means
    (*a*) Both movable and immovable property (*b*) Movable property
    (*c*) Immovable property (*d*) Removal property
34. "Distribution of material resources of the community as to sub-serve the common good" guaranteed under the Article 39B aim at the principle of _____ State.
    (*a*) Secular (*b*) Socialist
    (*c*) Sovereign (*d*) Democratic
35. Who said in the Constituent Assembly that the DPSP are like a 'Cheque on a bank payable at the convenience of the bank'?
    (*a*) K.T. Shah (*b*) Jawaharlal Nehru
    (*c*) B.R. Ambedkar (*d*) K.M. Munshi
36. Which one of the following wanted the DPSP to be the basis for all future legislation?
    (*a*) B.R. Ambedkar (*b*) Jawaharlal Nehru
    (*c*) K.M. Munshi (*d*) B.N. Rau
37. Which Amendment of the Constitution accorded precedence to all the DPSP over FRs?
    (*a*) 42nd (*b*) 44th
    (*c*) 39th (*d*) 24th
38. Which among the following articles guides the state to promote the welfare of the state?
    (*a*) 38 (*b*) 39
    (*c*) 40 (*d*) 41
39. Which Article provides for the separation of Judiciary from the Executive?
    (*a*) 50 (*b*) 51
    (*c*) 51A (*d*) 48
40. Which Article recognizes International Law under the Constitution?
    (*a*) 51 (*b*) 52
    (*c*) 48 (*d*) 49

41. In which case did the Supreme Court strike down the Provisions of the Constitution that accorded primacy to DPSP over FRs?
(*a*) Minerva Mills Case (*b*) Keshavananda Case
(*c*) Golak Nath Case (*d*) Maneka Gandhi Case

42. Which part of the Constitution aims at establishing a Welfare State in the country?
(*a*) DPSP (*b*) Preamble
(*c*) FRs (*d*) FDs

43. Under DPSP, the State is expected to provide free and compulsory education to all children up to the age (in years) of
(*a*) 14 (*b*) 16
(*c*) 18 (*d*) 24

44. Just and humane conditions of work and maximum living wages for workers is provided respectively under the Articles
(*a*) 42 & 43 (*b*) 39 & 41
(*c*) 40 & 41 (*d*) 43A & 44

45. The State is obligated to protect and improve the environment and safeguarding of forest and wildlife of the country under the Article
(*a*) 48A (*b*) 47
(*c*) 45 (*d*) 37

46. Protection and Improvement of environment and safeguarding of forest and wildlife under Article 48A is inserted into the Constitution by the ______ Amendment.
(*a*) 42nd (*b*) 44th
(*c*) 52nd (*d*) 36th

47. Which one of the following is a DPSP?
(*a*) The state shall endeavor to protect and improve the environment
(*b*) Untouchability is abolished and its practice in any form shall be punishable by law
(*c*) The state shall not discriminate against any person on grounds of religion, race, caste, sex or place of birth
(*d*) The state shall not deny to any person equality before the law

48. The 42nd Amendment made additions to DPSP with regard to the following three matters.
1. Participation of workers in the management of industry
2. Minimizing inequality in income and status
3. Protection of the environment
4. Free legal aid to the poor

Select the correct answer from the codes given below:
(*a*) 1, 3 and 4 (*b*) 1, 2 and 3
(*c*) 1, 2 and 4 (*d*) 2, 3 and 4

49. Consider the following statements regarding the DPSP.
1. The framers of the Constitution borrowed the DPSP from the Government of India Act, 1935
2. The DPSP aim at realizing the ideals of justice, liberty, equality and fraternity enshrined in the Preamble to the Constitution
3. The DPSP have to be kept in mind by the government while formulating policies and framing laws
4. The DPSP are justiciable

Select the correct answer from the codes given below:

(*a*) 2 and 3 (*b*) 1, 3 and 4

(*c*) 2, 3 and 4 (*d*) 2 and 4

50. Which one of the following DPSP is based on Gandhian Ideology?

1. Organization of Village Panchayats
2. Compulsory education for all children up to the age of 14 years
3. Prohibition on the use of intoxicating drinks except for medicinal purposes
4. To work for the development of weaker or backward sections of the society

Select the correct answer from the codes given below:

(*a*) 1, 3 and 4 (*b*) 1 and 2

(*c*) 2, 3 and 4 (*d*) 1, 2, 3 and 4

51. Which amendment of the Constitution sought to enhance the importance of the DPSP by providing that no law passed to give effect to DPSP contained in Articles 39 (b) and (c) shall be deemed to be void on the ground that it abridges the rights conferred by the Articles 14 and 19?

(*a*) 25th (*b*) 24th

(*c*) 42nd (*d*) 44th

52. Which of the following factors has been responsible for the slow implementation of the DPSP?

(*a*) All of these (*b*) Lack of resources with the government

(*c*) Lack of political will (*d*) Vastness of the country

53. Which characteristic of the DPSP provided in the Indian Constitution is incorrect?

(*a*) No law can be passed by legislature which is not in conformity with these principles

(*b*) Not enforceable by any court

(*c*) Moral guidelines for the Governors of the country

(*d*) Fundamental in the governance of the country

54. Which one of the following DPSP reflects Socialist Ideology?

(*a*) All of these

(*b*) To provide adequate means of livelihood to all

(*c*) To prevent concentration of wealth and means of production and to ensure equitable distribution of wealth and material resources

(*d*) To ensure a decent standard of living and leisure for all workers

55. The DPSP to be followed by the State for securing economic justice doe not include

(*a*) To secure Uniform Civil Code (*b*) To protect health and strength of the workers

(*c*) Equal pay for equal work

(*d*) Equal right of men and women to adequate means of livelihood

56. Which one of the following has been wrongly listed as a DPSP based on liberal principles?

(*a*) None of these has been wrongly listed

(*b*) Protection of monuments and places of artistic or historical importance

(*c*) Provision of a Uniform Civil Code for the country

(*d*) Separation of executive and judiciary

57. The DPSP

(*a*) Cannot be enforced in any court (*b*) Can be enforced in High Court

(*c*) Can be enforced only in Supreme Court

(*d*) Can be enforced relating to SCs and STs only

58. This is not one of the DPSP
   (*a*) Take stringent measures to eliminate corruption
   (*b*) To bring about prohibition of consumption of intoxicating drinks
   (*c*) Securing the level of nutrition
   (*d*) Securing equal pay for equal work for men and women
59. This is not a DPSP.
   (*a*) Secure just and efficient judiciary (*b*) Secure living wage
   (*c*) Provide free legal aid (*d*) Organize Village Panchayat
60. Free legal aid (Article 39A) is inserted under Indian Constitution by way of ____ Amendment.
   (*a*) 42nd (*b*) 44th
   (*c*) 24th (*d*) 25th
61. Village Panchayats (Article 40) are the best examples for India's ___ form of government.
   (*a*) Democratic (*b*) Republican
   (*c*) Sovereign (*d*) Secular
62. The Indian Constitution is silent as to which of the following DPSP?
   (*a*) Adult Education (*b*) Free legal aid to poor
   (*c*) Improving the standard of living of workers
   (d) Equal pay for equal work
63. Which one of following reasons has been wrongly listed for the slow implementation of DPSP?
   (*a*) Opposition from the society (*b*) Lack of resources with the government
   (*c*) Lack of political will (*d*) Difficulties arising due to vastness of the country
64. Which one of the following is not a DPSP?
   (*a*) None (*b*) Improvement of public health
   (*c*) Prohibiting the slaughter of cows (*d*) Maternity relief
65. Which one of the following DPSP did not form part of the original Constitution and was added subsequently through constitutional amendments?
   (*a*) All of these
   (*b*) Right of the workers to participate in the management of industries
   (*c*) To protect and improve the environment and to safeguard forests and wildlife
   (*d*) To minimize inequality in income, status, facilities and opportunities amongst individuals and groups

Chapterm 4: Fundamental Duties (FDs)

1. The concept of FDs are borrowed from the Constitution of
   (*a*) Russia (*b*) Ireland
   (*c*) Australia (*d*) America
2. Which Committee recommended for the inclusion of FDs in to the Constitution?
   (*a*) Sardar Swaran Singh (*b*) Ashok Mehta
   (*c*) Balwanth Rai Mehta (*d*) L.M. Singhvi
3. The FDs under the Indian Constitution are provided by
   (*a*) An Amendment to the Constitution (*b*) An Order of the President
   (*c*) An Order of the Supreme Court (*d*) A Legislation by the Parliament
4. FDs are applicable to all
   (*a*) Citizens (*b*) States
   (*c*) Foreigners (*d*) Persons

5. The FDs of the Indian citizens were
   (*a*) Added to the Constitution by 42nd Amendment (11.12.1976)
   (*b*) Enshrined in Original Constitution
   (*c*) Added to the Constitution by 44th Amendment
   (*d*) Added to the Constitution by 46th Amendment
6. The FDs of Indian Citizens were incorporated in the Constitution in
   (*a*) 1976 (*b*) 1952
   (*c*) 1979 (*d*) 1981
7. FD demands to
   (*a*) Abide by the Constitution (*b*) Work sincerely
   (*c*) Avoid corruption (*d*) Abide by moral rules
8. This is not a FD.
   (*a*) Not to indulge in corrupt practice
   (*b*) To develop scientific temper
   (*c*) To protect and improve natural environment
   (d) To abide by the Constitution
9. For the breach of FD, an action
   (*a*) Cannot be initiated in any Court
   (*b*) Can be initiated in Civil Court
   (*c*) Can be initiated in the Magistrate Court
   (*d*) Can be initiated either in the High Court or Supreme Court
10. What is the remedy available for the breach of FDs under the Constitution?
    (*a*) Filing writ petition (*b*) Filing Criminal complaint
    (*c*) Filing Civil suit (*d*) No remedy
11. FDs were incorporated in the Constitution to
    (*a*) Curb subversive and unconstitutional activities
    (*b*) Prevent misuse of FRs
    (*c*) Curb the growing power of executive (*d*) Make the FRs more meaningful
12. The FDs of citizens
    (*a*) Are contained in Part IV A of the Constitution
    (*b*) Lie scattered throughout the Constitution
    (*c*) Are contained in Schedule IX of the Constitution
    (*d*) None of these
13. Which one of the following is being included in the Part IV-A of the Constitution?
    (*a*) FDs (*b*) DPSP
    (*c*) Panchayat Raj System (*d*) FRs
14. FDs are enshrined under _____ Part of the Constitution.
    (*a*) IV A (*b*) IV
    (*c*) III (*d*) II
15. Under which Article the FDs are enshrined under the Indian Constitution?
    (*a*) 51A (*b*) 51
    (*c*) 52 (*d*) 50
16. The ratio between the length and breadth of the Indian National Flag is
    (*a*) 3:2 (*b*) 3:4
    (*c*) 2:3 (*d*) 1:2

17. Respecting our National Flag is a
   (*a*) FD (*b*) FR
   (*c*) DPSP (*d*) None of these
18. To respect the National Flag and National Anthem is
   (*a*) FDs of every citizen (*b*) FRs of every citizen
   (*c*) DP to the State (*d*) None of these
19. National Song 'Bande Matharam' was written in 1875 by Bankimchandra Chatterjee in his novel
   (*a*) Anand Math (*b*) Ananda Thirtha
   (*c*) Gitanjali (*d*) Geetha Govinda
20. India's National Anthem 'Jana gana mana' was adopted by the Constituent Assembly as the *National Anthem* of India on 24th January 1950 and was first sung on
   (*a*) 27th December 1911 (*b*) 15th August 1947
   (*c*) 26th January 1950 (*d*) 26th January 1949
21. The National Flag of India is a horizontal tri-color of deep Saffron (Kesari-representing courage and sacrifice) at the top, White (peace and truth) in the middle and deep Green (faith and chivalry) at the bottom in equal proportion and in the center Wheel (representing progression) was adopted by the Constituent Assembly of India on
   (*a*) 22.07.1947 (*b*) 20.07.1947
   (*c*) 15.08.1947 (*d*) 26.11.1949
22. The protection and improvement of environment including forest and wildlife of the country is enshrined in
   (*a*) Both (*b*) and (*c*) (*b*) FDs
   (*c*) DPSP (*d*) FRs
23. The duty to protect and improve the environment is enshrined under the Article
   (*a*) 51A (g) (*b*) 51A (f)
   (*c*) 51A (a) (*d*) 51A (b)
24. Which of the following is a FD of an Indian citizen?
   (*a*) To develop scientific temper (*b*) To cast his vote
   (*c*) To work for removal of literacy (*d*) To honor the elected leader
25. What is the main sanction behind the FDs?
   (*a*) Legal (*b*) Social
   (*c*) Moral (*d*) All of these
26. Which FD has been wrongly listed as a duty of Indian citizen as outlined in Article 51A?
   (*a*) To practice family planning and control population
   (*b*) To uphold and protect the sovereignty, unity and integrity
   (*c*) To promote harmony and the spirit of common brotherhood among people of India
   (*d*) To protect and preserve the natural environment
27. By what Amendment and with Year 'Child Education is compulsory between the ages of 06-14 years'?
   (*a*) 86 and 2002 (*b*) 86 and 2000
   (*c*) 68 and 2002 (*d*) 68 and 2000
28. Obligation of the parents/guardian to provide opportunities for the education to their children between 6 to 14 years of age is
   (*a*) FDs (*b*) FRs
   (*c*) DPSP (*d*) None of these

29. Which one of the following is/are FDs?
    (*a*) All (*b*) To safeguard the public property
    (*c*) To protect and improve environment (*d*) To uphold and protect the sovereignty of India
30. The FDs cannot be enforced by writs, they can be promoted by _____ method.
    (*a*) Constitutional (*b*) Legal
    (*c*) Statutory (*d*) Resolutionary
31. The original text of the Constitution doesn't contain FDs, however it is inserted by way of ____ Amendment.
    (*a*) 42nd (*b*) 44th
    (*c*) 24th (*d*) 1st
32. The 42nd Amendment introduced
    (*a*) FDs (*b*) FRs
    (*c*) DPSP (*d*) None of these
33. It is the duty of every citizen to promote harmony and the spirit of common brotherhood amongst all people of India under Article
    (*a*) 51A (e) (*b*) 51A (b)
    (*c*) 51A (c) (*d*) 51A (d)
34. FD under Article 51A (k) was inserted to the Constitution by ____ Amendment Act, 2002.
    (*a*) 86th (*b*) 85th
    (*c*) 84th (*d*) 83rd

Chapter 5: Union/Central Government

1. The President of Indian Union has the similar constitutional authority as the
   (*a*) British Monarch (*b*) President of USA
   (*c*) President of USSR (*d*) President of Egypt
2. The Supreme Court of India was created by
   (*a*) The Constitution (*b*) Act of Parliament, 1950
   (*c*) Indian Independence Act, 1947 (*d*) Indian Independence Act, 1951
3. The concept of Judicial Review has been borrowed from the Constitution of
   (*a*) Switzerland (*b*) USSR
   (*c*) USA (*d*) UK
4. The Seat of Supreme Court is
   (*a*) New Delhi (*b*) Kolkata
   (*c*) Mumbai (*d*) Chennai
5. Can a retired judge be asked to sit in the Supreme Court?
   (*a*) Yes (*b*) No
   (*c*) Never (*d*) Occasionally
6. Which of the following is not one of the three organs of the Union/State?
   (*a*) Press (*b*) Executive
   (c) Judiciary (*d*) Legislature
7. Which of the following is considered as the Fourth Estate?
   (*a*) Press (*b*) Assembly
   (*c*) Council (*d*) Parliament
8. The organ of the state which makes law is
   (*a*) Legislature (*b*) Executive
   (*c*) Judiciary (*d*) All

9. The organ of the state implement and execute laws is known as
(*a*) Executive (*b*) Legislature
(*c*) Judiciary (*d*) Parliament
10. 'Legislate' means
(*a*) Make law (*b*) Make constitutional amendment
(*c*) Form government (*d*) Put administrative machinery into action
11. 'Natural Justice' means
(*a*) Just, fair and reasonable action (*b*) Justice according to providence
(*c*) Justice not based on enacted law (*d*) Justice which is not based on technical formalities
12. Which of the following is not a function of judiciary?
(*a*) Catching criminals and punishing them (*b*) Acting as the guardian of citizen's rights
(*c*) Issuing writs (*d*) Settling conflict between State and Center
13. Article 254 of the Constitution deals with
(*a*) Dominance of Union laws over State laws in case of any conflict between the two
(*b*) Exclusive power of the Union government to make laws on any matter not enumerated in the Concurrent and State Lists
(*c*) Concurrent powers of the Union and States to legislate on matters enumerated in the List III
(*d*) Power of Parliament to increase the number of Judges
14. Under the Indian Constitution, the subjects of administration have been divided into
(*a*) Three lists (*b*) Four lists
(*c*) Five lists (*d*) Two lists
15. India is known as a Parliamentary Democracy because the
(*a*) Executive is responsible to the Parliament
(*b*) MPs are directly elected by the people
(*c*) President is not a MP
(*d*) Powers have been clearly distributed between Center and the States
16. In Parliamentary form of Government, the Council of Ministers are responsible to the
(*a*) Parliament (*b*) President
(*c*) Prime Minister (*d*) Supreme Court
17. The President of India is an integral part of the
(*a*) Parliament (*b*) LS
(*c*) RS (*d*) Union Cabinet
18. The Parliament may confer by law any functions on the authorities concerned except the
(*a*) President (*b*) Prime Minister
(*c*) Council of Ministers (*d*) Attorney General
19. All the Executive powers and the Defence forces of the Union shall be vested in the
(*a*) President (*b*) Prime Minister
(*c*) Home Minister (*d*) Defence Minister
20. In India, Mandamus will lie against
(*a*) Both Officers and Government (*b*) Only government
(*c*) Officers bound to do public duty (*d*) None
21. The power to establish new states in India rests with the
(*a*) Parliament (*b*) President
(*c*) Union Home Ministry (*d*) both (*a*) and (*b*) jointly

22. When can the President refer a matter to the Supreme Court for its opinion?
    (*a*) When a matter is of public importance
    (*b*) When emergency has been promulgated
    (*c*) When the Cabinet is not functioning properly
    (*d*) Whenever the President feels like it
23. Which of the following is not a writ issued only by a superior court to an inferior court?
    (*a*) Certiorari (*b*) Prohibition
    (*c*) Mandamus (*d*) None of these
24. The Supreme Court propounded 'The Theory of Basic Structure of the Constitution' in
    (*a*) Keshavananda Bharti case (*a*) Minerva Mills case
    (*c*) Golak Nath case (*d*) Gopalan vs. State of Madras
25. How many judges sat on the Bench to hear the landmark case of Keshavananda Bharti vs. State of Kerala in 1973?
    (*a*) 13 (*b*) 11
    (*c*) 9 (*d*) 7
26. Which of the following is not a constitutionally mandatory body? (Commission for)
    (*a*) Center-State Relations (*b*) National SC/ST
    (*c*) Planning (*d*) Election
27. The Appellate Jurisdiction of the Supreme Court does not involve in
    (*a*) Disputes arising out of pre-constitution treaties and agreements
    (*b*) Civil cases
    (*c*) Cases involving interpretation of the Constitution
    (*d*) Criminal cases
28. In India, the power of Judicial Review is enjoyed by the
    (*a*) Supreme Court only (*b*) High Courts
    (*c*) Lower Courts only (*d*) Supreme Court and High Court
29. The Chief Justice and other judges of the High Court are appointed by the
    (*a*) President (*b*) Governor
    (*c*) Chief Justice of India (*d*) Chief Minister
30. In criminal matters, the highest court of appeal in a district is the
    (*a*) Court of second class Magistrate (*b*) Court of first class Magistrate
    (*c*) High Court (*d*) Court of the Sessions Judge
31. A High Court for two or more states and or Union Territory may be established by
    (*a*) Law by Parliament (*b*) President
    (*c*) Chief Justice of India (*d*) Governor of the State
32. Golden Jubilee of Indian Parliament was celebrated on
    (*a*) 13.05.2002 (*b*) 12.06.2002
    (*c*) 15.08.2002 (*d*) 26.01.2002
33. Who is the integral part of the Parliament?
    (*a*) President of India (*b*) Prime Minister
    (*c*) Governor (*d*) Speaker
34. Who represents the Nation but does not rule the Nation?
    (*a*) President (*b*) Prime Minister
    (*c*) Council of Ministers (*d*) Speaker of LS

35. In the Presidential Election (Electoral College)
   (*a*) Parity between the Center and the States has been maintained
   (*b*) Center enjoys greater weightage
   (*c*) States are given greater weightage
   (*d*) None of these
36. Indian Constitution has distributed the powers between the Center and ______.
   (*a*) States (*b*) Districts
   (*c*) Territories (*d*) None of these
37. Who is the Chairman of the Rajya Sabha?
   (*a*) The Vice President (*b*) The President
   (*c*) The Prime Minister (*d*) None of these
38. The Speaker is elected by the members of ______.
   (*a*) Lok Sabha (*b*) Rajya Sabha
   (*c*) The Prime Minister (*d*) The President
39. The President of India is
   (*a*) Elected (*b*) Selected
   (*c*) Nominated (*d*) Appointed
40. Who elects the President of India?
   (*a*) By Electoral College (*b*) The Prime Minister
   (*c*) The Vice-President (*d*) None of these
41. How many times the President can seek re-election to his post?
   (*a*) Infinite times (*b*) Thrice
   (*c*) Twice (*d*) Once
42. Who acts as the President when neither the President nor the Vice-President is available?
   (*a*) Chief Justice of India (*b*) Speaker of LS
   (*c*) Chairman of RS (*d*) Attorney General of India
43. In the Presidential Election in India, every elected member of the Legislative Assembly of a State shall have as many votes as their multiples of one ______ in the quotient obtained by dividing the population of the state by the total number of elected members of the assembly.
   (*a*) Thousand (*b*) Lakh
   (*c*) Hundred (*d*) Ten
44. A Bill for the purpose of altering the boundaries of any State shall be introduced in either of the House of the Parliament with the recommendation of the ______.
   (*a*) President (*b*) Speaker of LS
   (*c*) Chairman of RS (*d*) Prime Minister
45. Which is the Committee recommended for the Re-organization of States?
   (*a*) Fazal Ali (*b*) Singhvi
   (*c*) Ashok Mehta (*d*) Swaran Singh
46. Which Act has been enacted by the Parliament by exercising its power under the Article 3 of the Constitution?
   (*a*) States Reorganization Act (*b*) Citizenship Act
   (*c*) People's Representation Act (*d*) Anti-Defection Law
47. States will be reorganized by the Parliament under the Article 3 of the Constitution on the
   (*a*) Linguistic basis (*b*) Population basis
   (*c*) Caste basis (*d*) Religion basis

48. A Bill for the purpose of reorganization of states shall be introduced in either of House of the Parliament with the prior approval of the
(*a*) President (*b*) Speaker of LS
(*c*) Chief Justice of India (*d*) Prime Minister
49. India opted for a federal form of government on the ground of
(*a*) Linguistic and regional diversity (*b*) Cultural integration
(*c*) Religion (*d*) Administrative convenience
50. Who is the Commander-in-Chief of all the Armed Forces?
(*a*) The President (*b*) The Vice-President
(*c*) The Prime Minister (*d*) Field Marshall
51. What is the eligibility, age and tenure of Office of President and Vice-President? (in years)
(*a*) 35 and 5 (*b*) 40 and 6
(*c*) 35 and 6 (*d*) 40 and 5
52. How many Members can be elected for LS and RS?
(*a*) 552 and 250 (*b*) 250 and 552
(*c*) 540 and 238 (*d*) 238 and 540
53. How many Anglo-Indian and other members can be nominated by the President to the LS & RS?
(*a*) 2 and 12 (*b*) 2 and 10
(*c*) 1 and 12 (*d*) 1 and 10
54. How many States and Union Territories are there in our country?
(*a*) 28 and 7 (*b*) 28 and 6
(*c*) 29 and 7 (*d*) 29 and 6
55. In which year, Delhi got the status of a State?
(*a*) 1993 (*b*) 1994
(*c*) 1995 (*d*) 1992
56. How many seats are reserved for the members of the Scheduled Tribes in the LS?
(*a*) 30 (*b*) 20
(*c*) 50 (*d*) 40
57. Which of the following became the 28th state of the Indian Union?
(*a*) Jharkhand (*b*) Chattisgarh
(*c*) Uttaranchal (*d*) Goa
58. Who will preside over the Joint Session of both the Houses of the Parliament?
(*a*) Speaker (*b*) President
(*c*) Prime Minister (*d*) Parliamentary Affairs Minister
59. Which of the following appointments is not made by the President of the Indian republic?
(*a*) Speaker of LS (*b*) Chief Justice of India
(*c*) Chief of Air Force (*d*) Chief Justice of High Court
60. The President will decide the question as to disqualification of the MPs in consultation with the
(*a*) Election Commissioner (*b*) Prime Minister
(*c*) Speaker (*d*) Vice President
61. Which Article empowers the President to give his assent to Bills?
(*a*) 111 (*b*) 100
(*c*) 123 (*d*) 200
62. Which Article authorizes the President to seek an advice from the Supreme Court?
(*a*) 143 (*b*) 134
(*c*) 124 (*d*) 142

63. In a Federation, the source of power for the States is the
    (*a*) Constitution (*b*) Electorate
    (*c*) Federal Court (*d*) Federal Legislature
64. How the Constitution of India has distributed the powers to different levels?
    (*a*) All of these (*b*) Central List
    (*c*) State List (*d*) Concurrent List
65. How many subjects are there in the Central, State and Concurrent Lists?
    (*a*) 97, 66 and 47 (*b*) 66, 97 and 47
    (*c*) 47, 66 and 97 (*d*) 47, 97 and 66
66. The Central, State and Concurrent Lists indicates division of
    (*a*) Legislative powers (*b*) Administrative powers
    (*c*) Financial powers (*d*) Judicial powers
67. Economic Planning is a subject in the
    (*a*) Concurrent List (*b*) Union List
    (*c*) State List (*d*) Special List
68. Railways is a subject under ____ List.
    (*a*) Union (*b*) State
    (*c*) Concurrent (*d*) Residuary
69. Lotteries organized by the State Government come under _____ List.
    (*a*) State (*b*) Union
    (*c*) Concurrent (*d*) Federal
70. Distribution of subjects between the Center and the States is enumerated under ____ Schedule.
    (*a*) 7th (*b*) 8th
    (*c*) 1st (*d*) 5th
71. Sarkaria Commission was appointed by the Government to report on
    (*a*) Center-State Relations (*b*) Electoral Reforms
    (*c*) Inter-State Disputes (*d*) Tribal Development
72. Planning in India derives its objectives from
    (*a*) DPSP (*b*) FDs
    (*c*) FRs (*d*) Preamble
73. Which of the taxes is exclusively assigned to Central Government by the Constitution?
    (*a*) Corporation Tax (*b*) Estate Tax
    (*c*) Taxes on Railways (*d*) Sales Tax
74. The other names for Rajya Sabha (Permanent Body) are
    (*a*) Upper House/House of States (*b*) Lower House/House of States
    (*c*) Upper House/House of People (*d*) Lower House/House of People
75. The other names for Lok Sabha (Temporary Body) are
    (*a*) Lower House/House of People (*b*) Upper House/House of People
    (*c*) Lower House/House of States (*d*) Upper House/House of States
76. The word 'Parliament' is derived from the French word 'Parler' which means
    (*a*) To talk (*b*) To vote
    (*c*) To pass Bill (*d*) To assemble
77. Parliament of India is composed of
    (*a*) LS, RS and President (*b*) LS and RS
    (*c*) LS and Council of Ministers (*d*) President, Council of Ministers

78. The first session of the Parliament after the General Election is
    (*a*) Mandatory (*b*) Directory
    (*c*) Discretionary (*d*) No such rule
79. The first session of the Parliament is called as ______ Session.
    (*a*) Budget (*b*) Winter
    (c) Monsoon (*d*) Primary
80. LS is superior to the RS because
    (*a*) All of these (*b*) It is directly elected
    (*c*) It alone controls the purse
    (*d*) It can oust the Council of Ministers through a vote of no-confidence
81. How many MPs of LS shall support a motion of 'No Confidence' in the government, before it can be admitted by the Speaker?
    (*a*) 50 (*b*) 55
    (*c*) 45 (*d*) 35
82. Which among the following is identified as the 'Democratic Chamber'?
    (*a*) LS (*b*) RS
    (*c*) Both LS and RS (*d*) State Legislative Council
83. Which among the following is described as 'Knowledge House'?
    (*a*) RS (*b*) LS
    (*c*) Both LS and RS (*d*) Legislative Assembly
84. Composition and function of RS points towards ______ Character.
    (*a*) Federal (*b*) Quasi-federal
    (*c*) Unitary (*d*) Quasi-unitary
85. What is the method of electing members of RS from Union Territories?
    (*a*) As law laid down by the Parliament (*b*) In direct election
    (*c*) Proportional representation (*d*) Universal adult franchise
86. The representation to the States in the RS is given by
    (*a*) In proportion to the state population (*b*) On the basis of equality
    (*c*) In proportion to the MLAs (*d*) In proportion to the territory of the state
87. Which of the following is not done by the Parliament?
    (*a*) Adjournment of the Houses of the Parliament
    (*b*) Prorogation of the Houses of Parliament
    (*c*) Summoning the Houses of the Parliament
    (*d*) Dissolving the LS
88. The President of India may from time to time
    (*a*) Dissolve the LS (*b*) Adjourn the RS
    (*c*) Dissolve the RS (*d*) Adjourn the LS
89. The President and Governors are immune from ____ during their term of Office.
    (*a*) Civil liability (*b*) Criminal liability
    (*c*) Both (*a*) and (*b*) (*d*) Economic liability
90. Which Article of the Constitution gives the protection to the President and Governors?
    (*a*) 361 (*b*) 352
    (*c*) 370 (*d*) 14
91. To contest for the election of LS, the person should be
    (*a*) Citizen of India (*b*) Resident of India for at least 10 years
    (*c*) Resident of India for at least 12 years (d) Resident of India for at least 05 years

92. An Ordinance promulgated by the President when one House is in session is
(*a*) Valid (*b*) Void
(*c*) Unlawful (*d*) Illegal

93. The Ordinance making power of the President is subjected to the control of the
(*a*) Parliament (*b*) Supreme Court
(*c*) Cabinet Minister (*d*) Prime Minister

94. An Ordinance can be promulgated on the subject mentioned in
(*a*) List I & List III (*b*) List II
(*c*) List I (*d*) List I, II & III

95. Parliament has exclusive power to make laws with respect to any matter enumerated in
(*a*) List I (*b*) List II
(*c*) List III (*d*) All of these

96. State Legislature has exclusive power to make laws with respect to any matter enumerated in
(*a*) List II (*b*) List I
(*c*) List III (*d*) All of these

97. If any matter is not enumerated either under the Concurrent List or under State List then who has the power to legislate on such matters?
(*a*) Parliament only (*b*) State Government only
(*c*) Panchayat Raj Institutions (*d*) Supreme Court

98. Who has the power to make laws on the subjects enumerated under List III of 7th Schedule?
(*a*) Both Parliament and State Legislature (*b*) Only Parliament
(*c*) Only State Legislature (*d*) Government of the State

99. A Resolution passed by the RS empowering the Parliament to legislate under List II on National interest should be supported by
(*a*) Two-third members present and voting (*b*) Two-third majority
(*c*) One-third members present and voting (*d*) Majority in the House

100. Parliament has power to legislate under the State List on the ground of national interest if
(*a*) RS passes a Resolution to that effect (*b*) LS passes a Resolution to that effect
(*c*) State LA passes a Resolution to that effect
(*d*) State LC passes a Resolution to that effect

101. A Resolution passed by the RS empowering the Parliament to legislate under State List shall remain in force for a maximum period of
(*a*) One year (*b*) Two years
(*c*) Six months (*d*) Ninety days

102. Law made by the Parliament on any subject is
(*a*) Uniformly applicable to all States
(*b*) Applicable to only those States which give consent
(*c*) Discretion of the state Governments (*d*) None of these

103. The law made by the Parliament
(*a*) Cannot be declared as extra-territorial (*b*) Can be declared as extra-territorial
(*c*) Can be declared as extra-territorial only by the Supreme Court
(*d*) Can be declared as extra-territorial by any High Courts

104. If the law made by the Parliament is inconsistent with the law made by the State Legislature under the List III, which law has the effect?
(*a*) Law made by the Parliament (*b*) Law made by the State Legislature
(*c*) Law which is former (*d*) Law which is later

105. A Fund which is utilized to meet the unforeseen expenditure is entitle as
   (*a*) Contingency Fund (*b*) Consolidated Fund
   (*c*) Unforeseen Expenditure Fund (*d*) None of these
106. The usual expenditure of the Government of India is charged from
   (*a*) Consolidated Fund (*b*) Contingency Fund
   (*c*) Sales Tax Fund (*d*) Income Tax Fund
107. The Custody of Contingency Fund of India is with the
   (*a*) President (*b*) Prime Minister
   (*c*) Finance Minister (*d*) Comptroller and Auditor General
108. What is the term of the Parliamentary Committees appointed by the President?
   (*a*) One year (*b*) Five Years
   (*c*) Six months (*d*) Till the LS is dissolved
109. A Select or Joint Committee of the two Houses of a Parliament is formed by
   (*a*) Speaker of the LS (*b*) Speaker of the LS and Chairman of the RS
   (*c*) Speaker in consultation with the President
   (*d*) Speaker in consultation with the Prime Minister
110. Which of the following has been wrongly listed as a Standing Joint Committee of the two Houses of the Parliament?
   (*a*) Committee on Government Assurances (*b*) Committee on Salaries and Allowances of MPs
   (*c*) Committee on Offices of Profit (*d*) Committee on Welfare of SCs and STs
111. Which of the following Committees of the Parliament has the largest membership?
   (*a*) Estimate Committee (*b*) Public Accounts Committee
   (*c*) Business Advisory Committee (*d*) Committee on Public Undertakings
112. Parliament Standing Committee for scrutiny of grants of various ministries comprises of
   (*a*) 30 members of LS and 15 members of RS
   (*b*) 25 members of LS and 10 members of RS
   (*c*) 20 members of LS and 10 members of RS
   (*d*) 10 members of LS and 05 members of RS
113. The Parliamentary Subject Committees (Number of Committees: 17) were introduced in 1993 on the recommendation of the
   (*a*) Rules Committee of the House (*b*) Joint Parliamentary Committee setup in 1990
   (*c*) Leaders of all political parties represented in Parliament (*d*) Minister for Parliamentary Affairs
114. The main advantage of the Standing Committee is the
   (*a*) Parliament is able to examine the grants of all ministries and departments in detail
   (*b*) Parliament is able to concentrate on the examination of the demands of some ministries
   (*c*) Parliament is absolved of the responsibility of examining the grants of all ministries and departments
   (*d*) None of these
115. One of the main advantages of the Standing Committee is
   (*a*) MPs of RS are able to exercise indirect control over financial matters
   (*b*) Members of Council of Ministers are able to serve on the Standing Committees
   (*c*) Discussion on the Budget is held simultaneously in the Parliament and the Standing Committees
   (*d*) None

116. The Standing Committee, apart from examining the grant of all ministries and departments, are able to examine
(*a*) All of these (*b*) Bills of technical nature
(*c*) Annual reports of ministries and departments
(*d*) Long-term policies
117. When an advance grant is made by Parliament pending regular passage of the Budget, it is called
(*a*) Vote of Account (*b*) Token Account
(*c*) Supplementary Account (*d*) Vote of Credit
118. Who is having the power to summon and dissolve the House of Parliament (LS)?
(*a*) President (*b*) Vice President
(*c*) Chief Justice of India (*d*) Prime Minister
119. Which Budget will be proposed first in the Parliament House?
(*a*) Railway (*b*) General Budget
(*c*) Financial (*d*) Vote of Credit
120. Usually, General Budget is presented to the Parliament on
(*a*) Last day of February (*b*) Last day of March
(*c*) First day of February (*d*) First day of March
121. The first session of the year commences with the address by the ______ in the Parliament.
(*a*) President (*b*) Vice-President
(*c*) Prime Minister (*d*) Speaker
122. The first hour of every sitting in both the Houses of Parliament is devoted to
(*a*) Question Hour (*b*) Zero Hour
(*c*) One Hour (*d*) Twin Hour
123. What are the timings followed for the Question Hour in the Parliament House?
(*a*) 11 to 12 (*b*) 12 to 1
(*c*) 10 to 11 (*d*) 1 to 2
124. What are the timings followed for the Zero Hour in the Parliament House?
(*a*) 12 to 1 (*b*) 2 to 3
(*c*) 11 to 12 (*d*) 1 to 2
125. The maximum duration of the Zero Hour (in minutes) in LS can be
(*a*) 60 (*b*) 30
(*c*) 120 (*d*) Unspecified
126. Zero Hour is
(*a*) The period immediately following the Question Hour when the members voice their concerns on various matters of public importance
(*b*) An hour when Money Bills are introduced
(*c*) The period exclusively reserved for introduction of private member
(*d*) The period of recess intervening between the two Bills sessions of the Parliament
127. The immediate hour after the Question Hour in LS is called as
(*a*) Zero Hour (*b*) Special Hour
(*c*) Answer Hour (*d*) Second Hour
128. Who presides over the joint sessions of Parliament?
(*a*) Speaker (*b*) Vice-President
(*c*) President (*d*) Prime Minister

129. What is the minimum age in years for becoming the MP at LS and RS?
(*a*) 25 and 30 (*b*) 30 and 25
(*c*) 18 and 25 (*d*) 25 and 18
130. Which of the following shall not be introduced in the RS?
(*a*) Money Bill (*b*) Union Budget
(*c*) Constitutional Amendment (*b*) Finance Bill
131. The system of Impeachment of the President is borrowed from the Constitution of
(*a*) Britain (*b*) Russia
(*c*) America (*d*) Canada
132. Who can be removed for violation of Constitution by a process called as Impeachment Motion?
(*a*) President (*b*) Prime Minister
(*c*) Council of Ministers (*d*) Chief Justice of India
133. The seat of a MP may be declared vacant, if he/she is, without the permission of the House absent from the meeting of that House for a period of ______ days.
(*a*) 60 (*b*) 30
(*c*) 90 (*d*) 45
134. Till now, any President has been removed under the Motion of Impeachment?
(*a*) No (*b*) Once
(*c*) Twice (*d*) Thrice
135. Under which Article of the Indian Constitution can the President be impeached?
(*a*) 61 (*b*) 76
(*c*) 75 (*d*) 356
136. Impeachment proceedings against the President shall be initiated in
(*a*) Either of the Houses (*b*) LS only
(*c*) RS only (*d*) None of these
137. The ground for the Impeachment of President is
(*a*) Violation of the Constitution
(*b*) Misbehavior with the foreign dignitaries
(*c*) Unable to discharge his duties due to old age
(*d*) Failure to follow the advice given by the Prime Minister
138. The Indian President can be impeached by the Parliament if
(*a*) He is charged with the violation of the Constitution
(*b*) He has grown quite old and does not possess the capacity to discharge the onerous duties of his Office
(*c*) He is suffering from an incurable disease
(*d*) He refuses to sign a Bill passed by the Parliament
139. Which one of the following takes part in the election of the President but has no role in his impeachment?
(*a*) State Legislative Assemblies (*b*) State Legislative Councils
(*c*) LS (*d*) RS
140. The salary/emoluments of whom of the following is exempted from income tax?
(*a*) President (*b*) Chief Justice of India
(*c*) Election Commissioner (*d*) Prime Minister

141. Which one of the following statements is correct?
   (*a*) President is not a part of Council of Ministers and hence not permitted to attend its meetings
   (*b*) President can attend meetings of the Council of Ministers during emergency
   (*c*) President is a part of the Council of Ministers but is not permitted to attend its meetings
   (*d*) President is not a member of Council of Ministers but can attend its meetings
142. A Bill presented in the Parliament becomes an Act after
   (*a*) The President has given his assent
   (*b*) The Supreme Court has declared it to be within the competence of Union Parliament
   (*c*) The Prime Minister has signed it
   (*d*) It is passed by the both the Houses
143. Who occupied the President's Office twice (two consecutive terms) in our country?
   (*a*) Rajendra Prasad (*b*) S. Radhakrishnan
   (*c*) V.V. Giri (*d*) A.P.J. Abdul Kalam
144. Veto is the power of the _______ to withhold or refuse assent to Legislation.
   (*a*) Executive (*b*) Legislature
   (*c*) Judiciary (*d*) All of these
145. Vice President of India draws salary in the designation of
   (*a*) Chairman of RS (*b*) Speaker of LS
   (*c*) Vice President (*d*) President in charge
146. Who will elect the Vice President of India?
   (*a*) MPs (RS & LS) (*b*) MPs (RS)
   (*c*) MPs (LS) (*d*) President
147. Which of the following is presided over by a non-member?
   (*a*) RS (*b*) LS
   (*c*) Vidhana Sabha (*d*) Vidhana Parishad
148. Full form of PIL is
   (*a*) Public Interest Litigation (*b*) Public Interest Legislation
   (*c*) Private Interest Litigation (*d*) Private Interest Legislation
149. PIL can be resorted to in case of injury due to
   (*a*) All of these (*b*) Breach of any public duty
   (*c*) Violation of the law (*d*) Violation of a constitutional provision
150. The Concept of Public Interest Litigation, which has become more popular in India in recent years, originated in
   (*a*) UK (*b*) USA
   (*c*) Australia (*d*) Canada
151. Who has the power to pardon in case of capital punishment?
   (*a*) President (*b*) Chief Justice
   (*c*) Prime Minister (*d*) Attorney General of India
152. Which Article empowers the President to grant pardon?
   (*a*) 72 (*b*) 73
   (*c*) 74 (*d*) 75
153. The pardoning power shall be exercised by the President on the advice of the
   (*a*) Home Minister (*b*) Prime Minister
   (*c*) Chief Justice of India (*d*) Vice-President

154. Who is authorized to transfer the judge of one High Court to another High Court?
(*a*) President (*b*) Chief Justice of India
(*c*) A Committee of Judges of the Supreme Court
(*d*) Union Law Minister
155. Which of the following constitutional post(s) is/are enjoyed for a fixed term?
(*a*) President (*b*) Prime Minister
(*c*) Chief Justice (*d*) Governor
156. The Constitution of India vests the executive powers of the Union Government in
(*a*) President (*b*) Prime Minister
(*c*) Council of Ministers (*d*) All three
157. Which Article empowers the President to appoint Prime Minister of India?
(*a*) 74 (*b*) 75
(*c*) 76 (*d*) 77
158. Joint Session of Parliament was held in
(*a*) All of these (*b*) Dowry Prohibition Bill, 1961
(*c*) Banking Service Commission Bill, 1978
(*d*) Prevention of Terrorism Ordinance, 2002
159. Joint Sittings of the two Houses of Parliament are hold for
(*a*) Resolution of deadlock between the two Houses on a non-money Bill
(*b*) Annual address by the President
(*c*) Special Address by the President (*d*) All of these
160. The House of People (LS) can be adjourned sine-die by the
(*a*) Speaker (*b*) Prime Minister
(*c*) President (*d*) Vice-President
161. The President of India is the
(*a*) Head of State (*b*) Head of the Government
(*c*) Head of State and Government (*d*) All of these
162. The President of India is
(*a*) Elected through Electoral college (*b*) Directly elected by the people
(*c*) Elected by the two Houses of Parliament at a joint sitting
(*d*) Elected by the LS
163. The President holds Office for a term of five years
(*a*) From the date on which he/she enters upon the Office
(*b*) From the date on which he/she is elected
(*c*) From the date determined by the Parliament
(*d*) From the date notified by the Election Commission
164. The practice of President addressing Parliament has been adopted from Constitution of
(*a*) UK (*b*) USA
(*c*) Russia (*d*) Canada
165. Which one of the following does not take part in the election of the President?
(*a*) Members-Legislative Councils (*b*) Elected Members-RS
(*c*) Elected Members-LS (*d*) All of these
166. The name of the candidate for the Office of the President of India has to be proposed by
(*a*) Any 50 members of the Electoral College
(*b*) Any 50 MPs
(*c*) 05 members of the Electoral College (*d*) Any 50 citizens

167. Who was the first President of the Indian Republic?
(*a*) Rajendra Prasad (*b*) S. Radhakrishnan
(*c*) Zakir Hussain (*d*) V.V. Giri

168. Which President held Office for two consecutive years?
(*a*) Rajendra Prasad (*b*) S. Radhakrishnan
(*c*) Zakir Hussain (*d*) V.V. Giri

169. Who among following got Bharat Ratna Award before becoming the President of India?
(*a*) Zakir Hussain (*b*) Rajendra Prasad
(*c*) S. Radhakrishnan (*d*) V.V. Giri

170. Who is the following enjoys the distinction of being the first Muslim President of India?
(*a*) Zakir Hussain (*b*) Fakkrudin Ali Ahmed
(*c*) Maulana Abul Kalam Azad (*d*) None

171. Which one of the following was elected President of India unopposed?
(*a*) Neelam Sanjeeva Reddy (*b*) Rajendra Prasad
(*c*) S. Radhakrishnan (*d*) K.R. Narayanan

172. Which one of the following political leaders successfully held the Office of the Chief Minister, Speaker of LS and President of India?
(*a*) Neelam Sanjeeva Reddy (*b*) Zail Singh
(*c*) Fakkrudin Ali Ahmed (*d*) None of these

173. Which one of the following Chief Justice of India had the distinction of having acted as President of India?
(*a*) Justice M Hidayatullah (*b*) Justice Mehar Chand Mahajan
(*c*) Justice P. N. Bhagwati (*d*) Justice Venkatachala

174. The election of the Office of the President is conducted by
(*a*) Election Commission (*b*) Speaker-LS
(*c*) Prime Minister (*d*) Minister of Parliamentary Affairs

175. Before entering upon Office, President has to take an oath or an affirmation, which is administered by
(*a*) Chief Justice of India (*b*) Chief Election Commissioner
(*c*) Vice President (*d*) LS Speaker

176. The procedure for the election of the President of India can be modified through an Amendment in the Constitution which must be passed by
(*a*) Two-thirds majority by both LS and RS and be ratified by the Legislatures of at least half of the member of states
(*b*) Two-thirds majority by RS
(*c*) Two-thirds majority by both LS and RS
(*d*) Two-thirds majority by LS

177. To amend the Constitution to change the procedure of election of the President of India, the Bill has to be passed by
(*a*) Special majority, ratified by more than half of the states
(*b*) Special majority and consented by the Chief Justice of India
(*c*) Special majority (*d*) Simple majority

178. The President can nominate two members of the LS to give representation to
(*a*) Anglo-Indians (*b*) Indian Christians
(*c*) Buddhists (*d*) Parses

179. The President, the Head of the State under the Parliamentary system prevailing in India, enjoys
(*a*) Only nominal powers` (*b*) No powers
(*c*) Limited but real powers (*d*) Absolute powers
180. The final authority to make a Proclamation of Emergency rests with
(*a*) President (*b*) Parliament
(*c*) Council of Ministers (*d*) Prime Minister
181. The President can grant pardon in
(*a*) All of these (*b*) All cases involving death sentence
(*c*) All offences against laws in the union and concurrent lists
(d) All cases of punishment by court martial
182. The President of India is not having
(*a*) Power to control Judiciary (*b*) Executive power
(*c*) Diplomatic power (*d*) Legislative power
183. Which one of the financial powers is enjoyed by the President?
(*a*) All of these (*b*) The President appoints a Finance Commission
(*c*) The President can advance money out of the Contingency Fund of India
(*d*) Money Bills can be introduced in the Parliament
184. The President can make laws through ordinances
(*a*) During the recess of the Parliament
(*b*) On certain subjects even when Parliament is in session
(*c*) Only on subjects contained in the concurrent list
(*d*) Under no circumstances
185. Where are disputes regarding election of President and Vice President filed and settled?
(*a*) Supreme Court (*b*) Election Commission
(*c*) Parliament (*d*) High courts
186. If the President wants to tender the resignation before expiry of normal term, he/she has to address the same to
(*a*) Vice President (*b*) Prime Minister
(*c*) Parliament (*d*) Chief Justice of India
187. The President of India is elected by
(*a*) Elected MLAs and MPs (*b*) People directly
(*c*) RS members (*d*) MPs (RS and LS)
188. To be eligible (age in years) for appointment as President, a candidate must be
(*a*) Over 35 (*b*) Over 60
(*c*) Over 65 (*d*) There is no age limit prescribed by Constitution
189. When does the President uses his discretion in appointing the Prime Minister?
(*a*) When no political party enjoys majority in LS
(*b*) When LS has been dissolved
(*c*) When the Prime Minister defects party from his party and joins another party
(*d*) Never
190. The Constitution prohibits to enact retrospectively
(*a*) Laws relating to thc election of the President
(*b*) Civil Law
(*c*) Criminal Law
(*d*) Laws relating to the women's right to property

191. What is the maximum age (in years) for election to the Office of the President?
(*a*) No age limit (*b*) 65
(*c*) 70 (*d*) 75

192. President can be impeached from Office on grounds of violating the Constitution by
(*a*) Two Houses of Parliament (*b*) Supreme Court
(*c*) High Court (*d*) LS

193. Impeachment proceedings against the President of India can be initiated
(*a*) In either of the Parliament (*b*) Only in LS
(*c*) By the Supreme Court (*d*) Only in RS

194. Impeachments proceedings can be initiated against the President in either of House of Parliament only if a resolution signed by _______ members of the House is moved.
(*a*) 25% of total (*b*) 20% of total
(*c*) 15% of total (*d*) 10% of total

195. This is not the legislative power of the President
(*a*) To grant pardon (*b*) Assent to legislation
(*c*) Summon each of the House (*d*) Nominate 12 members to RS

196. When the election of the President is declared void, all acts done by the President in the performance of the duties of his Office before the date of decision become
(*a*) Valid (*b*) Invalid
(*c*) Illegal (*d*) Unlawful

197. In the event of death or resignation of the President, the Vice President discharges the duties of the office of President
(*a*) For a maximum period of six months (*b*) For a maximum period of four months
(*c*) For a maximum period of one year (*d*) For the rest of the term

198. In case the Vice President is not available to discharge the duties of the Office of President, which official discharges these duties?
(*a*) Chief Justice of India (*b*) Prime Minister
(*c*) Speaker of LS (*d*) None of these

199. Who discharges the duties of the President, if both the President and Vice President are not available?
(*a*) Chief Justice of India (*b*) Speaker of LS
(*c*) Prime Minister (*d*) Chairman of RS

200. If the Office of the President, Vice President and Chief Justice of India falls vacant simultaneously, who succeeds to the Office of the President?
(*a*) Next Senior-most Judge of the Supreme Court
(*b*) Prime Minister
(*c*) Speaker of LS (*d*) Deputy Prime Minister

201. When the Office of the President falls vacant, the same must be filled within
(*a*) Six months (*b*) Four months
(*c*) Twelve months (*d*) Eighteen months

202. Who is legally competent to declare war or conclude peace?
(*a*) President
(*b*) Air Marshall
(*c*) Prime Minister and Council of Ministers
(*d*) Parliament

203. After a Bill has been passed by Parliament and sent to the President for his consideration
(*a*) He can sent it back for reconsideration (*b*) He can refuse to sign it
(*c*) He has to sign it (*d*) He can change certain clauses of the Bill
204. The President can make laws through ordinances
(*a*) During the recess of Parliament (*b*) On certain subjects when Parliament is in session
(*c*) Only on subjects contained in the Concurrent List
(*d*) Under no circumstances
205. Ordinance is promulgated by the
(*a*) President
(*b*) Prime Minister on advice of the Council of Ministers
(*c*) LS (*d*) RS
206. What financial power is enjoyed by the President?
(*a*) All these powers
(*b*) Certain Money Bills can originate in Parliament only on the recommendation of the President
(*c*) Only on the recommendation of the Governor
(*d*) He can appoint Finance Commission to recommend the distribution of taxes between Union and State Governments
207. Which one of the following officials is not appointed by the President? OR In the appointment of which one of the following officials, the President has no say?
(*a*) District and Sessions Judges (*b*) Judges of High Court
(*c*) Judges of Supreme Court (*d*) Attorney General of India
208. The President of India made use of his/her veto power only once in the
(*a*) Indian Post Office (Amendment) Bill (*b*) PEPSU Appropriation Bill
(*c*) Hindu Code Bill (*d*) Dowry Prohibition Bill
209. An ordinance promulgated by the President usually remains in force for
(*a*) Six weeks after the commencement of the next session of the Parliament
(*b*) Six weeks from the date of issue
(*c*) Six months from the date of issue
(*d*) Six months after the commencement of the next session of the Parliament
210. The President can promulgate an ordinance only when
(*a*) The Parliament is not in session
(*b*) The Bill was sponsored by the President but the Parliament refused to pass the same
(*c*) The Bill has been pending in the Parliament for a year
(*d*) There is disagreement between the two houses of the Parliament
211. Proclamation of President's Rule in a state can be made
(*a*) If the President, on receipt of a report from the Governor of a State or otherwise is satisfied that a situation has arisen in which the government of the state cannot be carried on in accordance with the provisions of the Constitution
(*b*) When the Governor and the Chief Minister of a state differ on a vital issue
(*c*) If the President, on receipt of a report from the Governor of a State, is satisfied that a situation is likely to arise in which the government of the state cannot be carried on in accordance with the provisions of the Constitution
(*d*) When a Bill introduced by the state government is defeated in the state legislature

212. The President can dismiss a member of the Council of Ministers
(a) On the recommendation of the Prime Minister
(*b*) With the consent of the Speaker
(*c*) At his discretion (*d*) He can't dismiss

213. The Presidential Address is prepared by
(*a*) The Prime Minister and his/her Cabinet
(*b*) The Special Secretary of the President
(*c*) The Ministry of Parliamentary Affairs (*d*) A Cabinet Minister of President's choice

214. Who among the following are appointed by the President of India?
1. State Governors
2. Chief Justice and Judges of High Courts
3. Chief Justice and Judges of Supreme Court
4. The Vice President
Select the correct answer from codes given below:
(*a*) 1, 2 and 3 (*b*) 1 and 2
(*c*) 2, 3 and 4 (*d*) 1, 3 and 4

215. The President of India is elected on the basis of
(*a*) Proportional representation by single-transferable vote
(*b*) Proportional representation
(*c*) Single member territorial representation
(*d*) None of these

216. Who will appoint the Attorney General of India?
(*a*) President (*b*) Chief Justice
(*c*) Prime Minister (*d*) Law Minister

217. The Vice President of India is
(*a*) Elected by MPs (LS & RS) at a joint sitting
(b) Elected by LS
(*c*) Elected directly by the people
(*d*) Elected by the same Electoral College which elects the President

218. Vice President of India can be removed from Office before expiry of his/her term by
(*a*) Two Houses of Parliament (*b*) President at his/her discretion
(*c*) RS with two-third majority
(*d*) President with the consent of the majority of the state legislatives

219. The Vice-President of India discharges the duties of President in the event
(*a*) All these situations (*b*) His resignation
(*c*) His absence due to illness (*d*) His death

220. The Vice President of India is the ex-officio Chairman of the
(*a*) RS (*b*) LS
(c) National Development Council (*d*) Planning Commission

221. Who decides disputes regarding the election of the Vice President?
(*a*) Supreme Court (*b*) Speaker
(*c*) President (*d*) Parliament

222. The Vice President discharges the duties of the President during his/her illness for a maximum period of
(*a*) Indefinitely (*b*) One year
(*c*) Six months (*d*) Three months

223. When the Vice President discharges duties of Office of President, he is entitled to
(*a*) Salary and allowances attached to the President's Office
(*b*) Salary of Vice-President as well as President
(*c*) Allowance of Rs.2500/- in addition to his own salary as Vice-President
(*d*) No salary

224. The Vice-President has
(*a*) Right to preside over RS (*b*) Executive power
(*c*) Legislative power (*d*) Power to grant pardon

225. No criminal proceedings shall be instituted during his term of Office against the
(*a*) Vice-President (*b*) Governor
(*c*) Prime Minister (*d*) Chief Minister

226. Among the four pairs given below, which one consists of correct combination of dignitaries who became Vice-Presidents after having held diplomatic positions?
(*a*) S. Radhakrishnan and G. S. Pathak (*b*) S. Radhakrishnan and Zakir Hussain
(*c*) S. Radhakrishnan and V. V. Giri (*d*) B. D. Jatti and K. R. Narayanan

227. Identify the correct order in which the following acted as Vice-President of India
(*a*) Zakir Hussain, Pathak, Jatti and Venkataraman
(*b*) Zakir Hussain, Venkataraman, Jatti and Pathak
(*c*) Jatti, Zakir Hussain, Pathak and Venkataraman
(*d*) Pathak, Jatti, Zakir Hussain and Venkataraman

228. Which one of the following Vice-Presidents resigned from his Office to contest for the Office of the President?
(*a*) Giri (*b*) Sanjeeva Reddy
(*c*) Fakhruddin Ali Ahmad (*d*) Both (b) and (c)

229. Who of the following held the Office of the Vice-President of India for two full terms?
(*a*) Radhakrishnan (*b*) Giri
(*c*) Zakir Hussain (*d*) Pathak

230. Who of the following became President of India without serving as Vice President?
(*a*) Sanjeeva Reddy (*b*) Venkataraman
(*c*) Giri (*d*) Zakir Hussain

231. Who is the first Chief Justice to be appointed as acting President of India?
(*a*) Hidayatullah (*b*) Giri
(*c*) Sanjeeva Reddy (*d*) Jatti

232. Which Article provides that there shall be the Prime Minister of India?
(*a*) 74 (*b*) 52
(*c*) 124 (*d*) 153

233. The Prime Minister is
(*a*) Head of Government (*b*) Head of State
(*c*) Head of State as well as Government (*d*) Constitutional Head

234. The Office of the Prime Minister
(*a*) Has been created by the Constitution
(*b*) Is based on conventions
(*c*) Has been created by parliamentary statute
(*d*) Is a combination of all of these

235. The Prime Minister is
   (*a*) Appointed by the President (*b*) Elected by the LS
   (*c*) Elected by the two Houses at a joint sitting
   (*d*) Elected by the LS and appointed by the President
236. Who is the real executive under the Indian Constitution?
   (*a*) Prime Minister (*b*) President
   (*c*) Chief Justice of India (*d*) Speaker of LS
237. Who is considered as the Chief Spokesperson (Spokesman) of the Union Government?
   (*a*) Prime Minister (*b*) President
   (*c*) Vice-President (*d*) Speaker of LS
238. Who is the Chairman of the Planning Commission and National Development Council?
   (*a*) Prime Minister (*b*) President
   (*c*) Vice-President (*d*) Speaker of LS
239. Generally, the Prime Minister is
   (*a*) Leader of the majority party in the LS (*b*) Senior most MP
   (*c*) A close friend of the President (*d*) Not a MP
240. The Prime Minister holds Office
   (*a*) As long as he enjoys confidence of Parliament
   (*b*) For a fixed term of five years
   (*c*) During the pleasure of President
   (*d*) As long as he enjoys confidence of the Council of Ministers
241. Generally the Prime Minister is
   (*a*) Member of LS (*b*) Member of RS
   (*c*) Member of RS and LS (*d*) Not a MP
242. Who announces the Government policies on the floor of the House?
   (*a*) Prime Minister (*b*) Speaker of LS
   (*c*) Finance Minister (*d*) Parliamentary Affairs Minister
243. Who recommends for the dissolution of LS?
   (*a*) Prime Minister (*b*) President
   (*c*) Parliamentary Affairs Minister (*d*) Speaker of LS
244. Who presides over the meetings of the Council of Ministers?
   (*a*) Prime Minister (*b*) President
   (*c*) Senior-most Minister (*d*) Speaker of LS
245. Who acts as the channel of communication between the President and Council of Ministers?
   (*a*) Prime Minister (*b*) Deputy Prime Minister
   (*c*) Speaker of LS (*d*) Senior-most Minister
246. Who is the keystone of the Indian Constitution?
   (*a*) Prime Minister (*b*) President
   (*c*) Speaker of LS (*d*) Chairman of RS
247. Who describes the Prime Minister of India as 'Primus Inter Pares' (first among equals)?
   (*a*) Lord Morely (*b*) K. M. Munshi
   (*c*) Harold Laski (*d*) Sir William Vernon
248. The members of Council of Ministers are appointed by the
   (*a*) President on the advice of the Prime Minister
   (*b*) President on the recommendation of the Parliament
   (*c*) Prime Minister (*d*) President at his/her discretion

249. A person can be member of the Council of Ministers without being a MP for a maximum period of _____ months.
(*a*) Six (*b*) Three
(*c*) One (*d*) Twelve

250. Who enjoys distinction of having been the Prime Minister of India for longest duration?
(*a*) Indira Gandhi (*b*) Jawaharlal Nehru
(*c*) Lal Bahadur Shastri (*d*) None of these

251. Who became the Prime Minister of India without becoming a Union Cabinet Minister?
(*a*) Deve Gowda (*b*) Charan Singh
(*c*) Inder Kumar Gujral (*d*) Morarji Desai

252. Which State of India has contributed the maximum Prime Ministers?
(*a*) Uttar Pradesh (*b*) Andhra Pradesh
(*c*) Gujarat (*d*) Both (a) and (b) equally

253. Maximum number of 'No-Confidence Motion' were admitted and discussed during the Prime Ministership of
(*a*) Narasimha Rao (*b*) Jawaharlal Nehru
(*c*) Morarji Desai (*d*) Indira Gandhi

254. The first Prime Minister of India was appointed by the
(*a*) Governor General (*b*) Viceroy
(*c*) M.K. Gandhiji (*d*) Committee headed by Rajendra Prasad

255. The Office of the Deputy Prime Minister
(*a*) Is an extra-constitutional growth (*b*) Was created under the Original Constitution
(*c*) Was created by 44th Amendment in 1979
(*d*) Was created by the 85th Amendment, 2002

256. Indian Constitution is silent on the concept of
(*a*) Deputy Prime minister (*b*) Deputy Chairman of RS
(*c*) Deputy Speaker of LS (*d*) Deputy Speaker of Legislative Assembly

257. Who enjoys the distinction of being the first Deputy Prime Minister of India?
(*a*) Sardar Vallabhai Patel (*b*) Jagjivan Ram
(*c*) Morarji Desai (*d*) L.K. Advani

258. Lal Krishnan Advani is the ______ Deputy Prime Minister.
(*a*) 7th (*b*) 5th
(*c*) 3rd (*d*) 4th

259. Which one of the following Motion can be moved by the Government?
(*a*) Confidence Motion (*b*) No-Confidence Motion
(*c*) Censure Motion (*d*) Semi-Confidence Motion

260. Which one of the following statement is correct? The Prime Minister of India
(*a*) Has full discretion in the choice of persons who are to serve as ministers in his Cabinet
(*b*) Is free to choose his ministers only from among those who are MPs of RS or LS
(*c*) Can choose his Cabinet colleagues after counseling by the President
(*d*) Has only limited powers in the choice of his cabinet colleagues

261. Which of the following enjoys the distinction of being the first recognized Leader of the Opposition in the LS?
(*a*) Y.B. Chavan (*b*) A.K. Gopalan
(*c*) Shyama Prasad Mukherjee (*d*) Indira Gandhi

262. A political party is accorded status of an Opposition Party in LS if it captures at least
(*a*) 10% of seats (*b*) 15% of seats
(*c*) 20% of seats (*d*) 18% of seats

263. 'Collective Responsibility of the Cabinet' means all ministers are collectively responsible to (OR) The Union Council of Ministers are responsible to
(*a*) LS (*b*) RS
(*c*) President (*d*) Prime Minister

264. Who enforces collective responsibility amongst the Council of Ministers?
(*a*) Prime Minister (*b*) President
(*c*) Speaker of LS (*d*) Parliament

265. The phrase under the Article 74 "There shall be Council of Ministers with the Prime Minister is its Head" is
(*a*) Mandatory (*b*) Directory
(*c*) Discretion of the President (*d*) Discretion of the LS

266. Who presides over the meetings of the Council of Ministers?
(*a*) Prime Minister (*b*) President
(*c*) Different ministers by rotation (*d*) Cabinet Secretary

267. The Council of Ministers is collectively responsible to
(*a*) Parliament (*b*) President
(*c*) Prime Minister (*d*) People

268. Who allocates portfolios among the Council of Ministers?
(*a*) President on the recommendation of Prime Minister (*b*) Prime Minister
(*c*) President (*d*) Speaker by draw of lots

269. A member of Council of Ministers can be dismissed by the President
(*a*) On the recommendation of the Prime Minister
(*b*) On his own
(*c*) On the recommendation of the LS (*d*) On the recommendation of the Parliament

270. The vote of 'No confidence' is passed against a Minister
(*a*) The whole Council of Ministers has to resign
(*b*) He has to tender his resignation
(*c*) Minister as well as Prime Minister
(*d*) None of these

271. Though the Council of Ministers is collectively responsible to the Parliament, the individual Ministers are responsible to
(*a*) President (*b*) Prime Minister
(*c*) Speaker (*d*) Vice-President

272. The President of India is removed from Office by
(*a*) Impeachment (*b*) No-Confidence Motion
(*c*) Dismissal Motion (*d*) Confidence Motion

273. The President of India is not bound by the aid and advice of the Council of Ministers in the matter of appointment of
(*a*) Union Ministers (*b*) Judges of Supreme and High courts
(*c*) Chairman and Members of UPSC (*d*) Governors of State

274. The Parliament of India consists of
(*a*) President, LS and RS (*b*) LS and RS
(*c*) LS, Speaker and Prime Minister (*d*) President and Prime Minister

275. Members of the LS are
(*a*) Directly elected by the people (*b*) Indirectly elected by the state legislatures
(*c*) Nominated by the President (*d*) None of these

276. How many seats have been reserved for the Union Territories in the LS?
(*a*) 20 (*b*) 25
(*c*) 40 (*d*) 50

277. The number of Ministers in the Central Government is fixed by the
(*a*) Parliament (*b*) Planning Commission
(*c*) President (*d*) Prime Minister

278. Seats are allocated to the various states in the LS on the basis of
(*a*) Their population (*b*) Their size and resources
(*c*) Their size, resources and population (*d*) Presidents words

279. Who among the following can initiate an amendment to the Indian Constitution?
(*a*) Either House of Parliament (*b*) Legislative Assembly in any State
(*c*) President (*d*) Any MP or State Legislature

280. Which State sends the maximum representatives to the LS?
(*a*) Uttar Pradesh (*b*) Madhya Pradesh
(*c*) West Bengal (*d*) Karnataka

281. The 42nd Amendment raised the term of the LS to _____ years.
(*a*) Six (*b*) Five
(*c*) Seven (*d*) Eight

282. The term of LS can be extended beyond its normal term of five years by the
(*a*) President during National Emergency only
(*b*) President during all types of Emergency
(*c*) President on the recommendation of Election Commission
(*d*) President at his/her discretion

283. The President can extend the life of the LS during a National Emergency in the first instance for a period of _______ months.
(*a*) One (*b*) Three
(*c*) Six (*d*) Twelve

284. The RS can be dissolved by
(*a*) Cannot be dissolved (*b*) President
(*c*) Vice-President (*d*) Prime Minister

285. The continuation of National Emergency beyond a period of six months is possible only with the approval of
(*a*) Parliament by special majority (*b*) Supreme Court
(*c*) Parliament by simple majority (*d*) High Court

286. What is the maximum gap in months permissible between two sessions of Parliament?
(*a*) Six (*b*) Three
(*c*) Nine (*d*) Twelve

287. Who can dissolve the LS before the expiry of its normal term of five years?
(*a*) President on the recommendation of the Prime Minister
(*b*) President
(*c*) Prime Minister
(*d*) President on the recommendation of the Speaker

288. Which of the following statements correctly describes a 'Hung Parliament'?
(*a*) A Parliament in which no party has a clear majority
(*b*) The Prime Minister has resigned but the Parliament is not dissolved
(*c*) The Parliament lacks the quorum to conduct business
(*d*) A lame duck Parliament

289. The President can call a joint session of the two houses of Parliament.
(*a*) All of these
(*b*) If a Bill passed by one House is rejected by the other
(*c*) If the Amendment proposed to a Bill by one House is not acceptable to the other
(*d*) If the house does not take any decision for six months on a Bill remitted by the other

290. In the RS, the states have been provided
(*a*) Representation on the basis of population
(*b*) Equal representation
(*c*) Representation on the basis of population and size
(*d*) Representation on the basis of size

291. The maximum number of representatives are sent to the RS by
(*a*) Uttar Pradesh (*b*) West Bengal
(*c*) Andhra Pradesh (*d*) Karnataka

292. The members of RS shall be elected by
(*a*) MLAs (*b*) MPs of LS
(*c*) Universal Adult Franchise (*d*) Secret Ballot

293. Who reserves the right to convene joint sessions of the LS and RS?
(*a*) President (*b*) Speaker of LS
(*c*) Chairman of RS (*d*) Prime Minister

294. Representatives of the Union Territories in the RS shall be chosen by the
(*a*) Parliament (*b*) President
(*c*) Chairman of RS (*d*) Lt. Governor of respective territory

295. Which one of the following is not a Central tax?
(*a*) Sales Tax (*b*) Income Tax
(*c*) Excise Duty (*d*) Customs Duty

296. A Money Bill can originate
(*a*) Only in the LS
(*b*) Only in the RS
(*c*) In either House of the Parliament
(*d*) Only in the joint sitting of the two Houses of the Parliament

297. Which Bill can be introduced in the Parliament only with prior approval of the President?
(*a*) Money Bills
(*b*) Bill pertaining to impeachment of President
(*c*) Bill pertaining to powers of the Supreme Court
(*d*) All of these

298. A Bill for which the President is bound to give his assent without sending it back for fresh consideration is
(*a*) Money Bill (*b*) Ordinary Bill
(*c*) Constitution Amendment Bill (*d*) Bill passed by both the Houses of Parliament
299. Which one of the following Bills must be passed by each House of the Indian Parliament separately, by special majority?
(*a*) Constitution Amendment Bill (*b*) Finance Bill
(*c*) Money Bill (*d*) Ordinary Bill
300. How many times the President can return a Non-Money Bill, passed by the Parliament for its consideration?
(*a*) Once (*b*) Twice
(*c*) Thrice (*d*) Never
301. The RS is a Permanent House but
(*a*) One-third of its members retire in two years
(*b*) One-third of its members retire in three years
(*c*) One-half of its members retire in two years
(*d*) One-half of its members retire in three years
302. A Money Bill passed by the LS can be delayed by the RS for a maximum period of
(*a*) 14 days (*b*) One month
(*c*) Two months (*d*) Tthree months
303. Which of the following sets of Bills is presented to the Parliament along with Budget?
(*a*) Finance Bill and Appropriation Bill (*b*) Finance Bill and Contingency Bill
(*c*) Contingency Bill and Appropriation Bill (*d*) Direct taxes Bill and Indirect taxes Bill
304. Salary of which one of the Officials is not charged on the Consolidated Fund of India?
(*a*) Prime Minister of India (*b*) CAG
(*c*) Chief Justice of India (*d*) President of India
305. A Union Minister must be a member of
(*a*) Parliament (*b*) Judiciary
(*c*) A State (*d*) Union Territory
306. The Prime Minister acts as a medium of communication between
(*a*) Ministry and President (*b*) President and Vice President
(*c*) Speaker and Deputy Speaker (*d*) LS and RS
307. Cabinet Ministers has to tender its resignation if a no-confidence vote is passed against it by
(*a*) LS (*b*) RS
(*c*) Two Houses at a joint sitting (*d*) Supreme Court
308. In which system, the government can be removed by way of 'No Confidence Motion'?
(*a*) Parliamentary (*b*) Federal
(*c*) Presidential (*d*) Unitary
309. Who will determine the rank of different Ministers in Union and State Council of Ministers?
(*a*) Prime Minister and Chief Minister (*b*) President and Governor
(*c*) Speaker of LS and Speaker of Vidhana Sabha
(*d*) Respective Parliamentary Affairs Minister
310. Which of the following powers is exclusively vested in the RS?
(*a*) To recommend the creation of new All India Services
(*b*) To initiate impeachment proceedings against President
(*c*) To remove the Vice President (*d*) All these powers

311. The RS can be dissolved before expiry of its term by the
   (*a*) None of these
   (*b*) President
   (*c*) Vice President
   (*d*) President on the recommendation of the Council of Ministers
312. Who is the first woman film star nominated or elected to RS?
   (*a*) Nargis Dutt (*b*) Vyjayanthimala
   (*c*) Hema Malini (*d*) Jayalalitha
313. No taxes can be levied or expenditure incurred without the approval of the
   (*a*) Parliament (*b*) Council of Ministers
   (c) President (*d*) All of these
314. Who decides disputes regarding the disqualification of MPs?
   (*a*) The President in consultation with Election Commission
   (*b*) Election Commission
   (*c*) The President (*d*) The concerned House
315. Election to the LS could not be held in Punjab in December 1984 due to
   (*a*) Uncertainties created by growing terrorist activities
   (*b*) Possibility of attack by the Pakistan
   (*c*) Decision of Akali Dal to boycott the elections
   (*d*) Outbreak of communal riots in the State
316. Who decides whether a Bill is a Money Bill or not? (OR) If any question arises whether a Bill is Money Bill or not, the decision of _____ is final.
   (*a*) Speaker (*b*) President
   (*c*) Prime Minister (*d*) Vice President
317. All Money Bills can be introduced
   (*a*) In LS only (*b*) In RS only
   (*c*) In either of the House (*d*) By the President
318. Who is the first Speaker of the LS who died in Office?
   (*a*) GMC Balayogi (*b*) MA Ayyangar
   (*c*) KD Hegde (*d*) None of these
319. Who presides over the LS if neither the Speaker nor the Deputy Speaker is available?
   (*a*) A Member appointed by President (*b*) A Senior-most Member of the LS
   (*c*) A Member chosen by the Council of Ministers
   (*d*) Deputy Chairman of RS
320. If there is a disagreement between the two Houses of the Parliament on any particular Bill
   (*a*) A Joint sitting of the two Houses of Parliament is convened
   (*b*) The President gives casting vote
   (*c*) Speaker of LS and Chairman of RS submits the Bill to the President
   (*d*) The Prime Minister intervenes and gives the final decision
321. In the Indian Constitution, the Budget is referred as
   (*a*) Annual Financial Statement (*b*) Annual Budget Statement
   (*c*) Annual Revenue Statement (*d*) Annual Expenditure Statement
322. During the discussions in Parliament, 'Guillotine' applies to
   (*a*) Demands for Grants (*b*) Vote on Account
   (*c*) Finance Bill (*d*) Appropriation Bill

323. Which Assembly is presided over by a non-member?
(*a*) Rajya Sabha (*b*) Lok Sabha
(*c*) State Assembly (*d*) All of these
324. The Chairman of the RS has
(*a*) A vote only in case of tie (*b*) A vote like any other MP of RS
(*c*) No vote because he is the Ex-officio Chairman of the House
(*d*) Two votes–an ordinary vote and casting vote
325. The Secretary General of the LS, who is the Chief of the LS Secretariat, is appointed by
(*a*) Speaker (*b*) President
(*c*) Minister of Parliamentary Affairs in consultation with the Speaker
(*d*) A Committee of the House, especially constituted for this purpose
326. The Parliament of India cannot be regarded as a sovereign body because
(*a*) All of these factors
(*b*) Its authority is confined to jurisdiction earmarked by the Constitution
(*c*) Laws passed by Parliament can be declared unconstitutional by the Supreme Court
(*d*) Of the presence of certain FRs of the citizens
327. The Parliament of India exercises control over administration
(*a*) Through parliamentary committees
(*b*) Through consultative committees of different ministries
(*c*) By obtaining periodic reports from administrators
(*d*) Through all of these
328. The speech made by a MP on the floor of House
(*a*) Cannot be questioned in any Court of Law
(*b*) Can be questioned in the High Court
(*c*) Can be questioned in the Supreme Court
(*d*) None of these
329. The Parliament works through numerous committees, whose members are
(*a*) Either appointed by the Speaker or elected by the House
(*b*) Appointed by the Speaker
(*c*) Appointed by the Council of Ministers (*d*) Appointed by the Parliamentary Affairs Minister
330. This is not the function of LS
(*a*) Judicial (*b*) Executive
(*c*) Financial (*d*) Legislative
331. The Speaker of the LS makes use of his/her casting vote only
(*a*) In case of tie i.e., when votes are equally divided
(*b*) To save the existing government
(*c*) In case of constitutional amendments (*d*) In case of emergency
332. LS passes vote on account to
(*a*) Meet the expenditure during the period between the introduction of budget and its passage
(*b*) To meet expenses on secret services
(*c*) To enable the government to meet unexpected expenditure
(*d*) None of these
333. LS Secretariat works under the direct supervision of the
(*a*) Speaker (*b*) Minister of Parliamentary Affairs
(*c*) President (*d*) None of these

334. Which state sends the maximum number of representatives to the RS?
(*a*) Uttar Pradesh (*b*) Madhya Pradesh
(*c*) Andhra Pradesh (*d*) West Bengal

335. A half-an-hour discussion can be raised in the House after giving notice to the
(*a*) Secretary General of the House (*b*) Presiding Officer
(*c*) Minister of Parliamentary Affairs (*d*) Concerned Minister

336. A MP enjoys immunity from prosecution for having said anything
(*a*) In the Parliament and its committees (*b*) During the session of the parliament anywhere
(*c*) At a press conference (*d*) None of these

337. Final decision whether a MP of LS has incurred disqualification under the Defection Law rests with
(*a*) Speaker (*b*) Election Commission
(*c*) Supreme Court (*d*) President

338. The Parliament or State Legislature can declare a seat vacant if a member absents himself without permission from the sessions for _____ days.
(*a*) 60 (*b*) 90
(*c*) 120 (*d*) 30

339. Who presides over the LS if neither Speaker nor Deputy Speaker is available?
(*a*) A member of the panel of Chairmen announced by Speaker
(*b*) A member nominated by President
(*c*) A member chosen by Council of Ministers
(*d*) The senior-most member of the LS

340. The function of the Pro-Temp Speaker is to
(*a*) Swear-in members and hold charge till a regular speaker is elected
(*b*) Conducts proceedings of the House in the absence of the speaker
(*c*) Officiate as speaker when speaker is unlikely to be elected
(*d*) Checks if election certificates of members are in order

341. Which one of the following are the Financial Committees of Parliament of India?
1. Public Accounts Committee
2. Estimate Committee
3. Committee on Public Undertakings
State the correct answer:
(*a*) 1, 2 and 3 (*b*) 1 and 2
(*c*) 1 and 3 (*d*) 1

342. The Public Accounts Committee submits its report to the
(*a*) Speaker (*b*) Comptroller and Auditor General
(*c*) President (*d*) Minister of Parliamentary Affairs

343. The Comptroller and Auditor General acts as friend, philosopher and guide of
(*a*) Public Accounts Committee (*b*) Estimate Committee
(*c*) Committee on Public Undertakings (*d*) All of these

344. Which one of the following motions is related with the Union Budget?
(*a*) Cut Motion (*b*) Censure Motion
(*c*) Adjournment Motion (*d*) Special Motion

345. Which of the following committees of Parliament is concerned with the regularity and economy of expenditure?
   (*a*) Public Accounts Committee (*b*) Estimate Committee
   (*c*) Committee on Privileges (*d*) All
346. Who of the following is considered the Custodian of the Parliament?
   (*a*) Speaker (*b*) Prime Minister
   (*c*) Leader of Opposition (*d*) Chief Whip of ruling party
347. A member, after being elected as Speaker of LS, generally
   (*a*) Cuts-off his connection with his party (*b*) Joins ruling party
   (*c*) Becomes Chief Spokesman of his party
   (*d*) Continues to be a member of party and seeks to promote its interest
348. Which one of the following is the correct definition of the term 'Whip'?
   (*a*) State in which all the members of the political party are required to be present in the Parliament and vote according to the instructions of the party
   (*b*) A document published by the government, containing full information on an issue of national importance
   (*c*) A situation in which all the members of a political party attend the session of Parliament but need not participate in voting
   (*d*) None of these
349. Who among the following may belong to RS but can speak in both the Houses?
   (*a*) Ministers who are MPs of RS
   (*b*) Nominated MPs of RS who are experts of a particular field
   (*c*) Deputy Chairman of the RS (*d*) Leader of the House in RS
350. Which one of the following statements regarding the Office of the Speaker is correct?
   (*a*) If he intends to resign, the letter of his resignation is to be addressed to the Deputy Speaker
   (*b*) He loses his Office if the House is dissolved before the end of the normal tenure
   (*c*) He is not be a member of the House at the time of election as Speaker, but must become the member of the House within six months of the date of election
   (*d*) He holds his Office during the pleasure of the President
351. Which of the following statement is correct?
   (*a*) The term of the LS can be extended by one year at a time
   (*b*) The term of the LS can be extended by the President for a full term of five years
   (*c*) The term of the LS can be extended by the President with the consent of the speaker for an unlimited period
   (*d*) The term of the LS cannot be extended beyond five years
352. Which one of the following LS enjoyed a term of more than five years?
   (*a*) 5th (*b*) 6th
   (*c*) 4th (*d*) 8th
353. The differences between the two Houses of Parliament are resolved through (OR) Disagreement between the two Houses of the Indian Parliament is finally resolved by which of the following processes?
   (*a*) A joint session of the two Houses
   (*b*) Mediatory efforts of the officers of the two Houses
   (*c*) A joint committee of the two Houses, specially constituted for this purpose
   (*d*) The mediation of the Ministry of Parliamentary Affairs

(*e*) Intervention of the Prime Minister of India
(*f*) Judgment by the Supreme Court
(*g*) Parliamentary Committee appointed by President of India

354. The quorum or minimum number of members required to hold the meeting of either House of Parliament is
(*a*) One-tenth (*b*) One-fifth
(*c*) One-fourth (*d*) One-third

355. Which of the following states sends the largest number of MPs to LS after Uttar Pradesh?
(*a*) Maharashtra (*b*) Madhya Pradesh
(*c*) Bihar (*d*) Karnataka

356. Which of the following statements is not correct?
(*a*) In the event of the dissolution of the LS, any Bill pending in the RS, but not passed by the LS, lapses
(*b*) In the event of the dissolution of the LS, any Bill pending in the RS, but passed by the LS, does not lapse
(*c*) In the event of the dissolution of the LS, any Bill passed by the LS and pending on the RS lapses
(*d*) In the event of the dissolution of the LS, any Bill pending in the LS lapses

357. Under the new committee system launched in April 1993, out of the 17 standing committees
(*a*) 06 are constituted by the Chairman of the RS and 11 by the Speaker of the LS
(*b*) 05 are constituted by the Chairman of the RS and 12 by the Speaker of the LS
(*c*) 08 are constituted by the Chairman of the RS and 09 by the Speaker of the LS
(*d*) All the committees are constituted jointly by the Chairman of the RS and the Speaker of the LS

358. The term 'closure' in Parliamentary terminology
(*a*) Stoppage of debate on a motion (*b*) The end of the session of the Parliament
(*c*) End of the day's proceedings (*d*) The end of budget session

359. 'No Confidence' motion against Council of Ministers can be introduced in the
(*a*) LS (*b*) RS
(*c*) Legislative Council (*d*) None of these

360. The Supreme Court of India consists of a Chief Justice and —— judges.
(*a*) 25 (*b*) 11
(*c*) 9 (*d*) 7

361. Who is the first Chief Justice of India?
(*a*) Harlal J. Kania (*b*) Patanjali Sasthri
(*c*) B.K. Mukherjee (*d*) S.R. Das

362. The following factor does not help to maintain independence of judiciary
(*a*) Highly attractive retirement benefits (*b*) Security of tenure
(*c*) No discussion in legislature on the conduct of judges
(*d*) Salary of judges cannot be reduced

363. The Principles of Natural Justice do not require
(*a*) Follow instructions strictly by superior officer
(*b*) Reasonable opportunity being heard
(*c*) Reasonable notice
(*d*) Decision on merits

364. The Supreme Court of India was set up
(*a*) By the Constitution (*b*) Under the Indian Independence Act, 1947
(*c*) Through an Act of Parliament in 1950 (*d*) Under the Government of India Act, 1935
365. Which is the highest Court of appeal in India?
(*a*) Supreme Court (*b*) High Court
(*c*) President's Court (*d*) Munsiff Court
366. Who interprets the Indian Constitution?
(*a*) Supreme Court (*b*) Parliament
(*c*) President (*d*) Founding Fathers
367. Which Article provides that laws laid down by Supreme Court is binding on all courts in India?
(*a*) 141 (*b*) 145
(*c*) 131 (*d*) 142
368. Which Article empowers the Supreme Court to review its own judgment?
(*a*) 137 (*b*) 136
(*c*) 131 (*d*) 32
369. The judges of the Supreme Court are appointed by the
(*a*) President in consultation with the Chief Justice of India
(*b*) President on the advice of the Prime Minister
(*c*) President on the advice of the Parliament
(*d*) Parliament
370. The judges of the Supreme Court hold Office till they attain the age (in years) of
(*a*) 65 (*b*) 62
(*c*) 70 (*d*) 60
371. One of the qualifications to become the Judge of the Supreme Court is
(*a*) In the opinion of the President, he must be a distinguished Jurist
(*b*) Practice in District level Court for at least 12 years
(*c*) Served as Judge of High Court for at least 3 years
(*d*) Practice in a High Court for at least 9 years
372. The Supreme Court holds its meetings at New Delhi, but it can meet elsewhere
(*a*) With the approval of the President (*b*) With the approval of the Parliament
(*c*) If a majority of judges so decide (*d*) On the request of the State Legislatures
373. For criminal misconduct, the Judge of the Supreme Court
(*a*) Can be prosecuted (*b*) Cannot be prosecuted
(*c*) Can be prosecuted with the consent of the President
(*d*) Can be prosecuted with the consent of the Chief Justice of India
374. The Judges of Supreme Court, after retirement, are not permitted to carry on practice before
(*a*) Any of these (*b*) Supreme Court of India
(*c*) High courts (*d*) District and Sessions courts
375. In the event of non-availability of Chief Justice of India, an Acting Chief Justice can be appointed by the
(*a*) President
(*b*) Union Law Minister
(*c*) Chief Justice of India
(*d*) President in consultation with Chief Justice of India

376. The judges of the Supreme Court
(*a*) Can be removed by the President on the recommendation of the Parliament
(*b*) Can be removed by the President on the recommendation of the Council of Ministers
(*c*) Can be removed by the President at his/her discretion
(*d*) Cannot be removed from the Office during their tenure

377. The judges of the Supreme Court can be removed on the ground of proved misbehavior by the _____ if the Parliament passes a resolution with two-third majority present and voting.
(*a*) President (*b*) Prime Minister
(*c*) Law Minister (*d*) Chief Justice of India

378. The Supreme Court of India is a court of record which implies that
(*a*) Both (*b*) and (*c*)
(*b*) All its decisions have evidentiary value and cannot be questioned in any court
(*c*) It has power to punish for its contempt
(*d*) It has to keep a record of all its decisions

379. The Supreme Court tenders advice to the President on a matter of law or fact
(*a*) Only if he seeks such advice (*b*) On its own
(*c*) Only if the matter relates to the FRs
(*d*) Only if the issue poses a threat to the unity and integrity of the country

380. The advice of the Supreme Court is
(*a*) Not binding on the President (*b*) Binding on the President
(*c*) Binding on President if it is tendered unanimously
(*d*) Binding in certain cases and not binding in others

381. All cases involving an interpretation of the Constitution fall within the
(*a*) Original jurisdiction of the Supreme Court
(*b*) Advisory jurisdiction of the Supreme Court
(*c*) Appellate jurisdiction of the Supreme Court
(*d*) Discretary power of Supreme Court

382. Power of the Supreme Court to decide disputes between the Center and States fall under its
(*a*) Original Jurisdiction (*b*) Advisory Jurisdiction
(*c*) Appellate Jurisdiction (*d*) Constitutional Jurisdiction

383. Original Jurisdiction of the Supreme Court of India relates to
(*a*) Disputes between Union and States (*b*) Writs directly filed in Supreme Court
(*c*) Criminal complaints directly filed in Supreme Court
(*d*) Civil suits directly filed in Supreme Court

384. The Supreme Court has Original Jurisdiction in
(*a*) All inter-state disputes (*b*) All disputes relating to international relations
(*c*) Disputes to which India and foreign states are parties
(*d*) In conflict between two foreign states

385. Under the Advisory Jurisdiction, the Supreme Court gives its opinion to
(*a*) President (*b*) Union Law Minister
(*c*) Planning Commission (*d*) Prime Minister

386. Appellate Jurisdiction of the Supreme Court does not include
(*a*) Appeals against writs (*b*) Special leave to appeal
(*c*) Appeals in criminal cases (*d*) Appeals in civil cases

387. Appellate Jurisdiction of the Supreme Court in appeal from High Court in regard to civil matters pertaining only to
(*a*) Substantial question of law (*b*) Mixed question of law and fact
(*c*) Question of law (*d*) Question of fact

388. Who has the power to enlarge the Jurisdiction of Supreme Court with respect to any matter contained under the Union List?
(*a*) Parliament (*b*) President
(*c*) Chief Justice of India (*d*) Prime Minister

389. Which of the following statement refers to 'Epistolary Jurisdiction' of the Supreme Court?
(*a*) Taking cognizance of the concerned matter through letter addressed to the Court
(*b*) Original Jurisdiction of the Supreme Court (Article 131)
(*c*) Enforcement of decrees and orders of the Supreme Court (Article 142)
(*d*) Advisory Jurisdiction of the Supreme Court (Article 143)

390. Who has the power to increase the number of judges of the Supreme Court?
(*a*) Parliament (*b*) Prime Minister
(*c*) President (*d*) Chief Justice of India

391. Ad hoc judges can be appointed in the Supreme Court by the
(*a*) Chief Justice of India with the prior consent of the President
(*b*) Chief Justice of India after consulting other Judges
(*c*) President on the advice of the Union Law Minister
(*d*) Union Law Minister, but such appointments must be ratified by the Parliament within two months

392. Ad hoc judges can be appointed to the Supreme Court
(*a*) If requisite number of judges are not available to hold the meating of the court
(*b*) If qualified candidates are not available for permanent apointment
(*c*) If some of the sitting Judges proceed on leave
(*d*) For the dismissal of accumulated cases

393. How many Judges of the Supreme Court have been removed from their Office before the expiry of their normal term through impeachment?
(*a*) None (*b*) One
(*c*) Two (*d*) Three

394. Which of the following has been wrongly listed as criteria for appointment as a Judge of the Supreme Court?
(*a*) Must have attained the age of 55 years
(*b*) Must in the opinion of the President, be a distinguished Jurist
(*c*) Must have been an Advocate of a High Court for not less than 10 years
(*d*) Must have been a Judge of a High Court for at least five years

395. Which conditions does not contribute to the independence of the Indian Judiciary?
(*a*) Once appointed, the judges cannot be removed from their Office before the date of retirement
(*b*) No change on salary and service conditions of judges can be made which operates against their interest after their appointment
(*c*) The salary and allowances are charged to the Consolidated Fund of India and are not subjected to parliamentary vote
(*d*) Retired judges are not permitted to carry on practice before any court or tribunal in India

396. Which of the following statements regarding Supreme Court of India is not correct?
(*a*) Acts as the protector of the DPSP
(*b*) Acts as the guardian of the Constitution
(*c*) Acts as the guardian of the liberties of the people of India
(*d*) Has final power to investigate disputes regarding election of the President and Vice President

397. Which of the following cases was connected with the Supreme Court's judgment in 1980 that the Amendments made to Articles 31 (c) and 368 are invalid?
(*a*) Keshavananda Bharti Case (*b*) Sajjan Singh Case
(*c*) Minerva Mills Case (*d*) Golak Nath Case

398. In which case did the Supreme Court restore the primacy of FRs over DPSP?
(*a*) Minerva Mills Case (*b*) Maneka Gandhi Case
(*c*) Keshavananda Bharti Case (*d*) Berubari Case

399. Any Act violating Article 13(2) of the Constitution shall be declared as Unconstitutional by
(*a*) Supreme Court (*b*) High Court
(*c*) President (*d*) Parliament

400. 'Appeal by Special Leave' means
(*a*) Supreme Court, granting in its discretion special permission to appeal from any judgment passed by any Court
(*b*) Supreme Court, granting special permission to appeal, though the time to appeal is barred by limitation
(*c*) Appeal permitted by the Supreme Court in matters relating to the election of the president
(*d*) Appeal permitted on payment of fine

401. The framers of Constitution borrowed the idea of Judicial Review from Constitution of
(*a*) USA (*b*) France
(*c*) UK (*d*) Japan

402. The framers of Constitution adopted the doctrine of Judicial Review
(*a*) To ensure proper working of the Federal System of the government
(*b*) To ensure proper working of the Parliamentary System of government
(*c*) To overcome the limitations of the rigid Constitution
(*d*) On account of all these factors

403. It became imperative for the framers of the Indian Constitution to adopt the doctrine of Judicial Review because of
(*a*) Adoption of Federal System of Government
(*b*) Its republican character
(*c*) Adoption of Parliamentary System of government
(*d*) A written Constitution

404. Which Amendment curtailed the Supreme Court/High Court's power of Judicial Review?
(*a*) 42nd (*b*) 44th
(*c*) 24th (*d*) 46th

405. The concept of 'Judicial Activism' gained currency in India in
(*a*) 1990s (*b*) 1980s
(*c*) 1970s (*d*) 1960s

406. Judicial Activism has led to increase in the powers of
(*a*) Judiciary (*b*) Legislature
(*c*) Executive (*d*) Press

407. The concept of Judicial Review is borrowed from the Constitution of
(*a*) USA (*b*) Russia
(*c*) Switzerland (*d*) UK

408. In India, power of Judicial Review is restricted because
(*a*) Constitution is supreme (*b*) Executive is supreme
(*c*) Legislature is supreme (*d*) Judges are transferable

409. While imparting justice, the Supreme Court relies on the principle of
(*a*) Procedure established by law (*b*) Due process of law
(*c*) Rule of law (*d*) None of these

410. On which list does the Union Government enjoy exclusive powers?
(*a*) Union List (*b*) State List
(*c*) Concurrent List (*d*) Special list

411. On which List do the states enjoy exclusive jurisdiction?
(*a*) State list (*b*) Concurrent list
(*c*) (*a*) and (*b*) (*d*) Union list

412. The subjects of National Importance were enumerated under
(*a*) Union list (*b*) State list
(*c*) Concurrent list (*d*) No such classification

413. Subjects like Defence and External Affairs are enumerated under
(*a*) List I (*b*) List II
(*c*) List III (*d*) Lists II and III

414. Subjects of Local Importance were enumerated under
(*a*) List II (*b*) List III
(*c*) List I (*d*) Lists I and II

415. The Constitution of India vests the Residuary powers in
(*a*) Union Government (*b*) States
(*c*) States and Union Government (*d*) Union Territories

416. Under the Constitution, Residuary Powers vested with the
(*a*) Union government (*b*) State government
(*c*) Supreme Court (*d*) President

417. In case of conflict between the Central and State laws on a subject in Concurrent List
(*a*) Law of the Center prevails (*b*) Law of the State prevails
(*c*) Both laws stand nullified (*d*) The law which has been passed first prevails

418. The concept of Concurrent List is borrowed from the Constitution of
(*a*) Australia (*b*) Ireland
(*c*) Canada (*d*) USA

419. At the time of accession to the Dominion, the States acceded only three subjects:
(*a*) Defence, Foreign Affairs and Communication
(*b*) Defence, Foreign Affairs and Planning
(*c*) Defence, Irrigation and Railways
(*d*) External Affairs, Planning and Transport and Communication

420. The Constitution of India has created
(*a*) Very strong center (*b*) Very weak center
(*c*) A center which is weak in normal times but very strong during emergencies
(*d*) No center

421. The Parliament can legislate on any subject in the state list
(*a*) In all these cases
(*b*) If two or more states make a request to Parliament to do so
(*c*) For the implementation of the international treaties or agreements
(*d*) If the RS declares by a two-thirds majority resolution that it is expedient to do so in national interest

422. The Central Government can issue directions to the State with regard to the subjects in
(*a*) All these Lists (*b*) Union List
(*c*) State List (*d*) Concurrent List

423. Which among the following subject is transferred from State List to Concurrent List by 42nd Constitutional Amendment?
(*a*) Education (*b*) Irrigation
(*c*) Agriculture (*d*) Local self-government

424. A Law passed by State Legislature on a Concurrent list gets precedence over Central Law if
(*a*) It was approved for the President (*b*) Majority of the State Legislature so decides
(*c*) The Supreme Court so decides (*d*) It was passed earlier than the Central Law

425. Water disputes between the States shall be decided by
(*a*) A Body appointed by Parliament (*b*) President
(*c*) High Court (*d*) Supreme Court

426. A tax shall not be levied or collected except by the authority of
(*a*) Law (*b*) President
(*c*) Prime Minister (*d*) Supreme Court

427. The main purpose to impose taxes is to
(*a*) Run the machinery of State (*b*) To balance accumulation of wealth
(*c*) To conduct elections (*d*) Uplift weaker sections

428. The Provisions regarding division of taxes between Union and State can be suspended
(*a*) During National Emergency (*b*) During Financial Emergency
(*c*) With the consent of majority of the State Legislature
(*d*) Cannot be suspended

429. The procedure for amendment of the Indian Constitution is
(*a*) Partly rigid and flexible (*b*) Very rigid
(*c*) Very flexible (*d*) Occasionally done

430. The Amendment procedure of the Constitution of India has been modeled on the Constitutional pattern of
(*a*) South Africa (*b*) USA
(*c*) Switzerland (*d*) Canada

431. Which Article of the Indian Constitution deals with the amendment procedure?
(*a*) 368 (*b*) 358
(*c*) 367 (*d*) 370

432. Which was the lengthiest Amendment to the Constitution?
(*a*) 42nd (*b*) 24th
(*c*) 44th (*d*) 46th

433. Which Amendment affirmed the right of the LS to amend any part of the Constitution?
(*a*) 24th (*b*) 42nd
(*c*) 39th (*d*) 43rd

434. The 24th Amendment became necessary as a result of the Supreme Court judgment in
(*a*) Golak Nath Case (*b*) Keshavananda Bharti Case
(*c*) Minerva Mills Case (*d*) Sajjan Singh Case
435. After a Bill is passed by the Parliament it is sent to the President for his assent, who can return it for reconsideration to LS. But if the Bill is re-passed and sent to the President for his assent, he
(*a*) Has to sign it
(*b*) Can send the Bill to the Parliament for reconsideration for second time
(*c*) He can submit the same to the people for referendum
(*d*) He can get it nullified through the Supreme Court
436. If Finance Minister fails to get Annual Budget passed in the LS, the Prime Minister can
(*a*) Submit resignation of his cabinet (*b*) Refer to it to the Joint Session of the Houses
(*c*) Compel the Finance Minister to resign (*d*) Form another Cabinet with different members
437. The Comptroller and Auditor General acts as the
(*a*) Guardian of public finances (*b*) Guardian of people's liberties
(c) Chief legal advisor of the government (*d*) All of these
438. The Comptroller and Auditor General is appointed by
(*a*) President (*b*) Prime Minister
(*c*) Parliament (*d*) President on the advice of Parliament
439. The Comptroller and Auditor General holds Office
(*a*) For a term of six years (*b*) For a term of five years
(*c*) During the pleasure of President (*d*) During the pleasure of the Parliament
440. The Comptroller and Auditor General can be removed from his Office before the expiry of his term by the
(*a*) President on the recommendation of the Parliament
(*b*) President on the advice of the Council ofMinisters
(*c*) President at his discretion (*d*) Prime Minister
441. The salary and allowances of the Comptroller and Auditor General are paid out of the
(*a*) Consolidated Fund of India (*b*) Contingency Fund of India
(*c*) Contingency Fund of concerned State (*d*) General Budget
442. The salary and allowances of the Comptroller and Auditor General are determined by the
(*a*) Parliament (*b*) Union Council of Ministers
(*c*) President in consultation with the Chief Justice of India
(*d*) Finance Minister
443. The Constitution secures the independence of the Comptroller and Auditor General by
(*a*) All of these
(*b*) Providing that his salary and service conditions shall not be changed to his disadvantage
(*c*) By giving the CAG complete control over his administrative staff
(*d*) Making the removal of CAG very difficult
444. The Comptroller and Auditor General performs
(*a*) Only audit functions (*b*) Only accounting functions
(*c*) Both accounting and audit functions (*d*) Accounting, audit and judicial functions
445. The Comptroller and Auditor General submits his annual report regarding the Center to
(*a*) President (*b*) Parliament
(*c*) Chairman of Planning Commission (*d*) Chief Justice of India

446. The Office of the Comptroller and Auditor General of India was created
(*a*) Under the Constitution (*b*) Through a resolution of Union Cabinet
(*c*) Through an enactment of the Parliament
(*d*) None of these

447. The Comptroller and Auditor General is intimately connected with the following Committee of the Parliament?
(*a*) Public Accounts Committee (*b*) Estimates Committee
(*c*) Committee of Public Undertakings (*d*) All of these

448. The Comptroller and Auditor General presents a detailed review of Union Accounts to the Union Finance Minister every
(*a*) Year (*b*) Three months
(*c*) Six months (*d*) Month

449. The Comptroller and Auditor General does not audit the accounts of
(*a*) Municipal Bodies (*b*) Government Companies
(*c*) State Government (*d*) Union Government

450. The Comptroller and Auditor General has to submit the Audit Report of the Central and State Governments before the
(*a*) President and Governor (*b*) Prime Minister and Chief Minister
(*c*) Union and State Finance Ministers (*d*) Parliament and Vidhana Sabha

451. Which one of the following is the most important item of expenditure of the Government of India on the revenue account?
(*a*) Interest payments (*b*) Pensions
(*c*) Subsidies (*d*) Defence

452. The Attorney General of India is the
(*a*) Highest Legal Officer of Union Government
(*b*) Highest Financial Officer of Union Government
(*c*) Highest Financial and Legal Officer of Union Government
(*d*) Defence Custodian

453. The Attorney General of India is appointed by the
(*a*) President (*b*) Chief Justice of India
(*c*) President on advice of Chief Justice of India
(*d*) Parliament

454. The Attorney General of India holds Office
(*a*) During the pleasure of the President (*b*) For life
(*c*) For a fixed term of six years
(*d*) As long as he enjoys the confidence of the Parliament

455. Which of the following duties/functions has been assigned to the Attorney General of India
(*a*) To render legal advice to Central Government
(*b*) To control state income and expenditure
(*c*) To arbitrate in disputes between Center and States (*d*) Both (*b*) and (*c*)

456. Who of the following acts as the Chief Legal Advisor to the Government of India?
(*a*) Attorney General (*b*) Union Law Minister
(*c*) Chief Justice of India (*d*) None

457. If the Attorney General of India wishes to tender his resignation before the expiry of his term, he has to address his resignation to the
(*a*) President (*b*) Speaker of LS
(*c*) Union Law Minister (*d*) Chief Justice of India
458. Who has the right to participate in proceedings of the Parliament even though he is not a MP?
(*a*) Attorney General of India (*b*) Comptroller and Auditor General
(*c*) Chief Election Commissioner (*d*) Chairman of UPSC
459. The three types of Civil Services envisaged under the Constitution are
(*a*) All India Services, Central Services and State Services
(*b*) Army, Navy and Air force
(*c*) Civil, Military and Paramilitary (*d*) None of these
460. Which one of the following is presided over by a non-member?
(*a*) RS (*b*) LS
(*c*) Vidhana Sabha (*d*) Vidhana Parishad
461. If the RS rejects a Money Bill, but follows
(*a*) The LS can sent the same for Presidential assent
(*b*) The President calls for a joint session for passing the Bill
(*c*) The LS may not consider it at all
(*d*) The LS may or may not accepts its recommendations
462. Which Article provides for the composition of Finance Commission?
(*a*) 280 (*b*) 290
(*c*) 250 (*d*) 260
463. The Finance Commission has a term of _____ years.
(*a*) 5 (*b*) 6
(*c*) 8 (*d*) 1
464. The Finance Commission consists of _____ number of members.
(*a*) 5 (*b*) 6
(*c*) 8 (*d*) 10
465. Who appoints the Finance Commission?
(*a*) President (*b*) Parliament
(*c*) Prime Minister (*d*) Finance Minister
466. The Report of Finance Commission shall be laid before the
(*a*) President (*b*) Prime Minister
(*c*) Finance Minister (*d*) LS
467. Grants-in-aid of revenue to the state is recommended by
(*a*) Finance Commission (*b*) Inter-state Council
(*c*) Planning Commission (*d*) National Development Council
468. Who finally approves the draft of Five-Year Plans?
(*a*) National Development Council (*b*) Finance Commission
(*c*) Planning Commission (*d*) Parliament
469. For those Union Territories without Legislative Councils of their own, laws are passed by the
(*a*) Parliament (*b*) President
(c) Union Ministry (*d*) Administrator
470. The day-to-day administration of the Union Territory is looked after by
(*a*) The President (*b*) Union Home Minister
(*c*) The Prime Minister (*d*) Lt. Governor

471. For Union Territories without legislative assemblies on their own, laws are passed by
(*a*) The Parliament (*b*) The Union Home Minister
(*c*) The President (*d*) Near by State

472. Which one of the following is the 28th State of the Indian Union?
(*a*) Jharkhand (*b*) Chattisgarh
(*c*) Uttaranchal (*d*) Nagaland

473. Which one of the following was a Union Territory before it was accorded the status of a full-fledged State?
(*a*) All of these (*b*) Himachal Pradesh
(*c*) Tripura (*d*) Manipur

474. Which one of the following has been wrongly listed as a Union Territory?
(*a*) Tripura (*b*) Chandigarh
(*c*) Pondicherry (*d*) Goa

475. Who is the competent to prescribe conditions for acquisition of citizenship?
(*a*) Parliament (*b*) Election Commission
(*c*) President (*d*) None of these

476. Which of the following is the Indian Constitution to Parliamentary procedures?
(*a*) Adjournment Motion (*b*) Cut Motion
(*c*) Zero Hour (*d*) Guillotine

477. What is the minimum duration in (years) of stay Presidential assentessential before a person can apply for Indian citizenship?
(*a*) 5 (*b*) 6
(*c*) 8 (*d*) 10

478. Who has the power to increase the salary and allowances of the President of India?
(*a*) Parliament (*b*) Prime Minister
(*c*) Union Council of Ministers (*d*) Speaker of LS

479. One-third of the members of the RS retire every _______ years.
(*a*) Two (*b*) Year
(*c*) Three (*d*) Four

480. 'Special majority' means more than
(*a*) Two-third majority (*b*) 50% majority
(*c*) 60% majority (*d*) 75% majority

481. 'Special leave' means
(*a*) Permission granted by the Supreme Court to appeal
(*b*) Leave granted only to Supreme Court judges before retirement
(*c*) Leave without salary (*d*) Leave with salary

482. 'Respite' means
(*a*) Awarding lesser punishment (*b*) Death due to drowning
(*c*) Death due to strangulation (*d*) Painless death

483. 'Violate' means
(*a*) Commit breach of law (*b*) Use force
(*c*) Overrule (*d*) Use violence

484. 'Interpret' means
(*a*) Ascertaining the meaning of a word
(*b*) Amending a law to make it more effective
(*c*) Passing a law by absolute majority (*d*) Interrupting in the exercise of legal right

485. Which one of the following has not been provided in the Constitution?
(*a*) Planning Commission (*b*) Public Service Commission
(*c*) Election Commission (*d*) Finance Commission

486. The Planning Commission is a
(*a*) Autonomous Body (*b*) Statutory Body
(*c*) Executive Body (*d*) Constitutional Body

487. Which of the following Offices has not been provided in the Constitution?
(*a*) Deputy Prime Minister (*b*) Deputy Speaker of Legislative Assembly
(*c*) Deputy Chairman of RS (*d*) Deputy Speaker of LS

488. Which Article of the Constitution provides protection to the Civil Servants?
(*a*) 311 (*b*) 315
(*c*) 312 (*d*) 288

489. Who has the power to create All India Services?
(*a*) Parliament (*b*) Prime Minister
(*c*) President (*d*) LS

490. Which Article of the Constitution authorizes the Parliament to create All India Services?
(*a*) 312 (*b*) 320
(*c*) 315 (*d*) 321

491. Parliament under the Article 312 gets the power to create All India Services when
(*a*) RS passes a Resolution with two-thirds majority
(*b*) LS passes a Resolution with two-thirds majority
(*c*) Majority of the State legislature requests the Parliament to do so
(*d*) Parliament can create such services *suo motto*

492. Which Article of the Constitution provides for the composition of Public Service Commission?
(*a*) 315 (*b*) 215
(*c*) 320 (*d*) 220

493. The members of Indian Administrative Services will be under the control of
(*a*) Ministry of Personnel (*b*) Home Minister
(*c*) Prime Minister (*d*) Rajya Sabha

494. The members of Indian Police Services will be under the control of
(*a*) Home Minister (*b*) President
(*c*) Prime Minister (*d*) Rajya Sabha

495. The members of Indian Forest Services will be under the control of
(*a*) Ministry of Environment & Forest (*b*) External Affairs Minister
(*c*) Prime Minister (*d*) Ministry of Foreign Affairs

496. Immediate control of the members of All India Services lies with the
(*a*) State Government (*b*) Central Government
(*c*) Local self-government (*d*) All of these

498. Members of All India Services hold office during the pleasure of the
(*a*) President (*b*) Prime Minister
(*c*) Speaker of LS (*d*) Chairman of RS

499. Which of the following All India Services does not included in the Constitution?
(*a*) All India Public Services (*b*) All India Judicial Services
(*c*) Indian Forest Services (*d*) Indian Administrative services

500. Which of the body which recruits persons to All India Services?
(*a*) Union Public Service Commission (*b*) State Public Service Commission
(*c*) Railway Recruitment Board (*d*) Staff Selection Commission

501. Chairman and Members of UPSC/KPSC shall hold Office for a term of __ years and tenure of __ years.
(*a*) 6/6 & 65/62 (*b*) 5/5 & 60/62
(*c*) 6/5 & 66/65 (*d*) 5/6 & 65/62

502. In the removal of which of the following officials does the Parliament play no role?
(*a*) Chairman of the Union Public Service Commission
(*b*) Judges of High Courts
(*c*) Judges of Supreme Court (*d*) Comptroller and Auditor General of India

503. Chairman and Members of UPSC/KPSC may resign their Office by submitting their resignation to the (OR) Chairman & Members of UPSC/KPSC can be removed on ground of proved misbehavior by the
(*a*) President/Governor (*b*) Prime Minister/Chief Minister
(*c*) Speaker of LS/Vidhana Sabha (*d*) Supreme Court/High Court

504. Salaries and Pension of the Chairman and members of UPSC shall be charged from the
(*a*) Consolidated Fund (*b*) Contingency Fund
(*c*) Public Accounts (*d*) Special Fund

505. UPSC/KPSC has to submit an Annual Report to the
(*a*) Parliament/Governor (*b*) Prime Minister/Chief Minister
(*c*) LS only/LA only (*d*) Finance Minister/Home Minister

506. Who enjoys the Rank of a Cabinet Minister of Indian Union?
(*a*) Deputy Chairman of Planning Commission
(*b*) Principal Secretary to Prime Minister
(*c*) Secretary to Union Government (*d*) Deputy Chairman of RS

507. Planning Commission was formed in the year
(*a*) 1950 (*b*) 1952
(*c*) 1949 (*d*) 1951

508. Who heads the National Integration Council?
(*a*) Prime Minister (*b*) President
(*c*) Speaker of LS (*d*) Vice-President

509. Recognition of States was done in the year 1956 on the ground of _____ basis.
(*a*) Linguistic (*b*) Population
(*c*) Caste (*d*) Religion

510. Which is the first State in India formed on Linguistic grounds?
(*a*) Andhra Pradesh (*b*) Jammu & Kashmir
(*c*) Karnataka (*d*) Tamil Nadu

511. Which Part of the Constitution incorporates special provisions to the State of J & K?
(*a*) XXI (*b*) XX
(*c*) XV (*d*) XI

512. The Provisions with regard to the UTs are incorporated under the Constitution by way of ____ Constitution Amendment Act.
(*a*) 7th (*b*) 1st
(*c*) 24th (*d*) 42nd

513. Every Union Territory (UT) shall be administered by the
(*a*) President (*b*) Parliament
(*c*) External Affairs Minister (*d*) Governor of neighboring states
514. The UT does not have
(*a*) Recognized Official language (*b*) Capital
(*c*) High Court (*d*) Administrator
515. Who has power to create Legislature or Council of Ministers or both for certain UT (Pondicherry)?
(*a*) Parliament (*b*) Prime Minister
(*c*) President (*d*) RS
516. Under Indian Constitution, the UT of Delhi is referred as
(*a*) National Capital Territory (*b*) Capital of India
(*c*) New Delhi (*d*) None of these
517. When did Delhi became UT?
(*a*) 1956 (*b*) 1952
(*c*) 1950 (*d*) 1947
518. The Administrator appointed under the Article 239 to the UT of Delhi is called
(*a*) Lieutenant Governor (*b*) Governor
(*c*) Governor General (*d*) Chief Minister of Delhi
519. Which of the following UT shall have LA?
(*a*) Delhi (*b*) Pondicherry
(*c*) Chandigarh (*d*) Daman & Diu
520. LA of Delhi shall have power to make laws for the whole of National Capital Territory with respect to the matter contained in
(*a*) Both List II & III (*b*) List II
(*c*) List III (*d*) List I
521. The Chief Minister of Delhi shall be appointed by the
(*a*) President (*b*) Parliament
(*c*) Prime Minister (*d*) Lieutenant Governor
522. The Council of Ministers of Delhi shall hold office during the pleasure of
(*a*) Prime Minister (*b*) President
(*c*) Parliament (*d*) Lieutenant Governor
523. The Council of Ministers of Delhi shall be collectively responsible to
(*a*) LA of Delhi (*b*) Parliament
(*c*) LS (*d*) President
524. The emergency provision for National Capital Territory of Delhi is enshrined under the Article
(*a*) 239A (*b*) 356
(*c*) 360 (*d*) 352
525. Who has the power to constitute a High Court to the UT?
(*a*) Parliament (*b*) Supreme Court
(*c*) President (*d*) Law Minister
526. Before 1956, the present day UT were characterized as
(*a*) Part C States (*b*) Part D States
(*c*) Part A States (*d*) Part B States
527. Parliament has delegated some legislative powers in relation to the UT to
(*a*) Union Government (*b*) Neighboring State Government
(*c*) Lieutenant Governor (*d*) Supreme Court

528. The aid and advice rendered by the Council of Ministers to the Administrator of the UT is
(*a*) Discretionary (*b*) Directory
(*c*) Mandatory (*d*) None of these

529. Who is authorized to appoint the Chief Minister of Delhi?
(*a*) President (*b*) Prime Minister
(*c*) Chief Justice of India (*d*) Lieutenant Governor

530. In 1954, Government of India introduced decorations (in form of the medals) Bharat Ratna, Padma Vibhushan, Padma Bhushan, and Padma Sri Awards under the Article
(*a*) 18 (*b*) 14
(*c*) 25 (*d*) 22

531. In 1996, the Supreme Court upheld the validity of the Civilians Awards, but recommended that the total awards to be given each year in all categories should be restricted to
(*a*) 50 (*b*) 40
(*c*) 60 (*d*) 75

Chapter 6: State Government

1. Who appoints the Governor of the State?
(*a*) The President (*b*) Chief Justice of India
(*c*) Chief Justice of State (*d*) Chief Minister

2. Membership of LA can vary between
(*a*) 60 - 500 (*b*) 70 - 400
(*c*) 100 - 300 (*d*) 100 - 400

3. What is the minimum age in years for becoming the MLC and MLA in the State?
(*a*) 30 and 25 (*b*) 35 and 30
(*c*) 40 and 35 (*d*) 45 and 40

4. What is the tenure in years of Office of MLA and MLC in the State?
(*a*) 5 and 6 (*b*) 5 and 5
(*c*) 6 and 6 (*d*) Indefinite

5. What is the eligibility age and tenure of Office of the Governor? (in years)
(*a*) 35 and 5 (*b*) 35 and 6
(*c*) 40 and 5 (*d*) 40 and 6

6. The State Legislature unless dissolved earlier shall continue for a period of _____ years.
(*a*) 5 (*b*) 6
(*c*) 4 (*d*) 2

7. The Legislative Council shall not be subjected to dissolution however one-third of its members shall retire after every _____ years.
(*a*) 2 (*b*) 3
(*c*) 4 (*d*) 5

8. Who appoints the Vice-chancellors of the universities?
(*a*) The Governor (*b*) Education Minister
(*c*) Chief Minister (*d*) President

9. Who is the Executive (Constitutional) Head of the State Government?
(*a*) The Governor (*b*) Chief Minister
(*c*) President (*d*) Prime Minister

10. The Executive powers of the State Government shall be exercised in the name of
    (*a*) The Governor (*b*) Chief Minister
    (*c*) President (*d*) Prime Minister
11. Generally, the Governor belongs to
    (*a*) Some other state (*b*) The neighboring state
    (*c*) The same state (*d*) IAS Officer
12. The Governor of a State acts as
    (*a*) Agent of President (*b*) Real Executive of a State
    (*c*) Advisor to Central Government (*d*) Secretary of President
13. The Governor of the State shall be appointed by the
    (*a*) President (*b*) Chief Minister
    (*c*) Prime Minister (*d*) Supreme Court
14. The Governor holds Office
    (*a*) During the pleasure of the President
    (*b*) As long as he/she enjoys the confidence of the Chief Minister
    (*c*) As long as he/she enjoys the confidence of the Council of Ministers of the State
    (*d*) During the pleasure of the Union Council of Ministers
15. As a matter of convention, while appointing the Governor of a State, the President consults
    (*a*) State Chief Minister (*b*) Chief Justice of India
    (*c*) President (*d*) All of them
16. The Governor is the part and parcel of the
    (*a*) State Legislature (*b*) State Judiciary
    (*c*) Union Judiciary (*d*) Parliament
17. The salary and allowances of the Governor are charged to
    (*a*) The Consolidated Fund of the State (*b*) The Consolidated Fund of India
    (*c*) The Contingency Fund of India (*d*) (a) and (b) in equal proportions
18. The emoluments of the ministers in the State Government are determined by
    (*a*) Legislative Assembly (*b*) The Chief Minister
    (*c*) The Governor (*d*) The President
19. The salaries and allowances of the Speaker of LA and Chairman of LC shall be determined by the
    (*a*) State Legislature (*b*) Parliament
    (*c*) LA (*d*) Governor
20. The emoluments, allowances and privileges of the Governor shall be determined by the
    (*a*) Parliament (*b*) Chief Minister
    (*c*) Prime Minister (*d*) President
21. If the Governor of a State wishes to relinquish Office before the expiry of his/her term, he/she has to address resignation to
    (*a*) President (*b*) Chief Minister
    (*c*) Prime Minister (*d*) Speaker of State Legislative Assembly
22. The Governor plays a dual role as an agent of the President and as the
    (*a*) Constitutional Head of the State (*b*) Agent of the Prime Minister
    (*c*) Agent of the Chief Justice of India (*d*) Agent of the Chief Minister of the State
23. The Governor of a State should
    (*a*) Not hold any other office of profit (*b*) Be resident of the state
    (*c*) Have completed the age of 45 years (*d*) Be a member of LS

24. The Governor may resign his/her Office by writing to
(*a*) President (*b*) Vice-President
(*c*) Chief Justice of India (*d*) Chief Justice of High Court
25. Can one person act as Governor of more than one State?
(*a*) Yes (*b*) No
(*c*) Only for a period of six months (*d*) Only for a period of three months
26. When a person acts as Governor of more than one State, his/her salary is
(*a*) Shared by the concerned States (*b*) Paid by the Union Government
(*c*) Charged on the Consolidated Fund of India
(*d*) Paid by the State named by the President
27. Which one of the following legislative powers is enjoyed by the Governor?
(*a*) All these powers (*b*) Can summon or prorogue the State Legislative
(*c*) Can appoint one-sixth the members of the Legislative Council
(*d*) Can nominate certain members of Anglo-Indian community to the Legislative Assembly
28. Who discharges the duties of the Office of Governor if it falls vacant due to death or resignation?
(*a*) Chief Justice of High Court (*b*) Chief Minister
(*c*) Speaker of State Legislative Assembly (*d*) President appoints a new Governor immediately
29. The Governor of a State is administered the oath of Office by (OR) The Governor before entering upon his Office has to administer his oath before the
(*a*) Chief Justice of High Court (*b*) Chief Justice of India
(*c*) President (*d*) Prime Minister
30. There is no provision for the impeachment of
(*a*) Governor (*b*) Chief Justices of High and Supreme Courts
(*c*) Vice-President (*d*) President
31. Which one of the following is correct regarding the Governor of a State?
(*a*) All of these
(*b*) He can recommend to the President to impose President's Rule in the State
(*c*) He has the power to issue ordinances when the legislature is not in session
(*d*) No Money Bill can be introduced in State Legislature without prior permission of Governor
32. The Governor can issue ordinances
(*a*) Only during the recess of the State Legislature
(*b*) Only when Chief Minister asks to do so
(*c*) Only in case of breakdown of constitutional machinery in the state
(*d*) Only after taking formal approval of the President
33. The ordinances issued by the Governor are subject to approval by the
(*a*) State Legislature (*b*) Chief Justice of High Court
(*c*) President (*d*) Chief Minister
34. A Governor
(*a*) May be transferred from one state to another state
(*b*) Cannot be transferred from one state to another state
(*c*) Can be transferred with his consent
(*d*) Can be transferred with the written consent of the President
35. The Governor has power to dissolve
(*a*) Legislative Assembly (*b*) Legislative Council
(*c*) Legislature (*d*) All

36. Who appoints and administers the oath for the Chief Minister and Council of Ministers?
(*a*) Governor (*b*) President
(*c*) Prime Minister (*d*) Chief Justice of High Court
37. The Contingency Fund of the State is operated by
(*a*) Governor (*b*) Chief Minister
(*c*) State Finance Minister (*d*) Union Finance Minister
38. The Governor is accountable for his/her actions to
(*a*) President (*b*) Prime Minister
(*c*) Council of Ministers of the State (*d*) State Legislature
39. Unless approved by the State Legislature, the ordinance issued by the Governor remains in force for a maximum period of
(*a*) Six months (*b*) Three months
(*c*) One year (*d*) Indefinitely
40. A Legislative Bill which did not receive the Governor's immediate assent was
(*a*) Jammu & Kashmir citizenship (*b*) Tamil Nadu Press Bill
(*c*) Assam citizenship (*d*) Bihar Prevention Detention
41. The District Judges and Magistrate of the Civil Courts shall be appointed by the
(*a*) Governor (*b*) Chief Minister
(*c*) High Court (*d*) Chief Justice of High Court
42. The High Court of Karnataka established in the year
(*a*) 1884 (*b*) 1944
(*c*) 1900 (*d*) 1947
43. The Guwahati High Court has territorial jurisdiction over ___ number of states.
(*a*) 7 (*b*) 6
(*c*) 3 (*d*) 2
44. Which High Court has four Principal Benches?
(*a*) Guwahati (*b*) Bombay
(*c*) Calcutta (*d*) Punjab & Haryana
45. The High Court for the territory of Andaman & Nicobar is the High Court of
(*a*) West Bengal (*b*) Tamil Nadu
(*c*) Kerala (*d*) Andhra Pradesh
46. The number of States under the Jurisdiction of a High Court shall be decided on the basis of
(*a*) Area and Population (*b*) Number of judges
(*c*) Number of cases (*d*) Discretion of Parliament
47. Who decides the number of judges in the High Court?
(*a*) President (*b*) Parliament
(*c*) Governor (*d*) State Legislature
48. High courts in India were first started (1862) at
(*a*) Bombay, Calcutta and Madras (*b*) Bombay and Delhi
(*c*) Calcutta and Delhi (*d*) Allahabad
49. The Governor can recommend imposition of President's Rule in the State
(*a*) At his discretion
(*b*) On the recommendation of the Council of Ministers
(*c*) On the recommendation of the state legislature
(*d*) Only on demand from the President

50. The term of LA can be extended for a period of ____ during the time of Emergency.
(*a*) One year (*b*) Two years
(*c*) One full term (*d*) No such extension
51. Governor will act under the following circumstance with advice of ministers while returning
(*a*) Appointing the Advocate General (*b*) Dissolving Legislative Assembly
(*c*) Recommending President's Rule (*d*) The Bill for reconsideration
52. Parliament or State Legislature can declare a seat vacant if the member is absent from the session for a period of _____ days without permission.
(*a*) 60 (*b*) 30
(*c*) 45 (*d*) 90
53. 'Bicameral' means
(*a*) Presence of two Houses in the State (*b*) Presence of one House in the State
(*c*) Presence of half House in the State (*d*) Presence of no House in the State
54. 'Unicameral' means
(*a*) Presence of one House in the State (*b*) Presence of two Houses in the State
(*c*) Presence of half House in the State (*d*) Presence of no House in the State
55. What is the system of Legislature in the State of Karnataka?
(*a*) Bicameral (*b*) Unicameral
(*c*) Cameral (*d*) None of these
56. Which state(s) is/are having Bicameral system?
(*a*) All of these (*b*) Karnataka
(*c*) Maharashtra (*d*) Uttar Pradesh
57. Which state(s) is/are having unicameral system?
(*a*) All of these (*b*) Andhra Pradesh
(*c*) Tamil Nadu (*d*) West Bengal
58. Which are the two states having common capital?
(*a*) Punjab and Haryana (*b*) Punjab and Himachal Pradesh
(*c*) Haryana and Uttaranchal (*d*) Uttaranchal and Himachal Pradesh
59. Sikkim was admitted as a full-fledged state of Indian Union in the year _____.
(*a*) 1975 (*b*) 1972
(*c*) 1978 (*d*) 1980
60. The Residuary power with respect to the Jammu & Kashmir rest with the
(*a*) State Government of J & K (*b*) Union Government
(*c*) Both (*a*) & (*b*) (*d*) Prime Minister
61. Who appoints the Governor of Jammu & Kashmir?
(*a*) President (*b*) Parliament
(*c*) Prime Minister (*d*) Legislature of J & K
62. Which of the following bodies can be abolished but not dissolved?
(*a*) State Legislative Council (*b*) RS
(*c*) Municipal Bodies (*d*) None of these
63. Who appoints the Chief Minister and Council of Ministers in the State?
(*a*) Governor (*b*) Chief Justice of High Court
(*c*) Chief Justice of India (*d*) President
64. Who appoints the Chief Justice and other judges of the High Court?
(*a*) President (*b*) Governor
(*c*) Prime Minister (*d*) Chief Justice of India

65. What is the retirement age in years for Chief Justice and other judges of High Court?
(*a*) 62 (*b*) 60
(*c*) 65 (*d*) 63
66. Salaries and other emoluments of the High Court judges shall be determined by the
(*a*) Parliament (*b*) State Legislature
(*c*) Governor (*d*) Chief Minister
67. Which Article of the Constitution empowers the High Court to issue writs of various kinds?
(*a*) 226 (*b*) 224
(*c*) 214 (*d*) 32
68. Writ Jurisdiction of the Supreme Court under Article 32 is not wider than that of the Writ Jurisdiction of the High Court under Article 226 because the High Court may exercise this power in relation to
(*a*) Violation of Fundamental & Legal Rights
(*b*) Civil & Criminal Matters
(*c*) FRs and Stay proceedings (*d*) None of these
69. Article 227 of the Indian Constitution deals with the
(*a*) High Court's power of superintendence over all courts and tribunals within its jurisdiction
(*b*) Judicial review
(*c*) Power of Speaker of LA (*d*) Election of Vice-President
70. Who has power to establish common High Court for two or more States and Union Territories?
(*a*) Parliament (*b*) Supreme Court
(*c*) President (*d*) RS
71. In Karnataka, the number of seats in Legislative Assembly and Legislative Council are
(*a*) 224 & 75 (*b*) 75 & 224
(*c*) 200 & 50 (*d*) 242 & 57
72. Who is having power to remove the Governor before expiry of the tenure?
(*a*) President (*b*) Prime Minister
(*c*) Chief Justice of State (*d*) Chief Minister
73. What is the retirement age in years of a High Court Judge?
(*a*) 62 (*b*) 60
(*c*) 64 (*d*) 58
74. The total members in the Legislative Council should not be less than (Article 171).
(*a*) 40 (*b*) 45
(*c*) 50 (*d*) 55
75. The LC is a permanent House, however, _____ number of members retire after every ____ years.
(*a*) One-third & 2 (*b*) One-third & 3
(*c*) Two-third & 2 (*d*) Two-third & 3
76. A Cabinet Minister of a State Government can be removed by the
(*a*) Chief Minister (*b*) Governor
(*c*) Cabinet (*d*) Chief Minister with consent of Cabinet
77. The Council of Ministers in the State remains in power for
(*a*) As long as it retains the confidence of Legislative Assembly
(*b*) Five years
(*c*) During the pleasure of the Governor (*d*) During the pleasure of the President

78. The State Council of Ministers has to tender their resignation if vote of no-confidence is passed against it by the
(*a*) LA (*b*) LC
(*c*) Governor (*d*) Joint session of both LA & LC
79. Who is the channel of communication between the Governor and the State Council of Ministers?
(*a*) Chief Minister (*b*) Speaker of LA
(*c*) Parliamentary Affairs Minister (*d*) Chairman of LC
80. Chief Minister of all the States are the members of
(*a*) National Development Council (*b*) Inter-State Council
(*c*) Finance Commission (*d*) Planning Commission
81. This is not the power of the Chief Minister.
(*a*) Control over State Judiciary (*b*) Chief Advisor to the Governor
(*c*) Control over the ministers (*d*) Formation of the Government
82. The Chief Minister of a State cannot take part in the election of President if he is
(*a*) A member of the Legislative Council of the State
(*b*) Heading a care-taker government in the State
(*c*) Not proved his majority in the Legislative Assembly
(*d*) Himself a candidate of President ship
83. If a member of LS is appointed as the Chief Minister of a State
(*a*) He must become a member of the State Legislature
(*b*) He continues to be a member of LS for six months but cannot vote in the House
(*c*) He ceases to be a member of the LS after 14 days
(*d*) None of these
84. What is the effect of the resignation or death of the Chief Minister of the State?
(*a*) Dissolves the LA (*b*) New Chief Minister takes oath
(*c*) Mid-term polls (*d*) None of these
85. Which tax is levied by the Union and collected and appropriated by the states?
(*a*) Stamp duties (*b*) Passenger & goods taxes
(*c*) Estate duty (*d*) Taxes on newspapers
86. Which category of professional people are entitled to elect their representatives to the State LC?
(*a*) Teachers of not lower than secondary school level in the state
(*b*) Doctors doing private practice in the state
(*c*) Chartered Accountants practicing in the state
(*d*) Lawyers practicing in the courts
87. The graduates constitute a separate constituency for the election of the specified number of members to
(*a*) State Legislative Council (*b*) State Legislative Assembly
(*c*) RS (*d*) LS
88. Legislative Council is
(*a*) Not dissolved (*b*) Dissolved after 3 years
(*c*) Dissolved after 5 years (*d*) Dissolved after 6 years
89. How many states in India have Legislative Councils?
(*a*) 5 (*b*) 4
(*c*) 6 (*d*) 7

90. Which among the following House cannot be dissolved but can be abolished?
(*a*) LC (*b*) LA
(*c*) RS (*d*) LS
91. Without certificate of High Court, an appeal can made to Supreme Court
(*a*) With the special leave of Supreme Court
(*b*) If the party is war widow
(*c*) If the party belongs to SC (*d*) If the party belongs to ST
92. What is meant by 'Court of Records'?
(*a*) The court that preserves all the records
(*b*) The court that maintains records of all lower courts
(*c*) The court that can punish for its contempt
(*d*) The court that is competent to give directions and issue writs
93. The Legislative Council in a State can be created or disbanded by the
(*a*) Parliament on the recommendation of the State Legislative Assembly
(*b*) Parliament
(*c*) State Legislative Assembly
(*d*) President on the recommendation of the State Governor
94. The Members of the State Legislature can claim immunity from _____ Proceedings.
(*a*) Civil (*b*) Criminal
(*c*) Civil and Criminal (*d*) Petty
95. The major part of following central revenues goes to various state governments in India?
(*a*) Excise duty (*b*) Gift tax
(*c*) Wealth tax (*d*) Income tax
96. Which of the following is the most important source of revenue of the states in India?
(*a*) Sales Tax (*b*) Professional Tax
(*c*) Land Revenues (*d*) Excise Duties
97. Who superintendents all subordinate courts in a State?
(*a*) High Court (*b*) Supreme Court
(*c*) Union Law Minister (*d*) Advocate General
98. Which one of the following High Courts has the territorial jurisdiction over Andaman and Nicobar Islands?
(*a*) Calcutta (*b*) Madras
(*c*) Andhra Pradesh (*d*) Orissa
99. Power to extend or restrict the jurisdiction of High Court vest with
(*a*) Parliament (*b*) President
(*c*) Supreme Court (*d*) Chief Justice of India
100. A temporary Judge of High Court can hold Office for a maximum period of
(*a*) Two years (*b*) One year
(*c*) Six months (*d*) Two months
101. Which one of the following Union Territories has a High Court of its own?
(*a*) Delhi (*b*) Pondicherry
(*c*) Chandigarh (*d*) Daman & Diu
(*e*) Lakshadweep

102. When there is no majority party in the State Legislative Assembly, the main consideration governing the appointment of a Chief Minister by Governor is the
(*a*) Ability of the person who is most likely to command a stable majority
(*b*) Largest political party in the Legislative Assembly
(*c*) The loyalty and support of the party members to their respective party programme
(*d*) None of these

103. If there is a dispute between two states
(*a*) Only Supreme Court has jurisdiction to decide that case
(*b*) High Court has jurisdiction to decide that case
(*c*) With the consent of both the states, High Court may decide that case
(*d*) If one of the states does not agree to approach the High Court, the dispute may be decided by the Supreme Court

104. Which of the following states are involved in disputes over sharing of river waters?
(*a*) All of these (*b*) Andhra Pradesh and Karnataka
(*c*) Karnataka and Tamil Nadu (*d*) Madhya Pradesh and Gujarat

105. Constitution empowers State Governments to make special law for
(*a*) Women and Children (*b*) Workers working in mines
(*c*) Farmers (*d*) Unemployed youths

106. The State Government does not enjoy any control over local bodies with regard to
(*a*) Personal matters (*b*) Financial matters
(*c*) Legislation (*d*) Grievances of citizens

107. The Speaker of the LA shall be elected by the
(*a*) Members of LA (*b*) Members of State Legislature
(*c*) Governor of State (*d*) Citizens of State

108. The Speaker of LA can vacate his Office by addressing his resignation to the
(*a*) Deputy Speaker of LA (*b*) Chief Minister
(*c*) President (*d*) Governor

109. Find out the correct response: 'After the State Legislature is dissolved the Speaker of LA'?
(*a*) Remains as Speaker until the 1st meeting of the LA after the
(*b*) Removed from the Office immediately dissolution
(*c*) He has to submit his resignation to the Deputy Speaker
(*d*) He can continue as Speaker for a period of 30 days

110. The Speaker of the LA shall be removed by the House by passing a resolution
(*a*) After 14 days clear notice passed by majority of all the members of the House
(*b*) Of a House passed by majority of total membership of the House
(*c*) Passed by two-third majority of Members present and voting
(*d*) Passed by one-third majority

111. Who among the following is described as the Custodian of State LA?
(*a*) Speaker (*b*) Leader of Opposition
(*c*) Chief Minister (*d*) Deputy Chief Minister

112. Who is the neutral in the affairs of the party politics?
(*a*) Speaker of LA (*b*) Chief Minister
(*c*) Home Minister (*d*) Finance Minister

113. The Speaker of LA enjoys
(*a*) Right to vote only in case of tie (*b*) No right to vote
(*c*) Right to vote like the other members (*d*) Special two votes

114. What is the minimum gap permissible between the two sessions of the Legislature?
(*a*) Six months (*b*) Three months
(*c*) Two months (*d*) Six weeks
115. The authority to allot the agenda of the State LA is
(*a*) Speaker of LA (*b*) Chairman of LC
(*c*) Chief Minister (*d*) Governor
116. Find out the correct response to the Ordinance promulgated by the Governor?
(*a*) Has the same force as the law made by the State Legislature
(b) Is more extensive than the law made by the State Legislature
(*c*) Is much narrower than the law made by the State Legislature
(*d*) It depends upon facts and circumstances of the case
117. What shall be the qualification of a person to be appointed as the Advocate General for the State?
(*a*) Qualified to be appointed as Judge of High Court
(*b*) Qualified to be appointed as Judge of District Court
(*c*) Qualified to be appointed as Judge of Supreme Court
(*d*) Has put in practice for at least five years in High Court
118. The Governor does not appoint
(*a*) Judges of High Court (*b*) Members of State Public Service Commission
(*c*) Chief Minister (*d*) Deputy Chief Minister
119. An Advocate General shall hold Office during the pleasure of the
(*a*) Governor (*b*) President
(*c*) Chief Minister (*d*) Prime Minister
120. Who has the power to create and abolish LC if the LA of State passes a resolution to that effect?
(*a*) Parliament (*b*) Governor
(*c*) President (*d*) Chief Minister
121. Which of the following taxes is levied by the State Government only?
(*a*) Entertainment Tax (*b*) Corporation Tax
(*c*) Income Tax (*d*) Wealth Tax
122. Goa got the status of statehood by the way of ____ Constitutional Amendment.
(*a*) 56th (*b*) 52nd
(*c*) 50th (*d*) 60th
123. Law with regard to Anti-defection is inserted by way of ____ Constitutional Amendment.
(*a*) 52nd (*b*) 50th
(*c*) 60th (*d*) 61st
124. Among the following Amendments, which is considered as Mini-Constitution?
(*a*) 42nd (*b*) 24th
(*c*) 44th (*d*) 25th
125. 73rd and 74th Constitutional Amendments is pertaining to
(*a*) Local Self-Government (*b*) Statehood to Goa
(*c*) Extension of reservation to SCs and STs
(*d*) Land Reforms
126. State Emergency (President's Rule) can be declared
(*a*) When the Government of the State cannot be carried in accordance with the provision of the Constitution
(*b*) When the party forming the ministry has a total rout in the election of LS

(*c*) When the State Government refuses to follow the direction given by the Supreme Court
(*d*) When the Chief Minister resigns

127. Which Article gives Special Provisions to the State of Jammu & Kashmir?
(*a*) 370 (*b*) 372
(*c*) 395 (*d*) 368

128. The President can make a Proclamation of Emergency in Jammu & Kashmir with the
(*a*) Concurrence of the State legislature (*b*) Concurrence of the Chief Minister
(*c*) Concurrence of the State Governor (*d*) Prior consent of the Parliament

Chapter 7: Constitutional Provisions for SCs & STs, Women, Children and OBCs

1. Which Article under the Constitution provides for the reservation of SCs and STs in the LS?
(*a*) 300 (*b*) 338
(*c*) 338A (*d*) 370

2. In which year was 'untouchability' abolished in India?
(*a*) 1950 (*b*) 1952
(*c*) 1954 (*d*) 1956

3. The following act does not amount to practicing untouchability
(*a*) Denying access to a home (*b*) Denying access to any shop
(*c*) Refusing admission to a hospital (*d*) Refusing to sell goods or render service

4. 'Self-incrimination' means Compelling a person to
(*a*) Be a witness against himself (*b*) Commit crime
(*c*) File complaint (*d*) Give evidence

5. The Constitution seeks to protect the interests of the SCs and STs by reserving seats for them in
(*a*) In (*b*) and (c) (*b*) Public services
(*c*) In legislatures (*d*) Defence services

6. Indian Constitution guarantees reservation to SCs and STs in
(*a*) LS and LA (*b*) LA only
(*c*) LS only (*d*) RS only

7. Seats for SCs and STs are not reserved in
(*a*) RS (*b*) LS
(*c*) LA (*d*) All of these

8. The Special Officer who looks into the working of the safeguards for SCs and STs is called
(*a*) Commissioner for SCs and STs (*b*) Commissioner for Welfare of Backward Classes
(*c*) Commissioner for Social Welfare
(*d*) Commissioner for Social Welfare and Family Planning

9. According to Marriage Act of 1954, the age is fixed at ____ years for men and ____ for women.
(*a*) 21 and 18 (*b*) 24 and 20
(*c*) 21 and 20 (*d*) 22 and 18

10. The year ____ was declared as the year of *women empowerment* to the promotion of the development of women.
(*a*) 2001 (*b*) 2000
(*c*) 2002 (*d*) 2003

11. Who are considered to be the vulnerable group?
(*a*) Women and Children (*b*) SCs
(*c*) STs (*d*) All of these

12. In which one of the following states is it constitutionally obligatory for the state to have a separate minister for tribal welfare?
(*a*) All these states (*b*) Bihar
(*c*) Madhya Pradesh (*d*) Orissa
13. The reservation for members of SCs and STs has been extended up to
(*a*) 2010 (*b*) 2005
(*c*) 2020 (*d*) 2015
14. Extension of reservation to SCs and STs for another 10 years is provided by way of __ Constitutional Amendment.
(*a*) 45th (*b*) 44th
(*c*) 86th (*d*) 90th
15. Reservation for the SCs and STs in the Parliament and State Assemblies was extended up to 2010 by the Amendment
(*a*) 79th (*b*) 64th
(*c*) 61st (*d*) 62nd
16. Concept of 'creamy layer', propounded by Supreme Court with regard to reservations, refers to
(*a*) Economically better-off people (*b*) OBCs
(*c*) Defence personnel (*d*) Non-residents Indians
17. What is the maximum percentage of jobs that can be reserved by a State for backward class people in the government jobs?
(*a*) 50% (*b*) 60%
(*c*) 65% (*d*) 70%
18. The Tamil Nadu Reservation Act, which provides for 69% reservation in the jobs and educational institutional in the State, was placed in the Ninth Schedule by the Amendment
(*a*) 76th (*b*) 75th
(*c*) 74th (*d*) 77th
19. Which Article provides for the National Commission of SCs/STs?
(*a*) 338/338A (*b*) 338A/338
(*c*) 339/340 (*d*) 340/339
20. The National Commission for SCs and STs has to submit an Annual report to the
(*a*) President (*b*) Parliament
(*c*) Ministry of HRD (*d*) LS
21. Which Article of the Indian Constitution empowers the President to appoint a Commission to investigate the conditions of backward classes in general and suggest ameliorative measures?
(*a*) 342 (*b*) 344
(*c*) 340 (*d*) 389
22. Certain seats shall be reserved for the SCs and STs in LS on the basis of their
(*a*) Population (*b*) Backwardness
(*c*) Representation in the House (*d*) Education
23. Minority Groups are recognized on the basis of their
(*a*) Population (*b*) Religion
(*c*) Race (*d*) Caste
24. Special provisions relating to the Minorities are guaranteed under the Part _____.
(*a*) XVI (*b*) XV
(*c*) XX (*d*) XIV

25. Jobs are reserved for SC and ST people
    (*a*) Both at the time of appointment and promotion
    (*b*) On the basis of their annual income
    (*c*) At the time of appointment (*d*) At the time of promotion
26. The Mandal Commission for backward classes was set up in
    (*a*) 1978 (*b*) 1987
    (*c*) 1986 (*d*) 1996
27. Which is the Commission appointed by the Government of India to investigate the conditions of socially and educationally backward classes of the society?
    (*a*) Mandal (*b*) Nanavathi
    (*c*) Singhvi (*d*) Narasimhan
28. Which of the following Prime Minister was in favor of implementation of the recommendation of the Mandal Commission?
    (*a*) V. P. Singh (*b*) Chandrashekar
    (*c*) P.V. Narasimha Rao (*d*) Both (*a*) and (*b*)
29. Who is empowered to nominate Anglo-Indian Community to LS/LA?
    (*a*) President/Governor (*b*) Prime Minister/Chief Minister
    (*c*) Speaker of LS/LA (*d*) None
30. How many members will be nominated by President/Governor from Anglo-Indian Community?
    (*a*) 2/1 (*b*) 1/2
    (*c*) 3/2 (*d*) 2/3
31. In which one of the following states, there is no reservation for the SCs for LS?
    (*a*) Jammu & Kashmir (*b*) Arunachal Pradesh
    (*c*) Meghalaya (*d*) All of these
32. Under the Provisions of which Article of the Constitution, the Government abolished the practice of untouchability?
    (*a*) 17 (*b*) 16
    (*c*) 18 (*d*) 20

Chapter 8: Emergency Provisions

1. Emergency Provisions were borrowed from the Constitution of
   (*a*) Germany (*b*) USA
   (*c*) Britain (*d*) Ireland
2. Emergency Provisions under Indian Constitution describes the nature of Indian Polity as
   (*a*) Unitary (*b*) Federal
   (*c*) Quasi-federal (*d*) Quasi-unitary
3. Which Article under the Constitution authorizes the President to proclaim an emergency?
   (*a*) 352 (*b*) 350
   (*c*) 250 (*d*) 324
4. Emergency Provisions are enshrined under _____ Part of the Constitution.
   (*a*) XVIII (*b*) XVII
   (*c*) XVI (*d*) XV
5. According to the Article 355, it is the duty of the Unio(b) on the basis of their annual incomen to protect states against
   (*a*) All of these (*b*) Constitutional breakdown
   (*c*) Internal disturbance (*d*) External aggression

6. The Indian Constitution is designed to work as a Unitary Government during the time of
   (*a*) Emergency (*b*) Normalcy
   (*c*) When the Parliament so desires (*d*) At the will of President
7. When the National Emergency is declared, the following Article is suspended?
   (*a*) 14 (*b*) 16
   (*c*) 18 (*d*) 19
8. While Proclamation of Emergency is in operation, the President cannot suspend certain FRs. They are
   (*a*) 20 and 21 (*b*) 14 and 15
   (*c*) 14 and 16 (*d*) 32
9. The final authority to make a Proclamation of Emergency rests with (OR) _____ is empowered to declare an Emergency
   (*a*) President (*b*) Prime Minister
   (*c*) Council of Ministers (*d*) Parliament
   (*e*) Supreme Court
10. President can proclaim an emergency with the recommendation of the
    (*a*) Union Cabinet (*b*) Prime Minister
    (*c*) LS (*d*) Vice-President
11. President can proclaim emergency on the recommendation of the Union Cabinet. Such recommendation shall be
    (*a*) Written recommendation (*b*) Oral recommendation
    (*c*) Majority in the House (*d*) Sincere request
12. How many types of emergencies are envisaged by the Constitution?
    (*a*) 3 (*b*) 4
    (*c*) 2 (*d*) None
13. Breakdown of Constitutional Machinery in a State is popularly known as
    (*a*) President's Rule (*b*) National Emergency
    (*c*) Financial Emergency (*d*) All of these
14. President's Rule can be imposed on the states
    (*a*) On failure of the constitutional machinery in a state
    (*b*) During the national emergency
    (*c*) During general elections (*d*) All
15. President's Rule at the Center is possible
    (*a*) During National Emergency (*b*) During political instability in the country
    (*c*) During general elections (*d*) At any time the President thinks it necessary
16. The President can declare National Emergency
    (*a*) On the recommendation of the Council of Ministers
    (*b*) On the recommendation of the Prime Minister
    (*c*) On the recommendation of the Parliament
    (*d*) On his/her own
17. Proclamation of National Emergency ceases to operate unless approved by the Parliament within (OR) Once the National Emergency is proclaimed, it should be approved by the Parliament within (OR) Proclamation issued under Article 352 shall be laid before the Parliament within
    (*a*) One month (*b*) Two months
    (*c*) Three months (*d*) Six months

18. Proclamation issued has been approved by the Parliament will be in force for a period of
(*a*) Six months (*b*) Three months
(*c*) One year (*d*) Two years
19. When the Proclamation of Emergency is in operation, Parliament has power to make laws for the whole or any part of the territory of India under
(*a*) List II (*b*) List I
(*c*) List III (*d*) All of these
20. When the Proclamation of Emergency is in operation, the Parliament has special powers to legislate under
(*a*) State List (*b*) Union List
(*c*) Concurrent List (*d*) Residuary List
21. The President can declare National Emergency
(*a*) Due to threat arising on account of foreign attack or armed rebellion
(*b*) Only in the event of foreign attack
(*c*) Only in the event of armed rebellion (*d*) None of these
22. President can proclaim an emergency on the ground of
(*a*) All of these (*b*) War
(*c*) Armed rebellion (*d*) External aggression
23. How many times has a National Emergency been declared so far by the President?
(*a*) Thrice (*b*) Twice
(*c*) Once (*d*) Never
24. The President can declare Constitutional Emergency in a State
(*a*) If he is satisfied that a situation has arisen in which the State government cannot be carried out on in accordance with the Constitution
(*b*) Only on the recommendation of Governor
(*c*) Only on the recommendation of the State Council of Ministers
(*d*) Only on the recommendation of the Union Council of Ministers
25. Which type of emergency has been declared the maximum number of times?
(*a*) Constitutional Emergency (*b*) National Emergency
(*c*) Financial Emergency (*d*) All three equal number of times
26. Which one of the following types of emergency has not yet declared, till now?
(*a*) Financial Emergency (*b*) National Emergency
(*c*) Constitutional Emergency (*d*) None
27. A National Emergency can remain in operation with the approval of Parliament for a
(*a*) Indefinite period (*b*) Maximum period of six months
(*c*) Maximum period of one year (*d*) Maximum period of three years
28. This is not a ground to declare National Emergency.
(*a*) Serious internal disturbance (*b*) War
(*c*) External aggression (*d*) Armed rebellion
29. To declare National Emergency, a decision must be taken by the
(*a*) Cabinet (*b*) LS
(*c*) RS (*d*) Both RS and LS
30. Financial Emergency can be proclaimed under the Article ____.
(*a*) 360 (*b*) 356
(*c*) 256 (*d*) 352

31. Who is empowered to proclaim the Financial Emergency?
    (*a*) President (*b*) Prime Minister
    (*c*) Parliament (*d*) Finance Minister
32. Financial Emergency can be proclaimed on the ground of
    (*a*) All (*b*) Financial stability
    (*c*) Credit of India (*d*) Any part of the Indian territory is threatened
33. The President can declare Financial Emergency
    (*a*) If there is a threat to the financial stability or credit of India
    (*b*) To meet the extraordinary expenses of conducting war
    (*c*) On the recommendation of the Comptroller and Auditor General
    (*d*) If a majority of a State Legislature so recommends
34. During a Financial Emergency, the President
    (*a*) Do all these things
    (*b*) Order the reduction of salaries of Supreme Court and High Court Judges
    (*c*) Order the reduction of salaries and allowances of all Central and State Civil Servants
    (*d*) Ask all States to reserve all the Money or Financial Bills passed by the State Legislature for his consideration
35. When the Financial Emergency is under operation, the Union is empowered to
    (*a*) Reduce the salaries of its employees (*b*) Increase the salaries of its employees
    (*c*) Discretion of the President (*d*) None of these
36. The three types of Proclamation of Emergency made by the President have to be placed before each House of Parliament for its approval within
    (*a*) One month in case of National Emergency and within two months due to breakdown of constitutional machinery and Financial Emergency
    (*b*) Six months
    (*c*) Two months (*d*) One month
37. Which one of the following emergencies can be declared by the President only on the receipt in writing of the decision of the Union Cabinet
    (*a*) Emergency due to war, external aggression or armed rebellion
    (*b*) Emergency due to breakdown of constitutional machinery in a State
    (*c*) Emergency due to threat to financial stability
    (*d*) All the above
38. When a Financial Emergency is proclaimed
    (*a*) Salaries and allowances of any class of employees may be reduced
    (*b*) Repayment of government debts will stop
    (*c*) Payment of salaries to public servants will be postponed
    (*d*) Union Budget will not be presented
39. If State fails to comply with the directives of the Central Government, the President can
    (*a*) Declare breakdown of the constitutional machinery in the State and assume responsibility for its governance
    (*b*) Send reserve police force to secure compliance with directions
    (*c*) Dissolve the State Legislature and order fresh elections
    (*d*) Can do either (*a*) or (*b*)

40. This is not a ground to declare State Emergency
(*a*) No clear majority
(*b*) Not complying with the direction given by the Central Government
(*c*) Disobeying the direction given by Supreme Court
(*d*) Failure to maintain law and order in State
41. When a State Emergency is declared, all or any of the functions of the State Government are assumed by the
(*a*) President (*b*) Governor
(*c*) Chief Minister (*d*) Union Cabinet
42. President made a Proclamation of Emergency on grounds of internal disturbances for first time in
(*a*) 1975 (*b*) 1965
(*c*) 1962 (*d*) 1950
43. When the State Emergency is in operation, the President can't interfere in the matters of
(*a*) State Judiciary (*b*) State Executive
(*c*) State Legislature (*d*) All of these
44. Who has the duty to protect states against external aggression and internal disturbance?
(*a*) Union Government (*b*) State Government
(*c*) Army (*d*) No such duty in federal states
45. For first time, the President make a Proclamation of Emergency under the Article 352 in
(*a*) 1962 (*b*) 1952
(*c*) 1965 (*d*) 1971

Chapter 9: Electoral Process

1. The Electoral System of India is largely based on the pattern of
(*a*) Britain (*b*) France
(*c*) USA (*d*) None of these
2. The details regarding the Electoral System of India
(*a*) Were provided by the Parliament through a number of laws
(*b*) Were laid down in the Constitution itself
(*c*) Were provided by the Election Commissioner and approved by the President in 1950
(*d*) Were prescribed through a Presidential ordinance in 1950
3. Who has the power to make necessary provisions with respect to elections?
(*a*) Parliament (*b*) President
(*c*) Election Commission (EC) (*d*) Parliament and respective Sate Legislatures
4. Who is competent to declare the elections to the LS?
(*a*) President (*b*) Chief Minister
(*c*) Union Cabinet (*d*) Election Commissioner
5. What is the outstanding feature (s) of the Electoral System of India?
(*a*) All of these (*b*) Based on Universal Adult Franchise
(*c*) Provides a single electoral body
(*d*) Political parties are an indispensable part of the process
6. Elections to LS and LA in India are conducted on the basis of
(*a*) Adult franchise (*b*) Single transferable vote
(*c*) Proportional representation (*d*) Limited suffrage

7. What is the system used to elect the President of India?
   (*a*) Proportional representation (*b*) Direct election
   (*c*) Secret ballot (*d*) Preferential system
8. Who is authorized to determine the territorial constituencies after each Census?
   (*a*) Parliament (*b*) President
   (*c*) EC (*d*) State Legislature
9. Which of the following provisions kept democracy alive in India?
   (*a*) Electoral provisions (*b*) DPSP
   (*c*) FDs (*d*) FRs
10. Chief Minister of a State is not eligible to vote in the Presidential Election if he is
    (*a*) Member of the LC of the State Legislature
    (*b*) Care-taker Chief Minister of the State
    (*c*) Yet to prove his majority on the floor of the House of the State Legislature
    (*d*) Himself is a candidate for such election
11. Voting age of citizens is changed from 21 to 18 years by ____ Constitutional Amendment Act.
    (*a*) 61st (*b*) 55th
    (*c*) 42nd (*d*) 7th
12. 61st Constitutional Amendment reduced the voting age from
    (*a*) 21 to 18 (*b*) 22 to 18
    (*c*) 21 to 19 (*d*) 21 to 20
13. Citizen of India have the right to cast his vote after attaining the age of _____ years.
    (*a*) 18 (*b*) 21
    (*c*) 24 (*d*) 16
14. Elections in India are held on the basis of
    (*a*) Single-member constituencies (*b*) Double-member constituencies
    (*c*) Multi-member constituencies (*d*) (*a*) and (*b*)
15. The Chief Election Commissioner (CEC)
    (*a*) Appointed by the President (*b*) Elected by the Parliament
    (*c*) Appointed by the Prime Minister (*d*) Appointed by the Union Home Minister
16. The Chief Election Commissioner holds Office
    (*a*) For a fixed term of five years (*b*) For a fixed term of six years
    (*c*) During the pleasure of the President (*d*) During the pleasure of the Parliament
17. The number of members in Election Commission (EC) including the Chairman is
    (*a*) 3 (*b*) 5
    (*c*) 7 (*d*) 9
18. Which Article under the Constitution gives power to EC to conduct elections?
    (*a*) 324 (*b*) 320
    (*c*) 234 (*d*) 335
19. The control and preparation of electoral rolls for Parliament and State Legislature vest with the
    (*a*) EC (*b*) Cabinet
    (*c*) Prime Minister (*d*) President
20. Election to Local Self-Government shall be conducted by
    (*a*) State EC (*b*) Regional EC
    (*c*) EC (*d*) Governor

21. Who will conduct the elections to posts of President and Vice-President?
(*a*) EC (*b*) Prime Minister
(*c*) Parliament (*d*) Both Parliament & State Legislature
22. EC does not conduct election to
(*a*) Speaker of LS (*b*) Members of State LA
(*c*) Members of Parliament (*d*) President
23. Who has been made responsible for free and fair elections in the country?
(*a*) Chief Election Commissioner (*b*) President
(*c*) Vice-President (*d*) Chief Justice of India
24. Elections to LS shall be held after every
(*a*) Five years (*b*) Six years
(*c*) Two Years (*d*) As soon as LS is dissolved
25. For election to LS, nomination papers can be filed by
(*a*) Any citizen whose name appears in the electoral roll
(*b*) Any citizen of India
(*c*) Citizen permitted by EC (*d*) Any person residing in India
26. The party system in India can be described as
(*a*) Multi-party (*b*) Bi-party
(*c*) Single-party (*d*) A mixture of all these
27. Which one of the following is a feature of the party system in India?
(*a*) All of these
(*b*) Political parties are largely based on language, religion, caste, etc.
(*c*) There are large number of regional parties in India
(*d*) There is a close resemblance in the policies and programmes of various political parties
28. In India, the citizens have been given the right to vote on the basis of
(*a*) Age (*b*) Education
(*c*) Property qualifications (*d*) Duration of stay in the country
29. Which categories of persons are not entitled to exercise vote through postal ballot?
(*a*) Indian nationals settled abroad (*b*) Civil servants on election duty
(*c*) Members of Armed Forces (*d*) Members of Foreign Services posted abroad
30. Which body gives recognition to political parties?
(*a*) EC (*b*) Election Board
(*c*) RS (*d*) LS
31. Main consideration which prompted government to convert EC into a multi-member body was
(*a*) To check the unbridled powers of the CEC
(*b*) To placate the opposition, which was greatly agitated with the then CEC
(*c*) To provide relief to the CEC (*d*) All the above
32. Who accords recognition to various political parties as national or regional parties?
(*a*) EC (*b*) President
(*c*) Parliament (*d*) President in consultation with the EC
33. To be recognized as a national party, a party must secure at least
(*a*) 4% of the valid votes in four or more states
(*b*) 10% of the valid votes in four or more states
(*c*) 15% of the valid votes in two states
(*d*) 25% of the valid votes in one state

34. To be recognized as a regional party, a party must secure at least
    (*a*) 4% of the valid votes in state
    (*b*) 25% of the valid votes in any one state
    (*c*) 15% of the valid votes in any one state
    (*d*) 10% of the valid votes in any one state
35. Which one of the following statements about the Election Commission is correct?
    (*a*) The members of the EC have equal powers with the CEC
    (*b*) The CEC has over-riding authority
    (*c*) The members of the EC are appointed by the CEC
    (*d*) Only those who can be appointed as Judges of a High Court can be appointed as members of EC
36. Which of the following is not the function of the EC?
    (*a*) Selecting candidates for contesting elections
    (*b*) Preparation of electoral rolls
    (*c*) Accordappointed by the CECing recognition to political parties
    (*d*) Allotting symbols to political parties
37. This is not the function of the EC.
    (*a*) Ascertain the suitability of candidates (*b*) Counting votes
    (*c*) Conduct of election (*d*) Preparation of election rolls
38. Election disputes shall be decided by
    (*a*) Election Commission (*b*) Parliament
    (*c*) High Court (*d*) Supreme Court
39. In terms of election laws in India, electioneering ceases in a constituency at least _____ hours before the commencement of the polling.
    (*a*) 48 (*b*) 36
    (*c*) 24 (*d*) 12
40. The Election Commission does not conduct election to the
    (*a*) Post of Prime Minister (*b*) Office of President
    (*c*) Office of Vice-President (*d*) Parliament
41. The Election Commission has no power to conduct election to the
    (*a*) Speaker of LS (*b*) Office of President
    (*c*) State Legislature (*d*) Parliament
42. The Election Commission is responsible for the conduct of elections to
    (*a*) All (*b*) Offices of President and Vice-President
    (*c*) State Legislatures (*d*) Parliament
43. The Election Commission of India enjoys
    (*a*) Constitutional basis
    (*b*) Statutory basis
    (*c*) Neither constitutional nor statutory basis
    (*d*) Legal basis
44. The Election Commission generally consists of the CEC and such other commissioners as
    (*a*) Determined by the President from time to time
    (*b*) Determined by the President from time to time
    (*c*) Prescribed by the Constitution
    (*d*) Recommended by the Chief Election Commissioner

45. CEC can be removed from Office before the expiry of the term by the
(*a*) President on the recommendation of the Parliament
(*b*) President on the recommendation of the Supreme Court
(*c*) President on the recommendation of Council of Ministers
(*d*) None

46. CEC shall be removed by the
(*a*) Parliament (*b*) President
(*c*) Supreme Court (*d*) Other Election Commissioners

47. Who of the following has voting rights?
(*a*) Adult resident citizen of a State (*b*) Adult literate citizen of a state
(*c*) Citizen of a state (*d*) Any inhabitant of a state

48. Who is responsible for keeping the voters' list up-to-date at all times?
(*a*) Election Commission (*b*) President
(*c*) Union Home Minister (*d*) All of these

49. The first general elections were held in India in (OR) When did first General Elections was held?
(*a*) 1951-52 (*b*) 1950-51
(*c*) 1949-50 (*d*) None of these

50. Which of the following general elections of India was spread over for 100 days?
(*a*) First (b) Fourth
(*c*) Seventh (*d*) Eighth

51. Which of the following features of the Electoral System of India has been wrongly listed?
(*a*) None of these
(*b*) Political parties are an indispensable part of the electoral process
(*c*) It provides a single electoral body (*d*) It is based on Universal Adult Franchise

52. The term 'Fourth Estate' refers to
(*a*) Press (*b*) Judiciary
(*c*) Parliament (*d*) Backward class residing in the state

53. The chief merit of proportional representation is
(*a*) Representation to all parties in the legislature according to their strength
(*b*) Elimination of minor parties and factions
(*c*) Equal opportunity for rural and urban people
(*d*) Equal opportunity for the poor and wealthy

54. In India, the system of proportional representation by means of single transferable vote is used in the election of
(*a*) President (*b*) Vice-President
(*c*) Speaker of LS (d) All of these

55. Regional election commissioners may be appointed by the
(*a*) President (*b*) Parliament
(*c*) EC (*d*) Governor

56. Regional election commissioners may be appointed by the President with the consultation of
(*a*) EC (*b*) Governor
(*c*) Prime Minister (*d*) Vice-President

57. Other Election Commissioner or Regional Election Commissioners shall be removed on the recommendation of the
(*a*) CEC (*b*) Governor
(*c*) President (*d*) Prime Minister

58. Which of the following LS was dissolved before the expiry of its nominal term and fresh elections held before the due date?
    (*a*) Fourth (*b*) Fifth
    (*c*) Third (*d*) None of these
59. The Parliamentary elections of 1999, which have been described as the longest elections of India, were spread over ______ weeks.
    (*a*) Four (*b*) Six
    (*c*) Eight (*d*) Ten
60. Which one of the following regional party emerged as the largest opposition party in the LS elections held in December, 1984?
    (*a*) Telugu Desam Party (*b*) DMK
    (*c*) AIADMK (*d*) None of these

Chapter 10 to 13: Engineering Ethics (Basics, Responsibility, Honesty, Integrity, Reliability, Risk, Safety and Liability)

1. Engineering Ethics is a
   (*a*) Preventive ethics (*b*) Developing ethics
   (*c*) Natural ethics (*d*) Scientifically developed ethics
2. Engineering Ethics
   (*a*) Stimulates the moral imagination
   (*b*) Provides up-to-date knowledge in the field of engineering
   (*c*) Stimulates to conduct research (*d*) Stresses on time management
3. Professional Ethics is
   (*a*) Set of rules relating to personal character of professionals
   (*b*) Traditional rules observed since a long time
   (*c*) Set of rules passed by professional bodies
   (*d*) Set of standards adopted by professionals
4. Professional Ethics takes in to account of the
   (*a*) Personal character of engineers (*b*) Temperament of engineers
   (*c*) Religious bent of mind of engineers (*d*) Social background of engineers
5. Engineering Profession is considered to be like a building, its foundation is
   (*a*) Honesty (*b*) Hard and sincere work
   (*c*) Expert engineering knowledge and skill (*d*) Sound common sense and expert knowledge
6. One of the aims in studying Engineering Ethics is to
   (*a*) Gain better insight into the profession (*b*) Know the secretes of the profession
   (*c*) Develop analytical skill (*d*) Understand the professional problems
7. One of the aims of Engineering Ethics is to
   (*a*) Stimulate the moral imagination
   (*b*) Inspire engineers to acquire in-depth knowledge in their field
   (*c*) Acquire new skills in Engineering, Testing and Research
   (*d*) Make engineers self-confident in discharging their duties
8. This is not the aim of studying Engineering Ethics.
   (*a*) Crimping (*b*) Cooking
   (*c*) Forging (*d*) Plagiarism

9. This is not the aim of studying Engineering Ethics
   (*a*) Addressing unclarity (*b*) Analyzing concepts
   (*c*) Engaging sense of responsibility (*d*) Procuring faultless results
10. Engineers shall issue public statements only
   (*a*) On their personal responsibility (*b*) Based on the reports sent by higher officers
   (*c*) In objective manner (*d*) In subjective manner
11. An engineer may not be held legally liable for causing harm, when the harm is caused
   (*a*) Internationally (*b*) Ignorantly
   (*c*) Negligently (*d*) Recklessly
12. One of the characteristic of Profession is
   (*a*) It gives scope to exercise one's skill (*b*) It gives monopoly on service
   (*c*) It provides opportunity to help the poor and needy
   (*d*) It demands high standard of honesty
13. One of the characteristics of profession is that
   (*a*) Usually it is having monopoly (*b*) It demands hard work
   (*c*) It is based on honesty (*d*) It is having tough competition
14. One of the views on responsibility of engineers is
   (*a*) They are absolutely reliable (*b*) They should do good works
   (*c*) They should take reasonable responsibility
   (*d*) They are strictly liable
15. One of the impediments to responsibility is
   (*a*) Self-deception (*a*) Rampant corruption at higher level
   (*c*) Interference by higher officers (*d*) Interference by politicians
16. This is not impediment to responsibility
   (*a*) Self-respect (*b*) Ignorance
   (*c*) Self-deception (*d*) Fear
17. Conflict of interest exists for an engineer when he is subject to
   (*a*) Loyalties (*b*) Professional impediments
   (*c*) Professional harassments (*d*) Threat
18. 'Professional Autonomy' means
   (*a*) Exercising independent and objective judgments
   (*b*) Liberty to express independent view
   (*c*) Liberty in selecting the work (*d*) Independent body controlling profession
19. It does not amount to misusing the truth
   (*a*) Biased professional information (*b*) Failure to seek-out the truth
   (*c*) Withholding information (*d*) Deliberation deception
20. One of the ways of misusing the truth is
   (*a*) Failure to seek out the truth (*b*) Exaggerating the truth
   (*c*) Making the confused statement (*d*) Making totally false statement
21. 'Good works' means
   (*a*) Work above and beyond the call of duty
   (*b*) Responsible work
   (*c*) Work involving high risk (*d*) Superior work done with great care and skill

22. 'Cooking' means
    (*a*) Retaining results which fit the theory (*b*) Making deceptive statements
    (*c*) Boiling under pressure
    (*d*) Misleading the public about the quality of the product
23. 'Cooking' is
    (*a*) Retaining the results to satisfy the theory discarding the rest
    (*b*) Using the actual data
    (*c*) Using falsified data (*d*) Both (*a*) and (*b*)
24. 'Forging' means
    (*a*) Inventing research data which are reported
    (*b*) Mixing material under high pressure
    (*c*) Signing in the name of some other person
    (*d*) Strengthening material by special process
25. An example for 'Forging' is
    (*a*) Mentioning of experiments to obtain data which were never conducted
    (*b*) Obtaining data by conducting an experiment
    (*c*) Referring to all research data (*d*) Both (*a*) and (*c*)
26. 'Egocentric tendencies' means
    (*a*) Interpreting situation from limited view (*b*) Superiority complex
    (*c*) Arrogant and irresponsible behavior (*d*) Habit of condemning the views of others
27. 'Group Thinking'
    (*a*) Is an impediment to responsibility (*b*) Leads to confusion and may cause loss
    (*c*) Is an impediment in the progress of work
    (*d*) Is useful to understand the different facts of the problem
28. 'Tight Couple' means
    (*a*) Binding two beams tightly (*b*) Erecting two pillars side by side
    (*c*) Process tightly coupled (*d*) Strong adhesive material
29. One process or function of one component that affect the other and spread the adverse effect to the entire system is observed in
    (*a*) Tight coupled (*b*) Loosely coupled
    (*c*) Complexly interactive (*d*) None
30. In _____ systems, risk estimation is difficult.
    (*a*) Complexly interactive (*b*) Tight coupled
    (*c*) Loosely coupled (*d*) Both (*b*) and (*c*)
31. A compound measure of the probability and magnitude of the adverse effect is known as
    (*a*) Risk (*b*) Benefit
    (*c*) Compensation (*d*) Both (*b*) and (*c*)
32. 'Lying' is
    (*a*) Intentionally conveying false or misleading information
    (*b*) Deception
    (*c*) Falsehood (*d*) Both (*b*) and (*c*)
33. 'Trimming' is
    (*a*) Smoothing of irregularities to make the data to appear accurate & precise
    (*b*) Retaining the entire data
    (*c*) consolidating the data (*d*) Both (*a*) and (*c*)

34. The principal obligation of engineers is to safeguard the public by
    (*a*) Spreading the information before the disaster takes place
    (*b*) Finding out the truth
    (*c*) Withholding the information (*d*) Deliberate deception
35. One of the characteristics of high-risk technologies susceptible to accident is Complex
    (*a*) Combinations (*b*) Working system
    (*c*) Interaction (*d*) Designs
36. One of the ways of reducing risk is
    (*a*) Tight coupling (*b*) Complex interaction
    (*c*) Normalization of deviance (*d*) Changing the working system
37. 'Minimalist View' means
    (*a*) A concept of responsibility (*b*) A narrow thinking
    (*c*) A ministerial view (*d*) A novel plan to minimize industrial loss
38. The basic attitude towards responsibility is
    (*a*) Minimalist (*b*) Recklessly causing harm
    (*c*) Negligently causing harm (*d*) Intentionally causing harm
39. They are not trade secrets.
    (*a*) Principles (*b*) Patterns
    (*c*) Formulas (*d*) Devices
40. Which of the following is not a trade secret?
    (*a*) Theorem (*b*) Equipment
    (*c*) Formulae (*d*) Pattern
41. The formulae of a soft drink is an example of
    (*a*) Trade secret (*b*) Patent
    (*c*) Copy right (*d*) Trade mark
42. Copy right protects the expression of ideas but not the
    (*a*) Ideas themselves (*b*) Deriving ideas
    (*c*) Predicting ideas (*d*) Both (*b*) and (*c*)
43. A company cannot have claim if the knowledge used is
    (*a*) Generic information (*b*) Stolen from the company
    (*c*) Used to create the same product (*d*) Both (*b*) and (*c*)
44. Which of the following is not conflict of interest as applied to making judgment?
    (*a*) Virtual (*b*) Apparent
    (*c*) Potential (*d*) Actual
45. A fault tree is used to
    (*a*) Assess the risk involved (*b*) Claim compensation
    (*c*) Take free consent (*d*) Improve safety
46. Risk estimation can be done by using
    (*a*) Event tree (*b*) Trimming
    (*c*) Cooking (*d*) Both (*b*) and (*c*)
47. The use of intellectual property of others without their permission or credit is referred as
    (*a*) Plagiarism (*b*) Trimming
    (*c*) Cooking (*d*) Forging
48. Which of the following is not preserved as an intellectual property?
    (*a*) Government regulations (*b*) Copy rights
    (*c*) Patents (*d*) Trade secrets

49. 'Acceptable Risk' means
    (*a*) Risk of harm equal to probability of producing benefit
    (*b*) Risk which is the natural part of the process
    (*c*) Inevitable risk (*d*) Risk which cannot be avoided
50. Allowing increased number of deviances from prescribed standards of safety and acceptable risk is referred to as
    (*a*) Normalizing deviance (*b*) Identification of risk
    (*c*) Estimation of risk (*d*) Probable risk
51. Lay public estimation of likelihood of low probability risks associated with causes of loss of lives is generally
    (*a*) Overestimation (*b*) Underestimation
    (*c*) Actual estimation (*d*) Rough estimation
52. In which of the following the competent technical knowledge of engineers is not required for certification in cases involving?
    (*a*) Legal matters (*b*) Defective goods
    (*c*) Accidents (*d*) Patent violation
53. An Expert Testimony does not demand
    (*a*) Adequate time for thorough investigation
    (*b*) Consulting extensively with the lawyer
    (*c*) Expert legal knowledge (*d*) Objective and unbiased demeanor
54. In issuing testimony, which of the following is not desired by an expert?
    (*a*) Not to maintain an objective and be biased
    (*b*) Be open to information, even during the course of the trial
    (*c*) Not to accept, if he cannot do so with good conscience
    (*d*) Not to accept, if there is no adequate time
55. Which of the following is not the concept of responsibility?
    (*a*) Utilitarian (*b*) Minimalist
    (*c*) Reasonable care (*d*) Good works
56. For an ethical engineer, responsibility is
    (*a*) Both legal and moral (*b*) Moral responsibility
    (*c*) Legal responsibility (*d*) Social responsibility
57. One's wish of being an ethical engineer is derived from
    (*a*) His wish of being an ethical person
    (*b*) His family members wish of him being an ethical person
    (*c*) His employers wish of him being an ethical person
    (*d*) All
58. What is morally wrong?
    (*a*) Cannot be measured as constitutionally right
    (*b*) Can be measured as constitutionally right
    (c) Can be legally right (*d*) Both (*b*) and (*c*)
59. A professional engineer take the help of CoE specifically when he enters into
    (*a*) Ethical crisis (*b*) Doubts
    (*c*) Confusion (*d*) Legal complications
60. The 'risk expert's approach is usually
    (*a*) Utilitarian (*b*) Biased
    (*c*) Favorable to employer (*d*) None

61. Risk as a maximizing benefit is understood by
   (*a*) Risk/benefit analysis (*b*) Straight-line analysis
   (*c*) Cost/benefit analysis (*d*) Break-even analysis
62. Conflicts of interest exists when an improper judgment is made by professional may not be due to
   (*a*) Protecting the public health (*b*) Temptations
   (*c*) Loyalties (*d*) Influences
63. It is not a kind of trademark
   (*a*) Goodwill (*b*) Symbols
   (*c*) Sounds (*d*) Designs
64. Conflict of interest may be
   (*a*) Potential (*b*) False
   (*c*) Created (*d*) Imaginary
65. Revealing confidential information means
   (*a*) Misusing the truth (*b*) Breach of contract
   (*c*) Criminal breach of trust (*d*) Violation of patent right
66. The professional ethics deals with _____ accepted by the professional group/community.
   (*a*) Ethical standards (*b*) Scientific standards
   (*c*) Moral standards (*c*) Social standards
67. The obligations and prerogatives associated with a specific role is referred to as
   (*a*) Role morality (*b*) Duty
   (*c*) Responsibility (*d*) Ethics
68. The codes of ethics can be taken as guidelines by the engineers to
   (*a*) Resolve the conflicts (*b*) Formulate the problem
   (*c*) Overcome the work pressure (*d*) Escape from the responsibility
69. No code will give ____ to get solutions for ethical problems.
   (*a*) An algorithm (*b*) Guidelines
   (*c*) Set of ideas (*d*) Ethical standards
70. Which of the following is not taken as the aim of engineering ethics?
   (*a*) Shifting of responsibility (*b*) Recognition of ethical issues
   (*c*) Moral imagination (*d*) Sense of responsibility
71. Responsibility is assigned as belonging to persons in
   (*a*) Both (*b*) and (c) (*b*) Rule
   (*c*) Morality (*d*) Obligation
72. Recklessly causing harm is
   (*a*) Not with an intention to cause harm but acting in the conscious awareness that harm is likely to take place
   (*b*) Unknowingly causing harm but failing to take due care
   (*c*) Purposely causing harm (*d*) Both (*b*) and (*c*)
73. As applied to responsibility, avoiding blame or being safe is the prime concern in
   (*a*) Minimalist approach (*b*) Considerable care
   (*c*) Both (*a*) and (*b*) (*d*) Good works view
74. Which of the following does not depict the attitude towards responsibility?
   (*a*) Protest (*b*) Good works
   (*c*) Reasonable care (*d*) Minimalist

75. In reasonable care concept of responsibility, the attention paid is to
    (*a*) Those who are at risk of being harmed
    (*b*) The employee
    (*c*) To client (*d*) Self
76. Engineers tempted by their own interest to act in contrary to the interest of others is
    (*a*) Self-interest (*b*) Self-deception
    (*c*) Ignorance (*d*) Fear
77. The thinking of betraying a willful lack of self-understanding is called
    (*a*) Self-deception (*b*) Self-interest
    (*c*) Ignorance (*d*) Egoism
78. Ignorance as a hurdle to responsibility is not due to
    (*a*) Fear (*b*) Overconfidence
    (*c*) Lack of imagination (*d*) Pressure and deadlines
79. The tendency of interpreting situations according their views and imposing views is
    (*a*) Egocentric (*b*) Self interest
    (*c*) Confined vision (*d*) Both (*b*) & (*c*)
80. Engineering CoE emphasize that the engineers should have ____ in discharging their duties.
    (*a*) Autonomy (*b*) Fidelity to employers
    (*c*) Obligation to public (*d*) Both (*b*) & (*c*)
81. ____ is not the symptom of group thinking.
    (*a*) Egocentric tendency (*b*) Mind guarding
    (*c*) Illusion of unanimity (*d*) Self-censorship
82. Tendency of shifting responsibility will logically come down if there is
    (*a*) Group-thinking (*b*) Microscopic vision
    (*c*) Fear (*d*) Both (*b*) & (*c*)
83. Which of the following is not advised by NSPE code to engineers?
    (*a*) Not to avoid deceptive acts (*b*) Not to use firm's name in dishonest business
    (*c*) To have professional obligations (*d*) To be honest
84. Which of the following qualities an ethically responsible engineer should not have with regard to risk?
    (*a*) Dishonest in assessing
    (*b*) Be aware of different approaches to the determination and risk
    (*c*) Not be deceiving (*d*) Aware of difficulty
85. The owner of 'Patent Right' retains his patent right for ____ years (OR) Patent holder does not allow others to use patented information for ____ years from date of filing.
    (*a*) 20 (*b*) 50
    (*c*) 75 (*d*) 100

SPECIAL ANNEXURE

The Constitution

The Constitution consists of the following:

1. The Preamble
2. Parts I to XXII covering Articles 1 to 395
3. Schedules 1 to 12
4. An Appendix. Part IX-The Panchayats and the Schedule XI (Article 243-G) have been incorporated under 73rd Constitution Amendment Act, 1992.

The Preamble

"We, the people of India, having solemnly resolved to constitute India into a Sovereign Socialist Secular Democratic Republic and to secure to all its citizens:

* JUSTICE, social, economic and political;
* LIBERTY of thought, expression, belief, faith and worship;
* EQUALITY of status and of opportunity; and to promote among them all
* FRATERNITY assuring the dignity of the individual and the unity and integrity of the Nation; ...

in our Constituent Assembly this twenty sixth day of November, 1949, do hereby adopt, enact and give to ourselves this Constitution".

The words 'Socialist, Secular' and 'the Unity and the Integrity of the Nation', were added by the Constitution (42nd Amendment) Act, 1976.

PART I: THE UNION AND ITS TERRITORY

1. Name and Territory of the Union.
   (*a*) India, that is Bharat, shall be a Union of States (Art. 1).
   (*b*) The States and Territories thereof shall be specified in the First Schedule (Art. 2).
   (*c*) The territories of India shall comprise-
      (c.i) The territories of the States;
      (c.ii) The Union Territories; and
      (c.iii) Such other territories as may be acquired.
2. Admission or establishment of new states.
3. Formation of new states and alteration of areas, boundaries or names of existing states.

Distribution of Powers

The Union has exclusive power to make laws on all matters in the List I of the Seventh Schedule (Union List). The States have exclusive power to make laws on all matters in the List II (State List). The Union and States have concurrent powers to legislate on any matter enumerated in List III (Concurrent List) (Article 246).

Residuary Powers: The Union has exclusive power to make laws on any matter not enumerated in the Concurrent List or State List (Article 248).

Overriding Powers: In case of any conflict between Union and State laws, The Union laws shall prevail (Article 254).

PART II: CITIZENSHIP

Indian Constitution, though federal in character, provides only Single Citizenship to the people of India. Citizenship rights, according to the Citizenship Act, 1955, are acquired:

(*a*) By birth, i.e. born on or after 26th January, 1950.
(*b*) By descent, i.e. either of whose parents was born in India, even if the person is born outside India on or after 26th January, 1950.
(*c*) By registration, i.e. who has been residing in India for 5 years (as required by the Citizenship Act, 1986) can acquire it by registering before the prescribed authority.
(*d*) By naturalization, i.e. a foreigner can apply to the Government of India for naturalization.
(*e*) By incorporation of territory, i.e. when new territories become part of the country, the Government of India shall specify the citizenship of people living there.

Citizenship could be lost on the grounds of
(*a*) Surrender—voluntarily surrendering it when the person possesses dual citizenship.
(*b*) Termination—when one acquire foreign citizenship.
(*c*) Deprivation—when acquired by fraud.

PART III: FUNDAMENTAL RIGHTS

These are granted to the citizens under Articles 12 to 35 of the Constitution. They are:

1. Right to Equality—before law; on the ground of religion, race, caste, sex, place of birth; employment; abolition of untouchability and titles.
2. Right to Freedom—of speech and expression; assemble peaceably and without arms; to form associations or unions; to move freely throughout the territory of India; to practice any profession or to carry any occupation, trade or business; of protection in respect of conviction for offences; of protection of life and personal liberty; of protection against arrest and detention in certain cases. Article 32(1)—The right to move Supreme Court by appropriate proceedings for enforcement of the rights conferred by this Part is guaranteed.
3. Right against Exploitation—prohibition of traffic in human beings and forced labor; prohibition of employment of children in factories, etc.
4. Right to Freedom of Religion—conscience and free profession, practice and propagation of religion. Right to—manage religious affairs; payment of taxes for promotion of any particular religion; attendance at religious instructions or religious worship in certain educational institutions.
5. Cultural and Educational Rights—protection of interest of minorities; to establish and administer educational institutions.
6. Right to Constitutional Remedies—
   (*a*) all citizens are guaranteed the right to move the Supreme Court or the High Courts by appropriate proceedings for enforcement of Fundamental Rights.
   (*b*) The Supreme Court can issue directions/orders/writs such as Habeas Corpus, Mandamus, Prohibition, Quo Warranto and Certiorari, for the enforcement of any rights conferred by the Part.
   (*c*) The right guaranteed by this Article cannot be suspended except as otherwise provided for by the Constitution. (The 16th and 24th Amendments have considerably limited the exercise of Fundamental Rights).

Habeas Corpus is an order calling on a person who has detained another to produce the latter before the Court in order to let the Court know on what ground he has been confined and to set him free if there is no legal justification for the imprisonment.

Mandamus commands a person to whom it is addressed to perform some public or quasi-public legal duty which he has refused to perform and the performance of which cannot be enforced by any other adequate legal remedy.

Quo Warranto is a proceeding whereby the Court enquires into the legality of the claim, which a party asserts to a public office, and to oust him from its enjoyment if the claim be not well founded.

Prohibition issues so long as proceedings are pending before a court or tribunal. If the court or tribunal has passed final orders in the matter, no prohibition will lie. Where an election tribunal had given its finding and finally decided the election petition it was held that prohibition would not lie.

Certiorari is an order issued against a Court or Tribunal to quash their decision-intended to secure the jurisdiction of an inferior court/tribunal.

PART IV: THE DIRECTIVE PRINCIPLES OF STATE POLICY

Articles 36 to 51 of the Constitution lay down 19 objectives. Directive Principles of State Policy enjoin the State to undertake within its means, a number of welfare measures. These are intended to assure citizens an adequate means of livelihood, raise the standard of living, improve public health, provide free and compulsory education for children, and assure that the operation of the economic system does not result in the concentration of wealth and means of production to the detriment of the common good. These are not enforceable by law like Fundamental Rights. Nevertheless, they are declared fundamental to the governance of the country.

Fundamental Duties: The 42nd Amendment Act (1976) has incorporated into the Constitution a new Chapter on Fundamental Duties under Part IV-A and the Article 51-A. The Duties for an Indian Citizen enshrined, include:

(*a*) To abide by the Constitution and respect its ideals and institutions, the National Flag and the National Anthem;

(*b*) To cherish and follow the noble ideals which inspired our freedom struggle;

(*c*) To uphold the sovereignty, unity and integrity of India;

(*d*) To render national service when called for;

(*e*) To promote harmony and spirit of common brotherhood amongst all Indians; and renounce practices derogatory to the dignity of women;

(*f*) To preserve the rich heritage of our composite culture;

(*g*) To protect and improve the natural environment including forests, lakes, and wild life and to have compassion for living creatures;

(*h*) To develop scientific temper, humanism and the spirit of enquiry and reform;

(*i*) To safeguard the public property and to abjure violence; and

(*j*) To strive towards excellence in all spheres of individual and collective activity so that the nation constantly rises to higher levels of endeavor and achievement.

PART V: THE UNION

Chapter I: The Executive

The President of India

The Union Executive consists of the President, the Vice President and the Council of Ministers with the Prime Minister at the Head to aid and advise the President.

The President

The President is elected by members of an electoral college consisting of elected members of both the Houses of Parliament and Legislative Assemblies of the states in accordance with the system of proportional representation by means of single transferable vote. To secure uniformity among the States *inter se* as well as parity between the States, as a whole, and the Union, suitable weightage is given to each vote. President must be a citizen of India, not less than 35 years of age and qualified for election of member of Lok Sabha. His term of office is five years and he is eligible for reelection. His removal from the office is to be in accordance with procedure prescribed in Article 61 of the Constitution. He may, by writing under his hand addressed to the Vice President, resign his office.

Executive power of the Union is vested in the President and is exercised by him either directly or through officers subordinates to him in accordance with the Constitution. Supreme command of defence forces of the Union also vests in him. The President summons, prorogues, addresses, sends messages to Parliament and dissolves the Lok Sabha; promulgates ordinances at any time, except when both Houses of Parliament are in session; makes recommendations for introducing financial and money bills and gives assent to bills; grants pardons, reprieves, respites or remission of punishment or suspends, remits or commutes sentences in certain cases. When there is a failure of constitutional machinery in a State, he can assume to himself all or any of the functions of the State Government. The President can proclaim emergency in the country if he is satisfied that a grave emergency exists whereby the security of India or any parts of its territory is threatened whether by war or external aggression or armed rebellion.

The Vice President

The Vice president shall be elected by the members of an electoral college consisting of the members of both the Houses of Parliament (Article 66-1). The Vice President may hold the office for five years (Article 67), and shall be the ex-officio Chairman of the Council of States (Article 64).

The Council of Ministers

There shall be a Council of Ministers with the Prime Minister at the head to aid and advice the President in the exercise of his functions (Article 74-1). The Prime minister shall be appointed by the President, and the other Ministers shall be appointed by the President, on the advice of the Prime Minister (Article 75-1). The ministers shall hold office during the pleasure of the President (Article 75-2).

The Council of Ministers (as at present constituted) consists of the Prime Minister and (1) Ministers who are members of the Cabinet (2) Ministers of State (Union Ministers) who are not members of the Cabinet and (3) Deputy Ministers.

A Secretary to Government is the Administrative Head of a ministry and the Principal Advisor of the Minister. When the volume of work in a ministry exceeds the manageable charge of the Secretary, one or more wings may be established under a Joint Secretary. A ministry is divided into divisions, branches and sections functioning under Deputy Secretaries, Under Secretaries and Section Officers respectively.

Chapter II: Parliament

Legislature of the Union, called Parliament, consists of the President and two Houses - the Council of States (Rajya Sabha) and the House of People (Lok Sabha) as in Article 79.

The Parliament House was designed by Sir Edwin Lutyens and Sir Herbert Baker. It was built at a cost of Rs.83.00 lakhs and inaugurated by Lord Irwin on 18th January, 1927. Parliament is a circular building with the Central Hall at the center. The three chambers for Lok Sabha, Rajya Sabha and the Library Hall radiate from the center. These chambers and the garden courts between them are in turn surrounded by a circular four-storeyed structure with rooms for Ministers, Parliamentary Committees, Party offices, press, etc. The Central Hall has witnessed historic moments. It is here that the Indian Constitution was framed between 09th December, 1946 and 24th January, 1950, when it served as the Constituent Assembly Hall. It was here again the power of reign was transferred on 15th August,

1947. Presidential address at the first Lok Sabha session after election, first session of the Budget session, joint sitting of both Houses and address by visiting Heads of States are held here.

The Lok Sabha Chamber is U-shaped with a seating capacity of 550 MPs. The Ruling party sits on the Speaker's right and the Opposition on his left side. Just below the Speaker's chair is the table of the Secretary General of the Lok Sabha. In front of him is a large table where the official reporters (work in five minute relay takes down verbatim the entire proceedings of the House) and other officials sit. This is the 'Table of the House' where documents, etc. are placed. The adjacent vacant place surrounding it is the 'Well' of the House. On the first floor are special galleries for the press, public, guests of the Speaker, Rajya Sabha members, diplomatic and distinguished visitors. A special place is reserved for the family and the guests of the President, Governors, visiting Heads of State and other visiting dignitaries, on the left side of the Speaker.

Rajya Sabha: The Council of States (Rajya Sabha) shall consist of not more than 238 elected representatives of States and Union Territories and 12 members to be nominated by the President (Article 80). The Council of States shall not be subject to dissolution but as nearly as possible one-third of its members shall retire, as soon as may be, after the expiry of 2 years. Elections to Rajya Sabha are indirect. Although the Constitution provides for 250 members it has now only 245 seats and of these, 233 are represented by the States and Union Territories.

Lok Sabha: The House of the People (Lok Sabha) shall consist of 552 members chosen by direct election from territorial constituencies. In this, 530 members from States, 20 from Union Territories and 2 are Presidential nominees from Anglo-Indian community (Article 81). It shall continue for 5 years (unless sooner dissolved) from the date of its meeting and no longer and the expiry of the said period of 5 years shall operate as dissolution of the House (Article 83). This mandatory provision of dissolution may be extended for a year due to emergency.

Parliament Committees

Broadly, they are of two types - Standing Committees (elected / appointed and their work goes on continuously) and Ad hoc Committees (appointed as the need arises and ceases to exist when the work is over). Among the Standing Committees, three are financial committees: (1) Public Accounts Committee (2) Estimate Committee and (3) Public Undertakings Committee. Ad hoc Committees are classified into two: (*a*) constituted by either two Houses on a motion adopted in that behalf or by Speaker/Chairman for an enquiry/report (for eg., Committees on conduct of certain members during President's address, Committees on Draft 5-year Plan, etc.) and (*b*) Select / Joint Committees on Bills (concerned with Bills and Procedures to be followed).

In a Parliamentary system like that of India, the Executive is subordinate to the Legislature. The Judiciary alone functions as an independent branch. (But in a Presidential system of government like that of the USA, the three branches of government-Legislature, Executive and Judiciary-are independent units).

Emergency Provisions: Part XVIII of the Constitution stipulates 3 kinds of Emergencies—National, State and Financial—which assign President of India more functions and powers. The Provisions of this Part mainly deals with extreme crisis (with respect to external attack, breakdown of constitutional machinery or financial instability) covering the country as a whole or any of its parts. Articles 352 to 360 discuss its Provisions.

PART IV: JUDICIARY

Chapter IV: Supreme Court of India

There shall be a Supreme Court of India, consisting of a Chief Justice (CJ) of India and other Judges

(Article124-1). The authorized strength of the Supreme Court Judges, including CJ is 26. The Parliament has the power to increase the number of Judges.

A Judge of the Supreme Court is to be appointed by the President after consultation with the CJ of the Supreme Court and shall hold office until the age of 65 years and can be removed from the office by the President, only after an address by each House of Parliament supported by more than two-thirds majority of members present and voting.

The Supreme Court has both Original and Appellate Jurisdictions. The Original Jurisdiction is limited to questions between the Government of India and the States, or between the States and to such other questions which involve "the existence or the extent of a legal right" (Article 131). The Appellate Jurisdiction extends overall the High Courts in India (Article 132).

High Courts

The Government of India have adopted a policy of having CJ of High Courts from the outside the States over which the Courts have jurisdiction.

The Attorney General

The President shall appoint a person who is qualified to be appointed as a Judge of the Supreme Court, to advise the Government of India on legal matters (Article 76). He has the right to speak and take part in the proceedings of either House and to be a member of any Parliamentary Committee but he is not entitled to vote (Article 88).

The Comptroller and Auditor General (CAG)

There shall be a CAG of India who shall be appointed by the President. He shall be only be removed from the office in like manner and on the like grounds as a Judge of the Supreme Court (Article 148-1). He exercises a general control over the accounts of the Union and State Governments (Article 149). He is not eligible for further office either of the Union or State Governments, once he has retired (Article 148-4).

Election Commission (EC)

It is to supervise and control all matters relating to elections to the Parliament and State Assemblies and to the Office of the President and Vice President (Article 324). It may consist of the Chief Election Commissioner (CEC) and such other Election Commissioners as the President may appoint from time to time. When any other Election Commissioner is appointed, the CEC shall function as the Chairman of EC. The CEC cannot be removed from office except in the same manner and on the same grounds as a Judge of Supreme Court (Article 324).

The States

The Governor of a State is the Executive Head of the State Government (Articles 155 & 156). He is assisted by a Council of Ministers, wit the Chief Minister at the Head (Article 163). The chief Minister is to be appointed by the Governor and other Ministers are to be appointed on the advice of the Chief Minister.

The Legislature of a State shall consist of the Governor and one or two Houses of Legislature, as the case may be (Article 168). The Legislative Assembly of a State or Vidhana Sabha may consist of not more than 500 and not less than 60 members (Article 170). (Bihar, Jammu & Kashmir-36 members, Karnataka, Maharastra and Uttar Pradesh, have two Houses: the Legislative Council or Vidhana Parishad and Assemoly). The total number of members in the Legislative Council, if any, shall not exceed one-third of the total number of members in the Legislative Assembly (Article 171) and in no case less than 40 members.

There shall be a High Court for each State, consisting of a CJ and such other Judges as the President may appoint (Articles 214 & 216). A Judge of the High Court can be removed from the office by the President, in the same manner as he may be remove a Judge of the Supreme Court (Article 217). The High Courts have Original Jurisdiction in such matters as writs and Appellate Jurisdiction over all subordinate courts in their jurisdiction. Every State shall have an Advocate General to advise the Government on legal matters (Article 165).

The Union Territories (UT)

It ordinarily has no Council of Ministers or Legislatures of their own. The Parliament may by law create for any of the UT a body, whether elected or partly nominated to function as a Legislature for the UT or a Council of Ministers or both (Article 239A).

PART IX: PANCHAYAT RAJ (PR)

PR institutions have been in existence in almost all States and UTs with variations in structural pattern, tenure and responsibilities entrusted to them.

Article 40 of the Constitution, as mentioned in the DPSP, lays down that the State shall take steps to organize village panchayats and endow them with such powers and authority as may be necessary to enable them to function as units of self-government. With a view to grant constitutional status to PR institutions, the Parliament passed the 73rd Constitutional Amendment Act in December 1992. it came into force on 24th April, 1993. it provides for a three-tier system (Grama/Village Panchayat, Panchayat Samithi and Zilla Parishad) for all States/UTs, except those having a population of less than 20 lakhs. Article 243 deals with its definitions and various provisions.

The Panchayats have been empowered by the 11th Schedule (Article 243G) to prepare plans and schemes in respect of 29 subjects for their economic development while ensuring social justice and implementation of various programmes.

(1) Agriculture, including Agriculture extension (2) Land Improvement, Implementation of Land Reforms, Land Consolidation and Soil Conservation (3) Minor Irrigation, Water Management & Watershed Development (4) Animal Husbandry, Dairying & Poultry (5) Fisheries (6) Social and Farm Forestry (7) Minor Forest Produce (8) Small Scale Industries including Food Processing (9) Khadi, Village & Cottage Industries (10) Rural Housing (11) Drinking Water (12) Fuel and Fodder (13) Roads, Culverts, Bridges, Ferries, Waterways and other means of communication (14) Rural Electrification and Non-Conventional Energy Sources (15) Poverty Alleviation Programme (16) Education, Adult & Non-formal Education, Technical Training and Vocational Training (17) Libraries and Cultural activities (18) Markets and Fairs (19) Health and Sanitation including Hospitals (20) Family Planning, Women and Child Welfare (21) Social Welfare including Handicapped (22) Welfare of Weaker Sections (23) Public Distribution System (24) Maintenance of Community Assets.

The Government of India passed a Law—"The Provisions of Panchayats (Extension to the scheduled Areas) Act, 1996" to provide for the extension of provisions of Part IX of the Constitution relating to the Panchayats to the Schedule V Areas (such as Andhra Pradesh, Bihar, Gujarat, Himachal Pradesh, Maharasthra, Madhya Pradesh, Orissa and Rajasthan).

Article 368 deals with Amendment of the Constitution. A Bill for Amendment must be passed in each House by a majority of the total membership of that House and by a majority of not less than two-thirds of the members present and voting. Amendments to certain parts of the Constitution, however, require ratification of the legislatures of not less than one-half of the States by resolutions to that effect.

There are 12 Schedules to the Constitution. The 9th Schedule was added by the 1st Amendment to the Constitution in 1951 and the 11th and 12th by the 73rd and 74th Amendments in 1992. With respect to Article 40, a new Part IX relating to the Panchayats has been inserted in the Constitution to provide for among other things, Grama Sabha in a village or group of villages; constitution of Panchayats at village and other levels; direct elections to all seats in Panchayat at the village and intermediate levels, if any and to the offices of the Chairpersons of the Panchayats at such levels; reservation of eats for SC & ST on proportion of their population for membership of Panchayat and office of the Chairpersons in Panchayat at each levels; reservation of one-third seats for women; fixing tenure of 5 years for Panchayats and holding election within a period of 6 months in the vent of super-session of any Panchayat.

In order to remove the inadequacies in the implementation and effectiveness in the Urban Local bodies, a new Part IX-A relating to the Municipalities has been incorporated in the Constitution to provide among the other things, Constitution of three types of Municipalities, i.e., Nagar Panchayat for areas in transition from a rural area, Municipal Council for smaller urban areas and Municipal Corporation for larger urban areas.

CONTENTS

Articles of Indian Constitution

PREAMBLE

PART I: THE UNION AND ITS TERRITORY

1. Name and Territory of the Union
2. Admission or Establishment of new States

2A. (Repealed)

3. Formation of new States and alteration of areas, boundaries or names of existing States
4. Laws made under Articles 2 & 3 to provide for the Amendment of the 1st & 4th Schedules and supplemental, incidental and consequential matters

PART II: CITIZENSHIP

5. Citizenship at the commencement of the Constitution
6. Rights of citizenship of certain persons who are migrated to India from Pakistan
7. Rights of citizenship of certain migrants to Pakistan
8. Rights of citizenship of certain persons of Indian origin residing outside India
9. Persons voluntarily acquiring citizenship of a foreign state not to be citizens
10. Continuance of the Rights of citizenship
11. Parliament to regulate the Rights of citizenship by law

PART III: FUNDAMENTAL RIGHTS

12. Definition
13. Laws inconsistent with or in derogation of the Fundamental Rights
14. *Right to Equality:* Equality before Law
15. Prohibition of discrimination on grounds of religion, race, caste, sex or place of birth
16. Equality of opportunity in matters of public employment
17. Abolition of Untouchability
18. Abolition of Titles
19. *Right to Freedom:* Protection of certain rights regarding freedom of speech, etc.

20. Protection in respect of conviction for offences
21. Protection of life and personal liberty
22. Protection against arrest and detention in certain cases
23. *Right against Exploitation:* Prohibition of traffic in human beings and forced labor
24. Prohibition of employment of children in factories, etc.
25. *Right to Freedom of Religion:* Freedom of conscience and free profession, practice and propagation of religion
26. Freedom to manage religious affairs
27. Freedom as to payment of taxes for promotion of any particular religion
28. Freedom as to attendance at religious instructions or worship in certain educational institutions
29. *Cultural and Educational Rights:* Protection of interest of Minorities
30. Right of Minorities to establish and administer educational institutions
31. (Repealed)

31A. Saving of laws providing for acquisition of estates, etc.

31B. Validation of certain Acts and Regulations

31C. Saving of laws giving effect to certain directive principles

31D. (Repealed)

32. *Right to Constitutional Remedies:* Remedies for enforcement of rights conferred by this Part

32A. (Repealed)

33. Power of Parliament to modify rights conferred by this Part in their application to their Forces, etc.
34. Restriction on rights conferred by this Part while martial law is in force in any area
35. Legislation to give effect to the provisions of this Part

PART IV: DIRECTIVE PRINCIPLES OF STATE POLICY

36. Definition
37. Application of the Principles contained in this Part
38. State to secure a social order for the promotion of welfare of the people
39. Certain principles of policy to be followed by the State

39A. Equal justice and free legal aid

40. Organization of Village Panchayats
41. Right to work, to education and to public assistance in certain cases
42. Provisions for just and humane conditions of work and maternity relief
43. Living wages, etc for workers

43A. Participation of workers in management of industries

44. Uniform Civil Code for the citizens
45. Provision for free and compulsory education for children
46. Promotion of educational and economic interests of SCs, STs and other weaker sections
47. Duty of the State to rise level of nutrition and the standard of living and to improve public health
48. Organization of agriculture and animal husbandry

48A. Protection and improvement of environment and safeguarding of forests and wildlife

49. Protection of monuments and places and objects of national importance
50. Separation of Judiciary from Executive
51. Promotion of International Peace and Security

PART IV A: FUNDAMENTAL DUTIES

51A. Fundamental Duties

PART V: THE UNION

Chapter I: The Executive: The President and the Vice President

52. The President of India
53. Executive power of the Union
54. Election of President
55. Manner of Election of President
56. Term of the Office of the President
57. Eligibility for re-election
58. Qualifications for election as President
59. Conditions of President's Office
60. Oath or Affirmation by the President
61. Procedure for impeachment of the President
62. Time of holding election to fill vacancy in the President's Office and the term of Office of person elected to fill causal vacancy
63. The Vice President of India
64. The Vice President to be ex-officio Chairman of the Council of States
65. The Vice President to act as President or to discharge his functions during casual vacancies in the Office, or during the absence, of President
66. Election of the Vice President
67. Term of Office of Vice President
68. Time of holding election to fill vacancy in the Office of Vice President and the term of Office of person elected to fill casual vacancy
69. Oath or Affirmation by the Vice President
70. Discharge of President's functions in other contingencies
71. Matters relating to, or connected with, the election of a President or Vice President
72. Power of President to grant pardons, etc. & to suspend, remit or commute sentences in certain cases
73. Extent of executive power of the Union
74. *Council of Ministers:* To aid and advise the President
75. Other provisions as to Ministers
76. Attorney-General of India
77. *Conduct of Government Business:* Conduct of Business of the Government of India
78. Duties of Prime Minister as respects the furnishing of information to the President, etc.

Chapter II: Parliament: General

79. Constitution of Parliament
80. Composition of the Council of States
81. Composition of the House of the People
82. Readjustment after each census
83. Duration of Houses of the Parliament
84. Qualification for membership of Parliament
85. Sessions of Parliament, Prorogation and Dissolution
86. Right of President to address and send messages to the Houses

87. Special address by the President
88. Rights of Ministers and Attorney General as respects Houses
89. *Officers of Parliament:* The Chairman and Deputy Chairman of the Council of States
90. Vacation and resignation of, and removal from, the Office of the Deputy Chairman
91. Power of Deputy Chairman or other person to perform the duties of Office of, or to act as, Chairman
92. Chairman and Deputy Chairman not to preside while a resolution for his removal from Office is under consideration
93. The Speaker and Deputy Speaker of the House of the People
94. Vacation and resignation of, and removal from, the Offices of Speaker and Deputy Speaker
95. Power of the Deputy Speaker or other person to perform duties of the Office of, or to act as, Speaker
96. Speaker or Deputy Speaker not to preside while a resolution for his removal from Office is under consideration
97. Salaries and allowances of the Chairman & Deputy Chairman and Speaker and Deputy Speaker
98. Secretariat of Parliament
99. *Conduct of Business:* Oath or Affirmation by the members
100. Voting in Houses, power of Houses to act notwithstanding vacancies and quorum
101. *Disqualifications of Members:* Vacation of seats
102. Disqualifications for membership
103. Decision on questions as to disqualifications of members
104. Penalty for sitting and voting before making oath or affirmation under Article 99 or when not qualified or when disqualified
105. *Powers, Privileges and Immunities of Parliament and its members:* All and Committees thereof
106. Salaries and allowances of Members
107. *Legislative Procedure:* Provisions as to introduction and passing of Bills
108. Joint sitting of both Houses in certain cases
109. Special procedure in respect of Money Bills
110. Definition of "Money Bills"
111. Assent to Bills
112. *Procedure in Financial Matters:* Annual Financial Statement
113. Procedure in Parliament with respect to estimates
114. Appropriation Bills
115. Supplementary, additional or excess grants
116. Votes of account, votes of credit and exceptional grants
117. Special Provisions as to Financial Bills
118. *Procedure Generally:* Rules of procedure
119. Regulation by law of procedure in Parliament in relation to financial business
120. Language to be used in Parliament
121. Restriction on discussion in Parliament
122. Courts not to inquire into proceedings of Parliament

Chapter III: Legislative Powers of the President

123. Powers of President to promulgate Ordinances during recess of Parliament

Chapter IV: The Union Judiciary

124. Establishment and constitution of Supreme Court
125. Salaries, etc. of Judges
126. Appointment of Acting Chief Justice
127. Appointment of Adhoc Judges
128. Attendance of retired Judges at sittings of the Supreme Court
129. Supreme Court to be a Court of Record
130. Seat of Supreme Court
131. Original Jurisdiction of the Supreme Court
131A. (Repealed)
132. Appellate Jurisdiction of Supreme Court in appeals from High Courts in certain cases
133. Appellate Jurisdiction of Supreme Court in appeals from High Courts in regard to Civil matters
134. Appellate Jurisdiction of Supreme Court in regard to Criminal matters
134A. Certificate for appeal to the Supreme Court
135. Jurisdiction and powers of the Federal Court under existing law to be exercisable by Supreme Court
136. Special leave to appeal by the Supreme Court
137. Review of judgments or orders by the Supreme Court
138. Enlargement of jurisdiction of the Supreme Court
139. Conferment on the Supreme Court of powers to issue certain writs
139A. Transfer of certain cases
140. Ancillary powers of the Supreme Court
141. Law declared by the Supreme Court to be binding on all courts
142. Enforcement of decrees and orders of the Supreme Court and orders as to discovery, etc.
143. Power of President to consult the Supreme Court
144. Civil and judicial authorities to act in aid of the Supreme Court
144A. (Repealed)
145. Rules of Court, etc.
146. Officers and servants and expenses of the Supreme Court
147. Interpretation

Chapter V: Comptroller and Auditor General of India

148. Comptroller and Auditor General of India
149. Duties and powers of the Comptroller and Auditor General of India
150. Form of accounts of the Union and States
151. Audit Reports

PART VI: THE STATES

Chapter I: General

152. Definition

Chapter II: The Executive: The Governor

153. The Governor of the States
154. Executive power of State
155. Appointment of Governor

156. Term of Office of Governor
157. Qualifications for appointment as Governor
158. Conditions of Governor's Office
159. Oath or Affirmation by the Governor
160. Discharge of the functions of the Governor in certain contingencies
161. Power of Governor to grant pardons, etc. and to suspend, remit or commute sentences in certain cases
162. Extent of Executive power of the State
163. *Council of Ministers:* Council of Ministers to aid and advise the Governor
164. Other provisions as to Ministers
165. The Advocate General for the State
166. *Conduct of Government Business:* Conduct of the Business of the State Government
167. Duties of Chief Minister as respects the furnishing of information to Governor, etc.

Chapter III: The State Legislature

168. *General:* Constitution of Legislatures in States
169. Abolition or creation of Legislative Councils in States
170. Composition of the Legislative Assemblies
171. Composition of the Legislative Councils
172. Duration of State Legislatures
173. Qualification for membership of the State Legislature
174. Sessions of the State Legislature, prorogation and dissolution
175. Right of Governor to address and send messages to the House (s)
176. Special address by the Governor
177. Rights of Ministers and Advocate General as respects the Houses
178. *Officers of the State Legislatures:* Speaker and Deputy Speaker of the Legislative Assembly
179. Vacation and resignation of, and removal from, the Offices of Speaker and Deputy Speaker
180. Power of the Deputy Speaker or other person to perform the duties of the office of, or to act as, Speaker
181. Speaker or Deputy Speaker not to preside while a resolution for his removal from office is under consideration
182. The Chairman and Deputy Chairman of the Legislative Council
183. Vacation and resignation of, and removal from, the Offices of Chairman and Deputy Chairman
184. Power of the Deputy Chairman or other person to perform duties of Office of, or to act as, Chairman
185. Chairman or Deputy Chairman not to preside while a resolution for his removal from office is under consideration
186. Salaries and allowances of Speaker and Deputy Speaker and Chairman and Deputy Chairman
187. Secretariat of State Legislature
188. *Conduct of Business:* Oath or Affirmation by the members
189. Voting in Houses, power of Houses to act notwithstanding vacancies and quorum
190. *Disqualification of Members:* Vacation of seats
191. Disqualification of Membership
192. Decision on questions as to disqualification of Members
193. Penalty for sitting and voting before making Oath or Affirmation under Article 188 or when not qualified or when disqualified

194. *Powers, Privileges and Immunities of State Legislatures and their members:* All and Committees thereof
195. Salaries and allowances of the members
196. *Legislative Procedure:* Provisions as to introduction and passing of Bills
197. Restriction on powers of Legislative Council as to Bills other than Money Bills
198. Special procedure in respect of Money Bills
199. Definition of "Money Bills"
200. Assent to Bills
201. Bills reserved for consideration
202. *Procedure in Financial matters:* Annual Financial Statement
203. Procedure in Legislature with respect to estimates
204. Appropriation Bills
205. Supplementary, additional or excess grants
206. Votes on account, votes of credit and exceptional grants
207. Special provisions as to Financial Bills
208. *Procedure Generally:* Rules of Procedure
209. Regulation by law of procedure in the State Legislature in relation to financial business
210. Language to be used in the Legislature
211. Restriction on discussion in the Legislature
212. Courts not to inquire into proceedings of the Legislature

Chapter IV: Legislative Power of the Governor

213. Power of Governor to promulgate Ordinances during recess of Legislature

Chapter V: High Courts in the States

214. High Courts for States
215. High Courts to be Courts of Record
216. Constitution of High Courts
217. Appointment and conditions of the Office of a Judge of a High Court
218. Application of certain provisions relating to Supreme Court to High Courts
219. Oath or Affirmation by Judges of High Courts
220. Restriction on practice after being a permanent Judge
221. Salaries, etc. of Judges
222. Transfer of a Judge from one High Court to another
223. Appointment of Acting Chief Justice
224. Appointment of additional and acting Judges

224A. Appointment of retired Judges at sittings of High Courts

225. Jurisdiction of existing High Courts
226. Power of High Courts to issue certain writs

226A. (Repealed)

227. Power of superintendence over all courts by the High Court
228. Transfer of certain cases to High Court

228A. (Repealed)

229. Officers and servants and the expenses of High Courts
230. Extension and jurisdiction of High Courts to Union Territories
231. Establishment of common High Court for two or more States

232. (Repealed)

Chapter VI: Subordinate Courts

233. Appointment of District Judges
233A. Validation of appointments of, and judgments, etc delivered by, certain District Judges
234. Recruitment of persons other than District Judges to the judicial service
235. Control over Subordinate Courts
236. Interpretation
237. Application of the provisions of this Chapter to certain class (s) of Magistrates

PART VII: THE STATES IN PART B OF THE 1ST SCHEDULE

238. (Repealed)

PART VIII: THE UNION TERRITORIES

239. Administration of Union Territories
239A. Creation of local Legislatures or Council of Ministers or both for certain UTs - Special provisions with respect to Delhi
239AA. Provision in case of failure of constitutional machinery
239AB. Power of Administrator to promulgate Ordinances during recess of Legislature
240. Power of President to make regulations for certain UTs
241. High Courts for UTs
242. (Repealed)

PART IX: THE PANCHAYATS

243. Definitions
243A. Grama Sabha
243B. Constitution of Panchayats
243C. Composition of Panchayats
243D. Reservation of seats
243E. Duration of Panchayats
243F. Disqualifications for membership
243G. Powers, authority and responsibilities of Panchayats
243H. Powers to impose taxes by, and Funds of, the Panchayats
243I. Constitution of Finance Commission to review financial position
243J. Audit of accounts of Panchayats
243K. Elections to the Panchayats
243L. Application to UTs
243M. Part not to apply to certain areas
243N. Continuance of existing laws and Panchayats
243-O. Bar to interference by courts in electoral matters

PART IX A: THE MUNICIPALITIES

243P. Definitions
243Q. Constitution of Municipalities
243R. Composition of Municipalities
243S. Constitution and composition of Wards Committees, etc.
243T. Reservation of seats

243U. Duration of Municipalities
243V. Disqualifications for membership
243W. Powers, authority and responsibilities of Municipalities
243X. Powers to impose taxes by, and Funds of, the Panchayats
243Y. Constitution of Finance Commission to review financial position
243Z. Audit of accounts of Municipalities
243ZA. Elections to the Municipalities
243ZB. Application to UTs
243ZC. Part not to apply to certain areas
243ZD. Committee for District planning
243ZE. Committee for Metropolitan planning
243ZF. Continuance of existing laws and Municipalities
243ZG. Bar to interference by Courts in electoral matters

PART X: THE SCHEDULED AREAS AND TRIBAL AREAS

244. Administration of The Scheduled Areas and Tribal Areas
244A. Formation of an autonomous State comprising certain tribal areas in Assam and creation of local Legislature or Council of Ministers or both thereof

PART XI: RELATIONS BETWEEN THE UNION AND THE STATES

Chapter I: Legislative Relations (Distribution of Legislative Powers)

245. Extent of laws made by Parliament and by the State Legislatures
246. Subject-matter of laws made by Parliament and by the State Legislatures
247. Power of Parliament to provide for the establishment of certain additional courts
248. Residuary powers of Legislation
249. Power of Parliament to legislate with respect to a matter in the State List in the national interest
250. Power of Parliament to legislate with respect to a matter in the State List if a Proclamation of Emergency is in operation
251. Inconsistency between the laws made by Parliament under Articles 249 & 250 and laws made by State Legislatures
252. Power of Parliament to legislate for two or more States by consent and adoption of such legislation by any other State
253. Legislation for giving effect to international agreements
254. Inconsistency between the laws made by Parliament and laws made by the State Legislatures
255. Requirements as to recommendations & previous sanctions to be regarded as matters of procedure only

Chapter II: Administrative Relations (General)

256. Obligation of the States and the Union
257. Control of the Union over States in certain cases
257A. (Repealed)
258. Power of the Union to confer powers, etc. on States in certain cases
258A. Power of the States to entrust functions to the Union
259. (Repealed)
260. Jurisdiction of the Union in relation to territories outside India

261. Public Acts, Records and Judicial proceedings
262. *Disputes relating to Waters:* Adjudication of disputes relating to Waters of Inter-State rivers or river valleys
263. *Coordination between States:* Provisions with respect to an Inter-State Council

PART XII: FINANCE, PROPERTY, CONTRACTS AND SUITS

Chapter I: Finance (General)

264. Interpretation
265. Taxes not to be imposed save by authority of law
266. Consolidated Funds and Public Accounts of India and of the States
267. Contingency Fund
268. *Distribution of revenues between the Union and States:* Duties levied by the Union but collected and appropriated by the State
269. Taxes levied and collected by the Union but assigned to the States
270. Taxes levied and distributed between the Union and States
271. Surcharge on certain duties and taxes for purposes of the Union
272. (Repealed)
273. Grants in lieu of export duty on jute and jute products
274. Prior recommendation of President required to Bills affecting taxation in which States are interested
275. Grants from the Union to certain States
276. Taxes on professions, trades, callings and employments
277. Savings
278. (Repealed)
279. Calculation of "Net Proceeds", etc.
280. Finance Commission
281. Recommendations of the Finance Commission
282. *Miscellaneous Financial Provisions:* Expenditure defrayable by Union or a State out of its revenues
283. Custody, etc. of Consolidated Funds, Contingency Funds and Moneys credited to Public Accounts
284. Custody of Suitors' deposits and other money received by public servants and courts
285. Exemption of property of the Union from State Taxation
286. Restrictions as to imposition of tax on the sale or purchase of goods
287. Exemption from taxes on electricity
288. Exemption from taxation by States in respect of water or electricity in certain cases
289. Exemption of property and income of a State from Union taxation
290. Adjustment in respect of certain expenses and pensions

290A. Annual payment to certain Devaswom Funds

291. (Repealed)

Chapter II: Borrowing

292. Borrowing by the Government of India
293. Borrowing by the States

Chapter III: Property, Contracts, Rights, Liabilities, Obligations and Suits

294. Succession to property, assets, rights, liabilities and obligations in certain cases
295. Succession to property, assets, rights, liabilities and obligations in other cases
296. Property accruing by escheat or laps or as *bona vacantia*
297. Things of value within territorial waters or continental shelf and the resources of the exclusive economic zone to vest in the Union
298. Power to carry on trade, etc.
299. Contracts
300. Suits and Proceedings

Chapter IV: Right to Property

300A. Persons not to be deprived of property save by authority of law

PART XIII: TRADE, COMMERCE AND INTERCOURSE WITHIN THE INDIAN TERRITORY

301. Freedom of trade, commerce and intercourse
302. Power of Parliament to impose restrictions on trade, commerce and intercourse
303. Restrictions on the Legislative powers of the Union and States with regard to trade and commerce
304. Restrictions on trade, commerce and intercourse among States
305. Saving of existing laws and laws providing for State monopolies
306. (Repealed)
307. Appointment of authority for carrying out the purposes of Articles 310 and 304

PART XIV: SERVICES UNDER THE UNION AND THE STATES

Chapter I: Services

308. Interpretation
309. Recruitment and conditions of service of persons serving the Union or a State
310. Tenure of Office of persons serving the Union or a State
311. Dismissal, removal or reduction in rank of persons employed in civil capacities under Union or a State
312. All India Services

312A. Power of Parliament to vary or revoke conditions of service of Officers of certain services

313. Transitional Provisions
314. (Repealed)

Chapter II: Public Service Commissions

315. Public Service Commissions for the Union and States
316. Appointment and term of Office of Members
317. Removal and suspension of a Member of a Public Service Commission
318. Power to make regulations as to conditions of service of Members and Staff of the Commission
319. Prohibition as to holding of offices by the members of Commission on ceasing to be such members
320. Functions of Public Service Commissions
321. Power to extend functions of Public Service Commissions
322. Expenses of Public Service Commissions
323. Reports of Public Service Commissions

PART XIV A: TRIBUNALS

323A. Administrative Tribunals
323B. Tribunals for other matters

PART XV: ELECTIONS

324. Superintendence, direction and control of elections to be vested in an Election Commission
325. No person to be ineligible for inclusion in, or to claim to be included in a special, electoral roll on grounds of religion, race, caste or sex
326. Elections to the House of the People and to the Legislative Assemblies of States to be on the basis of adult suffrage
327. Power of Parliament to make provision with respect to elections to Legislatures
328. Power of State Legislature to make provision with respect to elections to such Legislatures
329. Bar to interference by courts in electoral matters
329A. (Repealed)

PART XVI: SPECIAL PROVISIONS RELATING TO CERTAIN CLASSES

330. Reservation of seats for SCs and STs in the House of the People
331. Representation of the Anglo-Indian community in the House of the People
332. Reservation of seats for SCs and STs in the State Legislative Assemblies
333. Representation of the Anglo-Indian community in the State Legislative Assemblies
334. Reservation of seats and special representation to cease after 60 years
335. Claims of SCs and STs to services and posts
336. Special provision for Anglo-Indian community in certain services
337. Special provision with respect to educational grants for the benefit of Anglo-Indian community
338. National Commission for Scheduled Castes (SCs)
338A. National Commission for Scheduled Tribes (STs)
339. Control of the Union over the administration of Scheduled Areas and the welfare of STs
340. Appointment of a Commission to investigate the conditions of backward classes
341. Scheduled Castes
342. Scheduled Tribes

PART XVII: OFFICIAL LANGUAGE

Chapter I: Language of the Union

343. Official language of the Union
344. Commission and Committee of Parliament on Official language

Chapter II: Regional Languages

345. Official language or languages of a State
346. Official language for communication between one State and another or between a State and Union
347. Special provision relating to language spoken by a section of the population of a State

Chapter III: Language of the Supreme Court, High Courts, etc.

348. Language to be used in the Supreme Court and High Courts and for Acts, Bills, etc.
349. Special procedure for enactment of certain laws relating to language

Chapter IV: Special Directives

350. Language to be used in the representations for redress of grievances
350A. Facilities for instruction in mother-tongue at primary stage
350B. Special Officer for Linguistic Minorities
351. Directive for development of the Hindi Language

PART XVIII: EMERGENCY PROVISIONS

352. Proclamation of Emergency
353. Effect of Proclamation of Emergency
354. Applications of provisions relating to distribution of revenues while a Proclamation of Emergency is in operation
355. Duty of the Union to protect States against external aggression and internal disturbances
356. Provisions in case of failure of constitutional machinery in States
357. Exercise of Legislative powers under Proclamation of Emergency issued under Article 356
358. Suspension of provisions of Article 19 during emergencies
359. Suspension of the enforcement of the rights conferred by Part III during emergencies
359A. (Repealed)
360. Provisions as to Financial Emergency

PART XIX: MISCELLANEOUS

361. Protection of President and Governors and Rajprakukhs
361A. Protection of publication of proceedings of Parliament and State Legislatures
361B. Disqualification for appointment on remunerative political post
362. (Repealed)
363. Bar to interference by courts in disputes arising out of certain treaties, agreements, etc.
363A. Recognition granted to Rulers of Indian States to cease and privy purses to be abolished
364. Special provisions as to major ports and aerodromes
365. Effect of failure to comply with, or to give effect to, directions given by the Union
366. Definitions
367. Interpretation

PART XX: AMENDMENT OF THE CONSTITUTION

368. Power of Parliament to amend the Constitution and procedure therefor

PART XXI: TEMPORARY, TRANSITIONAL AND SPECIAL PROVISIONS

369. Temporary power to the Parliament to make laws with respect to certain matters in the State List as if they were matters in the Concurrent List
370. Temporary provisions with respect to the state of Jammu & Kashmir
371. Special provision with respect to the States of Maharashtra and Gujarat
371A. Special provision with respect to the State of Nagaland
371B. Special provision with respect to the State of Assam
371C. Special provision with respect to the State of Manipur
371D. Special provision with respect to the State of Andhra Pradesh
371E. Establishment of Central University in Andhra Pradesh
371F. Special provision with respect to the State of Sikkim
371G. Special provision with respect to the State of Mizoram
371H. Special provision with respect to the State of Arunachal Pradesh

371-I. Special provision with respect to the State of Goa
372. Continuance in force of existing laws and their adaptation
372A. Power of the President to adapt laws
373. Power of President to make order in respect of persons under preventive detention in certain cases
374. Provisions as to Judges of the Federal Court and proceedings pending in the Federal Court or before His Majesty in Council
375. Courts, authorities and officers to continue to function subject to the provisions of the Constitution
376. Provisions as to Judges of High Courts
377. Provisions as to Comptroller and Auditor General of India
378. Provisions as to public Service Commissions
378A. Special provisions as to duration of Andhra Pradesh Legislative Assembly
379-91. (Repealed)
392. Power of the President to remove difficulties

PART XXII: SHORT TITLE, COMMENCEMENT, AUTHORITATIVE TEXT IN HINDI AND REPEALS

393. Short title
394. Commencement
394A. Authoritative Text in the Hindi language
395. Repeals

SCHEDULES

1st Schedule: (Under Articles 1 and 4) It gives a List of the States and Territories comprising the Union. **States** 1. Andhra Pradesh 2. Assam 3. Bihar 4. Gujarat 5. Kerala 6. Madhya Pradesh 7. Tamil Nadu 8. Maharashtra 9. Karnataka 10. Orissa 11. Punjab 12. Rajasthan 13. Uttar Pradesh 14. West Bengal 15. Jammu & Kashmir 16. Nagaland 17. Haryana 18. Himachal Pradesh 19. Manipur 20. Tripura 21. Meghalaya 22. Sikkim 23. Arunachal Pradesh 24. Mizoram 25. Goa **Union Territories** 1. Delhi 2. Andaman & Nicobar Islands 3. Laccadive, Minicoy and Amindivi Islands 4. Dadra and Nagar Haveli 5. Daman and Diu 6. Pondicherry and 7. Chandigarh.

2nd Schedule: (Under Articles 59-3, 65-3, 75-6, 97, 125, 148-3 & 158-3) consists of 5 Parts, A to E.

Part A fixes the remuneration and emoluments payable to the President and Governors. Part B has been deleted by the Constitution (7th Amendment) Act of 1956. Part C contains provisions as to the Speaker and the Deputy Speaker of the House of the People and the Chairman and Deputy Chairman of the Council of the States and the Speaker of the Legislative Assembly and the Chairman and Deputy Chairman of the Legislative Council. Part D contains provisions as to emoluments of the Judges of the Supreme Court and of the High Courts. Part E contains provisions as to the Comptroller and Auditor General of India.

3rd Schedule: (Under Articles 75-4, 99, 124-6, 148-2, 164-3, 188 and 219) contains forms of Oaths and Affirmations.

4th Schedule: (Under Articles 4-1 and 20) allocates seats for each State and the Union Territory, in the Council of States.

5th Schedule: (Under Article 244-1) provides for the administration and control of Scheduled Areas. This Schedule provides for the Amendment by a simple majority of Parliament and takes it out of the ambit of Article 368 (Amendment of the Constitution).

6th Schedule: (Under Articles 214-2 and 275-1) provides for the administration of Tribal Areas in Assam, Meghalaya and Mizoram. This is the lengthiest Schedule which goes into the details of the administration in the Tribal Areas concerned. This Schedule can also be amended by a simple majority of the Parliament.

7th Schedule: (Under Article 246) gives three Lists: (1) Union List contains 97 subjects in which the Union Government has exclusive authority; (2) State List contains 66 subjects which are under the exclusive authority of State Governments; and (3) Concurrent List contains 47 subjects, where the Union and States has concurrent powers.

8th Schedule: (Under Articles 344-1 and 351-1) gives a List of 18 languages recognized by the Constitution: Assamese; Bengali, Gujarati, Hindi, Kannada, Kashmiri, Malayalam, Marathi, Oriya, Punjabi, Sanskrit, Sindhi, Tamil, Telugu, Urdu, Konkani, Manipuri and Nepali.

9th Schedule: (Under Article 31-B) was added by the Constitution (1st Amendment) Act 1951. It contains Acts and Orders relating to land tenures, land tax, railways, industries, etc. passed by the State Governments, and the Union Government which are beyond the jurisdiction of Civil Courts.

10th Schedule: (Under Articles 101, 102, 191 and 192). It contains the Anti-defection Act.

11th Schedule: (Under Article 243-G) mentions functional areas or subjects that are necessary for implementation of schemes for economic development and social justice in each Panchayat. To mention few–agriculture, social forestry, small scale industry, roads, rural housing, PDS, education, health & sanitation, poverty-alleviation, non-conventional energy sources, etc.

12th Schedule: Mentions three types of municipal committees–Nagar Panchayats for transitional area, Municipal Council for smaller urban areas and Municipal Corporations for large urban areas.

Constitutional Amendments

One of the peculiar features of the Indian Constitution is that various parts of it call for various processes of Amendments. The methods of Amendments are three, according to the subject matter of the Article concerned. (1) Articles that may be amended by a simple majority of the Parliament. These are mainly matters of detail like those provided in the Schedules. (2) Articles that may be amended by two-thirds majority of both the Houses of Parliament. These are comparatively important matters. (3) Articles that require not only a two-thirds majority of Parliament but also ratification by at least one-half of the State Legislatures.

Articles of the third category are specifically mentioned. They are the following: Articles concerning the election of the President (Articles 54 & 55), the powers of the Union Cabinet (Article 73), the powers of State Cabinets (Article 162), the High Courts in Union Territories (Article 241), the establishment of Supreme Court (Chapter IV, Part V), Constitution and powers of High Courts (Chapter V, Part VI). Relations between the Union & State Legislatures (Chapter I, Part IX), the Lists –Union List, State List and Concurrent List–in the 7th Schedule, the representation of States in Parliament and the provisions of Article 368 itself (Part XX).

Article 368 (Part XX) lays down the general procedure for the Amendments. But Articles that require a only a simple majority in the Parliament do not fall in this category. Such Articles are indicated by a special clause attached to each of them which specifically excludes the operation of the Article 368 (Refer Article 21, 6th Schedule). Amendment of all other Articles comes within the scope of Article 368.

1. (1950) This Amendment has permitted rcasonable restrictions to be imposed by law on the exercise of the right of freedom of speech and expression in the interest of friendly relations with foreign states, or public order.

2. (1952) Amended Article 81 with a view to readjusting the scale of representation in the House of the People, necessitated by the completion of the 1951 census.
3. (1954) Substituted entry 33 of the Concurrent List in the 7th Schedule by a new one including food stuffs, cattle fodder, raw cotton and jute as additional items whose production and supply can be controlled by the Central Government if found expedient in the public interest.
4. (1955) The Amendment provides that when the State compulsorily acquires private property for a public purpose, the scale of compensation prescribed by the authorized legislation could not be called in question in a court.
5. (1955) Empowers the President to fix a time limit for State Legislatures to express their views on proposed central laws affecting the area, boundaries, etc. of their respective states.
6. (1956) Added a new entry to the Union List in the 7th Schedule relating to taxes on sale and purchase of goods in the course of Inter-State transactions.
7. (1956) It was passed for the reorganization of the States. It involved not only the establishment of new states and alterations in the state boundaries but also the abolition of the three categories of the States and classification of certain areas as Union Territories.
8. (1960) Extended the special provision relating to the reservation of seats for the Scheduled Tribes and the representation of Anglo-Indians in the House of the People and State Legislative Assemblies, for the further period of 10 years from 26th January, 1960.
9. (1960) Amended the 1st Schedule to the Constitution in order to give effect to the transfer of certain territories to Pakistan in pursuance of the agreements entered between the Governments of India and Pakistan in September 1958.
10. (1961) Incorporated former Portuguese enclaves of Dadra and Nagar Haveli within India and provided for their administration by the President.
11. (1961) Obviated the necessity of a Joint meeting of the Houses of Parliament by forming them into an Electoral College for the election of the Vice President. It also amended Article 71 so as to make it clear that the election of the President or Vice President shall not be challenged on the ground of any vacancy, for whatever reason, in the appropriate Electoral College.
12. (1962) It was passed to include the territories of Goa, Daman and Diu as a Union Territory in the 1st Schedule to the Constitution and to empower the President to make regulations for the peace, progress and good government of these areas.
13. (1962) Created Nagaland as the 16th State in the Indian Union.
14. (1962) Conferred necessary legislative powers on Parliament to enact laws for the creation of Legislature and Council of Ministers in Union Territories. Former French establishments of Pondicherry, Karaikal, Mahe and Yanam were specified in the Constitution as the UT of Pondicherry.
15. (1963) Empowers the President of India, in consultation with the Chief Justice of India to make final decisions on the dispute about High Court's Judge age. It also shortened the procedure for disciplinary action against the State employees.
16. (1963) Empowered the State to enact any legislation, imposing reasonable restrictions in the exercise of fundamental rights by the citizens, so as to protect the sovereignty and integrity of India.
17. (1964) Provided that if the State acquires land which is under the personal cultivation of the owner and within the ceiling limit, compensation has to be paid at the market value of the property so acquired.

18. (1966) Provided for the linguistic reorganization of the Punjab into Punjabi-speaking State called Punjab and a Hindi-speaking State called as Haryana. It further provided that the word 'State' in Clauses (a) to (e) of Article 3 includes a UT and clarified that the Parliament had the power to form a new State or UT by combining any part of a State or UT with any part of any State or UT.
19. (1966) Clarifies the duties of Election Commission.
20. (1966) Validated the appointment of certain District Judges, irregularly appointed.
21. (1967) Includes Sindhi language in the 8th Schedule to the Constitution.
22. (1969) Empowered the Parliament to carve a new State (Meghalaya) out of Assam.
23. (1969) Provided for the extension of the reservation of seats for Scheduled Castes and Tribes and the nomination of the members of the Anglo-Indian community for another 10 years.
24. (1971) Affirmed the Parliament's power to amend the any part of the Constitution, including the Fundamental Rights by amending the Articles 368 and 13 of the Constitution. This neutralized the decision in Golak Nath case. A peculiar feature of the Amendment was that the President was bound to give assent to amending Acts, when they were presented to him, thus making the Presidential assent an automatic Act.
25. (1971) Barred the jurisdiction of courts over acquisition laws in regard to the adequacy of the amount paid in lieu of takeover. The word 'Compensation' in the case of takeover was deleted and the word 'amount' substituted.
26. (1971) This amendment withdrew the recognition given to former rulers of Princely States and abolished the privy purses granted to them.
27. (1971) Under this Amendment, two new Union Territories, Mizoram and Arunachal Pradesh, were setup.
28. (1972) Deleted the Article 314 of the Constitution, which gave protection to the ICS Officers' conditions of service and privileges.
29. (1972) Included the Kerala Land Reforms (Amendment) Act, 1969 and the Kerala Land Reforms (Amendment) Act, 1971, in the 9th Schedule to the Constitution so as to protect these Acts from the judicial review.
30. (1972) Curtailed the number of appeals to the Supreme Court. Formerly appeals to the Supreme Court were decided on the basis of the valuation of the subject matter. The Amendment made only such cases which involve a substantial question of law, appealable to the Supreme Court.
31. (1973) Increased the upper limit of the elective seats in the Lok Sabha from 525 to 545.
32. (1973) Implemented the 6-point programme for Andhra Pradesh.
33. (1974) Invalidated the acceptance of resignations by the members of the Legislatures and Parliament, which were made under duress or coercion, or any other kind of involuntary resignations.
34. (1974) Provided constitutional protection to 20 land reform Acts passed by the various states, by including them in the 9th Schedule to the Constitution.
35. (1974) Provided for the Associate State status to Sikkim.
36. (1975) Made Sikkim a State of the Indian Union as the 22nd State.
37. (1975) Provided for Legislative Assembly and a Council of Ministers for the UT of Arunachal Pradesh.
38. (1975) Declaration of Emergency by the President and the promulgation of the Ordinances by the President, Governors and Administrative Heads of UTs were made non-justiciable (beyond the purview of the judiciary).

39. (1975) Placed the election of the President, Vice President, Prime Minister and Speaker beyond judicial scrutiny.
40. (1976) Amended Article 297 and declared that all land, minerals and other things of value underlying the ocean within the territorial waters or the continental shelf or exclusive economic zone of India shall vest in the Union and shall be held for the purpose of the Union.
41. (1976) Raised the retiring age of State Public Service Commission members from 60 to 62. This does not affect members of the UPSC who retire at the age of 65.
42. (1976) The main features of the Amending Act may be summarized as follows:
    (*a*) The Preamble has been altered from 'Sovereign Democratic Republic' to 'Sovereign Socialist, Secular, Democratic, Republic' and 'unity of the nation' into 'unity and integrity of the nation'.
    (*b*) The Directive Principles of the Constitution given precedence over the Fundamental Rights, wherever they came into conflict.
    (*c*) Similarly, the prevention or prohibition of anti-national activities takes precedence over Fundamental Rights.
    (*d*) Certain fundamental Duties are laid down which have to be observed by all citizens. Non-compliance with or refusal to observe the duties shall be punishable by law. No court shall question the validity of such actions.
    (*e*) Number of seats in the Lok Sabha and the State Assemblies which are based on population shall remain frozen as in the 1971 census till 2001 A.D.
    (*f*) The duration of the Lok Sabha and the State Assemblies is increased from 5 to 6 years.
    (*g*) The quorum for the Lok Sabha and the State Assemblies prescribed in the Constitution has been removed which means that a quorum is no longer a constitutional necessity.
    (*h*) The Parliament may decide what offices are offices of profit under the government or what amounts to corrupt practice in disqualifying an elected member from any House of Legislature.
    (*i*) Rights and privileges of members and Committees of Legislatures are to be decided by the concerned Houses from time to time.
    (*j*) Proclamation of Emergency may be made applicable to any part of the country (instead of the whole country). Similarly emergency can be lifted from any part of the country while it remains in force in other parts.
    (*k*) The duration of the Presidential proclamation taking over the State Government shall be one year instead of six months.
    (*l*) The union has the power to deploy armed forces to any State and to delimit cantonment areas in the State. The State cannot exercise any power in the disposition of the armed forces or the administration of the cantonment areas.
    (*m*) No court can question the competence of the Parliament to amend the Constitution.
    (*n*) The Supreme Court alone can adjudicate on the validity of any Central Law and the High Courts can adjudicate on the validity of the State Laws. If the validity of any State Law is dependent on the validity of any Central Law or vice versa, then the Supreme Court can adjudicate on them. In any case, any decision on the constitutional invalidity has to be made by a two-third majority of sitting Judges where the number is not less than 5. If the number of Judges is less than 5, the judgment has to be unanimous. It is also provided that the High Courts have no power to make an interim order, where it will impede or obstruct any enquiry or action by the government.

(*o*) The President's liability to act in accordance with the advice of the Council of Ministers has been made practically mandatory.

43. (1977) Which received the Presidential assent on 03rd April, 1978 (i) omit some Articles added by the 42nd Amendment and (ii) alters the other Articles and restores the Jurisdiction of Supreme Court and High Courts to review any legislation in the States.
44. (1978) Makes Right to Property not a fundamental one, prevents declaration of emergency on account of internal strikes and empowers for declaration of emergency only if there is armed rebellion. It also places restriction on preventive detention.
45. (1980) extends the safeguards in respect of reservation of seats in Parliament and State Assemblies for Scheduled Castes and Tribes as well as for the Anglo-Indians for a period of 10 years.
46. (1982) Tax levied on the consignment of the goods in the course of inter-state trade or commerce is assigned to the states.
47. (1984) Intended to provide for the inclusion of certain land reform Acts in the 9th Schedule to the Constitution.
48. (1984) This was an Amendment to Clause 5(q) Article 356 of the Constitution for the continuation of the President's Rule in the Punjab for another year.
49. (1984) Gives constitutional security to the autonomous District Councils functioning in the State of Tripura.
50. (1984) (i) the members of the Forces charged with the protection of property belonging to, or in the charge or possession of the State; or (ii) persons employed in any bureau or other organization established by the State for the purposes of intelligence or counter intelligence; or (iii) persons employed in, or in connection with, the telecommunication systems setup for the purposes of any Force, bureau or organization were brought within the ambits of Article 33.
51. (1984) Replaces the section dealing "Scheduled Castes and Tribes except in the tribal areas of Assam, Nagaland, Meghalaya, Arunachal Pradesh and Mizoram" with "the Scheduled Tribes except the Scheduled Tribes in the autonomous district of Assam"–in the Articles 330 and 332.
52. (1985) Effected by a Bill popularly called Anti-Defection Bill, was to curb defection by disqualification. The following are the features of the Act:
    1. A Member of Parliament or State Legislature belonging to any political party shall be disqualified for being a member of that House: (a) if he has voluntarily given up his membership of such political party; or (b) if he votes or abstains from voting in such House contrary to any direction issued by the political party to which he belongs or by any person or authority authorized by it in this behalf without obtaining in either case, the prior permission of such political party, persons or authority, and such voting or abstention hasn't been condoned by such political party, person or authority within 15 days from the date of such voting or abstention.
    2. An elected member of House who has been elected as such otherwise than as a candidate setup by any political party shall be disqualified for being a member of the House if he joins any political party after such elections.
    3. A nominated member of a House shall be qualified for being a member of the House if he joins any political party after the expiry of 6 months from the date on which he takes his seat after complying with the requirements of the Article 99 or, as the case may be Article 188.

53. (1986) Inserted a new Article 371G conferring full Statehood on Mizoram.
54. (1986) Amended Part D of the Schedule II giving effect to the increases of salaries of the Chief Justice and Judges of Supreme Court and High Courts. An enabling provision for changes in the salaries of Judges in future by Parliament by Law was made in Articles 125 and 221.
55. (1986) Conferred full Statehood on Arunachal Pradesh.
56. (1987) Sought to make a special provision for the setting up of new State of Goa. Consequently, Daman and Diu were separated from the former to form a UT.
57. (1987) Amended Article 332 of the Constitution providing for special arrangements with regard to reservation for Scheduled Tribes in the North-eastern states of Arunachal Pradesh, Nagaland, Mizoram and Meghalaya, until readjustment of seats on the basis of the first census after 2000 A.D.
58. (1987) Authorizes the President to publish an authoritative translation of the Constitution.
59. (1988) Empowered the government to impose emergency in the Punjab on the grounds that India's integrity was threatened by the internal disturbances.
60. (1988) Empowered the State Governments to increase the ceiling on Professional Tax from Rs. 250.00 to Rs. 2500.00 per person per annum.
61. (1989) Lowered the voting age to 18 from 21 years.
62. (1989) Provided for the extension by another 10 years of reservation of seats in the Parliament and State Assemblies for Scheduled Castes and Tribes and reservation for Anglo-Indian community by nomination.
63. (1989) Repealed Amendment 359A empowering government to impose emergency in the Punjab.
64. (1990) Sought extension of President's Rule in Punjab for another six months.
65. (1990) To setup National Commission for Scheduled Castes and Tribes.
66. (1990) To bring land reforms within the purview of 9th Schedule of the Constitution.
67. (1990) Extension of President's Rule in Punjab.
68. (1991) Extends President's Rule in Punjab.
69. (1991) Delhi made National Capital Territory.
70. (1992) Some changes in the Amendment No. 69.
71. (1992) 8th Schedule of the Constitution amended to include Konkani, Manipuri and Nepali.
72. (1992) Article 332 amended to determine the number of reserved seats for STs in the State Assembly of Tripura, until readjustment of seats made on the basis of census 2000.
73. (1993) Part IX relating to Panchayats inserted in the Constitution to provide Grama Sabha, constitution of Panchayats at village and other levels, direct elections to all seats, fixing the tenures, reservations for SC & ST and 33% seats for women, etc.
74. (1993) A new Part IX-A relating to Municipalities i.e. Nagar Panchayats, Municipal Councils and Municipal Corporations.
75. (1994) Article 332 (Part XIV-A) amended to give timely relief to the rent litigants by setting up State-level Rent Tribunals to reduce the tiers of appeals, and to exclude jurisdiction of all courts except Supreme Court under the Article 136.
76. (1994) Aims at the reservation of seats in the educational institutions and reservation of appointments or posts in public services for Backward Classes, SCs and STs. The Supreme Court, on 16th November, 1992 ruled that the total reservations under the Article 16-4 should not exceed 50%.

77. (1995) Article 16-4A provides reservations in promotion for the SC and ST.
78. (1995) The Amendments to Acts placed in the 9th Schedule are immunized from legal challenge, through a number of amending Acts along with few principal Acts so that its implementation becomes smooth.
79. (1999) Government extends the reservation of seats for SC, ST and Anglo-Indians in the Lok Sabha and Legislative Assemblies for next 10 years.
80. (2000) Deals with an alternative scheme for sharing taxes between Union and States.
81. (2000) Provides that the unfilled vacancies of a year reserved for SC/ST kept for being filled up in a year as per Article 16, shall be considered separately for filling vacancies in succeeding year and the previous list will not be considered for filling the 50% quota of the respective year.
82. (2000) Provides that nothing in the Article 355 shall prevent the State from making any provisions in favor of the members of SC/ST for relaxation in qualifying marks with respect to examination/job/promotion.
83. (2000) The Act amended Article 243M to provide that no reservations in Panchayats be made in favor of SC/ST in Arunachal Pradesh where the whole population is tribal.
84. (2001) The Act amended provisions to the Articles 82 and 170-3 to readjust the territorial constituencies in the States, without altering the number of seats allotted to each State in House of People and Assemblies, including the SC/ST constituencies 1991.
85. (2001) Amended Article 16-4A to provide for consequential seniority in promotion by virtue of rule of reservation for the government servants belonging to SCs and STs.
86. (2002) Provides for insertion of a new Article 21A that the State shall provide free and compulsory education to all children of age of 6 to 14 years in such manner as the State may, by law, determine. A new Fundamental Duty under 51A (k) has also added to make it the responsibility of parent or guardian to provide opportunities for education between the age of 6 to 14 years.

Table of Precedence (Indian/State Governments)

1. President
2. Vice President
3. Prime Minister
4. Governors of States within their respective States
5. Former Presidents

5*a*. Deputy Prime Minister

6. Chief Justice of India; Speaker of Lok Sabha
7. Cabinet Ministers of the Union; Chief Ministers of the States within their respective States; Deputy Chairman, Planning Commission; Former Prime Ministers; Leaders of the Opposition in Rajya Sabha and Lok Sabha

7*a*. Holders of the Bharat Ratna Decoration

8. Ambassadors extraordinary and plenipotentiary and High Commissioners of Common Wealth countries accredited to India; Chief Ministers of States outside their respective States; Governors of States outside their respective States
9. Judges of Supreme Court

9*a*. Chief Election Commissioner; Comptroller & Auditor General

10. Deputy Chairman, Rajya Sabha; Deputy Chief Ministers of States; Deputy Speaker, Lok Sabha; Members of Planning Commission; Ministers of State of the Union and any other Minister in the Ministry of Defence for defence matters

11. Attorney General of India; Cabinet Secretary; Lieutenant Governors within their respective UTs
12. Chiefs of Staff holding the rank full General or equivalent rank
13. Envoys extraordinary and Ministers plenipotentiary accredited to India
14. Chairman and Speaker of State Legislatures within their respective States; Chief Justice of High Courts within their respective jurisdiction
15. Cabinet Ministers in the States within their respective States; Chief Ministers of Union Territories within their respective UTs; Deputy Ministers of the Union
16. Officiating Chiefs of Staff holding the rank of Lieutenant General or equivalent rank
17. Chairman, CAT; Chairman, Minorities Commission; Chairman, SC & ST Commission; Chairman, UPSC; Chief Justices of High Courts outside their respective jurisdiction; Puisne Judges of High Courts within their respective jurisdictions
18. Cabinet Ministers in States outside their respective States; Chairman and Speaker of State Legislatures outside their respective States; Chairman, MRTP Commission; Deputy Chairman and Deputy Speaker of State Legislatures within their respective States; Ministers of UTs within their respective UTs; Speaker of Legislative Assemblies in UTs within their respective UTs
19. Chief Commissioner of UTs not having Council of Ministers, within their respective UTs; Deputy Ministers in States within their respective States; Deputy Speaker of Legislative Assemblies in UTs, within their respective UTs
20. Deputy Chairman and Deputy Speakers of State Legislatures outside their respective States; Ministers of States outside their respective States; Puisne Judges of High Courts outside their respective jurisdictions
21. Members of Parliament
22. Deputy Ministers in States outside their respective States
23. Army Commanders/Vice Chief of the Army Staff or equivalent in other Services; Chief Secretaries to State Governments within their respective States; Commissioner for Linguistic Minorities; Commissioner for SC and ST; Members, Minorities Commission; Members, SC/ST Commission; Officers of the rank of full General or equivalent rank; Secretaries of Government of India (including Officers holding this office ex-officio); Secretary, Minority Commission; Secretary, SC/ST Commission; Secretary to President; Secretary to the Prime Minister; Secretary, Rajya and Lok Sabhas; Solicitor-General; Vice Chairman, CAT
24. Officers of the rank of Lt. General or equivalent rank
25. Additional Secretaries to the Government; Additional Solicitor-General; Advocate Generals of States; Chairman, Tariff Commission; Charged Affairs and acting High Commissioners a pied and interim; Chief Ministers of UTs outside their respective UTs; Chief Secretaries of the State Governments outside their respective States; Deputy CAG; Deputy Speakers of Legislative Assemblies in UTs outside their respective UTs; Director, CBI; Director General, BSF; Director General, CRPF; Director, IB; Lt. Governors outside their respective UTs; Members, CAT; Members, MRTP Commission; Members, UPSC; Ministers of UTs outside their respective UTs; Principal Staff Officers of the Armed Forces and the Officers of the rank of Major; General or equivalent rank; Speakers of Legislative Assemblies in UTs and Chairman, Delhi Metropolitan Council outside their respective UTs
26. Joint Secretaries to the Government of India and Officers of equivalent rank; Officers of the rank of Major General or equivalent rank

ANNEXURE: CODE OF ETHICS

Code of Ethics (CoE)

For Corporate Members of The Institution of Engineers (India), Kolkata-IEI

Preamble

Ethics deal with moral duty and obligation and give rise to a set of values which in turn are used to judge the appropriateness of a particular conduct or behavior. These are the basic principles by which the members of a professional body are to be guided in their daily professional work and decision-making.

To uphold the concept of the professional conduct amongst its Corporate Members, the IEI had introduced the Professional Conduct Rules on August 30, 1944, which were replaced by the code of Ethics for Corporate Members from October 15, 1954. This Code was further revised on August 12, 1962.

The engineering organizations world over have updated their CoE to give greater emphasis to responsibilities to society and to strengthen statements regarding responsibilities to the environment.

Similar to the actions taken by engineering associations in other nations, consistent with the changing needs of the profession and to recognize the environmental responsibilities to the public as well, the IEI Council had again revised the CoE for the Corporate Members of the Institution on June 29, 1997.

The CoE is based on broad principles of truth, honesty, justice, truth-worthiness, respect and safeguard of human life and welfare, competence and accountability which constitutes the values every Corporate Member of IEI must recognize and uphold.

The Code

A Corporate Member

- Shall practice his profession with integrity, conscience, dignity and honor and follow the best traditions of the profession.
- Shall be aware that the principles of ecosystemic inter-dependence, diversity maintenance, resource recovery and interrelational harmony form the basis of our continued existence and that each of these poses a threshold of sustainability that should not be exceeded.
- Shall hold paramount the safety, health and welfare of the people and protection of the environment and promote health and safety within the workplace.
- Shall offer services, advise on or undertake engineering assignments only in the areas of his competence and furnish correct information of his qualifications and experience to concerned clients.
- Shall uphold and maintain confidentiality and respect for secrets confided in him by the clients, employers and employees in connection with any professional work undertaken by him.
- Shall keep informed and updated in his area of professional activity and strive to provide opportunities for professional development of his subordinates.
- Shall conduct without consideration of caste, creed, sect, social status and shall not perform and act against the interest of the nation.
- Shall present clearly to all concerned the possible consequences of ignoring, overruling or discarding technological and engineering decisions or judgments without proper justification.
- Shall not directly or indirectly injure the professional reputation of another Corporate Member.

- Shall not accept any unauthorized commission, discount, allowance or profit, direct or indirect, to himself in connection with any work under his charge or for any professional business entrusted to him.
- Shall not act in a manner which may injure the reputation of the image of the institution or may cause damage to the Institution financially or otherwise.

Accreditation Board for Engineering and Technology, New York
(Formerly Engineers' Council for Professional Development)

Faith of the Engineer

I am an Engineer, in my profession I take deep pride, but without vain-glory; to it I owe solemn obligations that I am eager to fulfill.

As an Engineer, I will participate in none but honest profession. To him that has engaged my services, as employer or client, I will give the utmost of performance and fidelity.

When needed, my skill and knowledge shall be given without reservation for the public good. From special capacity springs the obligation to use it well in the service of humanity; and I accept the challenge that this implies.

Jealous of the high repute of my calling, I will strive to protect the interests and the good name of any engineer that I know to be deserving; but I will not shrink, should duty dictate, from disclosing the truth regarding anyone that, by unscrupulous act, has shown himself unworthy of the profession.

Since the Age of Stone, human progress has been conditioned by the genius of my professional forbears. By them have been rendered usable to mankind Nature's vast resources of material and energy. By them have been vitalized and turned to practical account the principles of science and the revelations of technology. Except for this heritage of accumulated experience, my efforts would be feeble. I dedicate myself to the dissemination of engineering knowledge, and, especially to the instruction of younger members of my profession in all its arts and traditions.

To my fellows I pledge, in the same full measure I ask of them, integrity and fair dealing, tolerance and respect, and devotion to the standards and the dignity of our profession; with the consciousness, always, that our special expertness carries with it the obligation to serve humanity with complete sincerity.

The Fundamental Principles

Engineers uphold and advance the integrity, honor and dignity of the engineering profession by:

- Using their knowledge and skill for the enhancement of human welfare;
- Being honest and impartial, and serving with fidelity the public, their employees and clients;
- Striving to increase the competence and prestige of the engineering profession; and
- Supporting the professional and technical societies of their disciplines.

The Fundamental Canons

Engineers shall

- Hold paramount the safety, health and welfare of the public in the performance of their professional duties.
- Perform services only in the areas of their competence.
- Issue public statements only in an objective and truthful manner.
- Act in professional matters for each employer or client as faithful agents or trustees, and shall avoid conflicts of interest.

- Build their professional reputation on the merit of their services and shall not compete unfairly with others.
- Act in such a manner as to uphold and enhance the honor, integrity and dignity of the profession.
- Continue their professional development throughout their careers and shall provide opportunities for the professional development of those engineers under their supervision.

Model Guide for Professional Conduct
American Association of Engineering Societies

Preamble

Engineers recognize that the practice of engineering has a direct and vital influence on the quality of life for all people. Therefore, engineers should exhibit high standards of competency, honesty and impartiality; be fair and equitable; and accept a personal responsibility for adherence to applicable laws, the protection of the public health, and maintenance of safety in their professional actions and behavior. These principles govern professional conduct in serving the interests of the public, clients, employers, colleagues and the profession.

The Fundamental Principle

The engineer as a professional is dedicated to improving competence, service, fairness and the exercise of well-founded judgment in the practice of engineering for the public, employers and clients with fundamental concern for the public health and safety in the pursuit of this practice.

Canons of Professional conduct

- Engineers offer services in the areas of their competencies and experience, affording full disclosure of their qualifications.
- Engineers consider the consequences of their work and societal issues pertinent to it and seek to extend public understanding of those relationships.
- Engineers are honest, truthful and fair in presenting information and in making public statements reflecting on professional matters and their professional role.
- Engineers engage in professional relationships without bias because of race, religion, sex, age, national origin or handicap.
- Engineers act in professional matters for each employer or client as faithful agents or trustees, disclosing nothing of a proprietary nature concerning the business affairs or technical processes of at present or former client or employer without specific consent.
- Engineers disclose to affected parties known or potential conflicts of interest or other circumstances which might influence-or appear to influence-judgment or impair the fairness or quality of their performance.
- Engineers are responsible for enhancing their professional competence throughout their careers and for encouraging similar actions by their colleagues.
- Engineers accept responsibility for their actions; seek and acknowledge criticism of their work; offer honest criticism of the work of others; properly credit the contributions of others; and do not accept credit for work not theirs.
- Engineers perceiving a consequence of their professional duties to adversely affect the present or future public health and safety shall formally advise their employers or clients and, if warranted, consider further disclosure.

- Engineers act in accordance with all applicable laws and the rules of conduct, and lend support to others who strive to do likewise.

Declaration of Rotarians in Businesses and Professions

The Declaration of Rotarians in Businesses and Professions was adopted by the Rotary International Council on Legislation in 1989 to provide more specific guidelines for the high ethical standards called for in the Object of Rotary:

As a Rotarian engaged in a business or profession, I am expected to:

- Consider my vocation to be another opportunity to serve;
- Be faithful to the letter and to the spirit of the ethical codes of my vocation, to the laws of my country, and to the moral standards of my community;
- Do all in my power to dignify my vocation and to promote the highest ethical standards in my chosen vocation;
- Be fair to my employer, employees, associates, competitors, customers, the public, and all those with whom I have a business or professional relationship;
- Recognize the honor and respect due to all occupations which are useful to society;
- Offer my vocational talents: to provide opportunities for young people, to work for the relief of the special needs of others, and to improve the quality of life in my community;
- Adhere to honesty in my advertising and in all representations to the public concerning my business or profession; and
- Neither seeks from nor grant to a fellow Rotarian a privilege or advantage nor normally accorded others in a business or professional relationship.

IMPORTANT CASES

Case 1: Maneka Gandhi vs. Union of India (1978)

The fact situation in this case was as follows:

Section 10(3)(c) of the Passport Act authorizes the Passport authority to impound a Passport if it deems it necessary to do so in the interest of the sovereignty and integrity of India, the security of India, friendly relations of India with any foreign country, or in the interest of the general public. Maneka's passport was impounded by the central Government under the Passport Act in the interest of the general public.

Maneka filed a writ petition challenging the order on the ground of violation of her Fundamental Rights under Article 21. One of the major grounds of challenge was that the order impounding the Passport was null and void as it had been made without affording her an opportunity to being heard in her defence.

The court laid down a number of propositions seeking to make Article 21 much more meaningful than hitherto.

- The court reiterated the proposition that Articles 14, 19 and 21 are not mutually exclusive. A law prescribing a procedure for depriving a person of 'personal liberty' has to meet the requirements of Article 19. Also the procedure established by law in Article 21 must answer the requirement of Article 14 as well.
- The expression 'Personal liberty' in Article 21 was given an expansive interpretation. The expression 'Personal liberty' ought not be read in a narrow and restricted sense so as to exclude those attributes of personal liberty, which are specifically dealt with in Article 19. The right to travel abroad falls under Article 21.

- The most significant and creative aspect of Maneka case is the re-interpretation by the Court of the expression 'procedure established by law' used in article 21. Article 21 would no longer mean that law could prescribe some semblance of procedure, however arbitrary or fanciful, to deprive a person of his personal liberty. It now means that the procedure must satisfy certain requisites in the sense of being fair and reasonable.

The procedure cannot be arbitrary unfair or unreasonable.

As the right to travel abroad falls under art 21, natural justice must be applied while exercising the power of impounding a Passport under the Passport Act. Although the Passport Act does not expressly provide for the requirement of hearing before a passport is impounded, yet the same has to be implied therein.

Case 2: Sunil Batra vs. Delhi Administration (1980)

The Court has given several directives to improve many aspects of prison administration and condition of prisoners. In this case, the Court has pointed out that its powers under Art. 32 are free from the rigid restraints of the traditional English writs. Prison torture is not beyond the reach of the Supreme Court under Article 32. For this purpose, the Court treats letters from prisoners as writ petitions. In this case, the judicial process was set in motion by a letter written by a prisoner to a Judge of the Supreme Court complaining of the brutal attack by the prison staff on a fellow prisoner. Forsaking all procedural formalities, "since freedom was at stake", the letter was treated by the Court as a petition for the writ of Habeas Corpus.

Case 3: Hussainara Khatoon vs. Home Secretary–State of Bihar (1979)

Hussaainara Khatoon case of the Bihar under trials started with an article written in Indian Express. An advocate then filed a petition under Article 32 in the Supreme Court to protect the personal liberty of the under trials. The Supreme Court has laid great emphasis on speedy trial of criminal offences and has emphasized: "It is implicit in the broad sweep and content of Article 21". A fair trial implies a speedy trial. No procedure can be 'reasonable fair or just' unless that procedure ensures a speedy trial for determination of the guilt of such person. The Supreme Court has directed release of all under trials who have been in jail for periods longer than the maximum term of imprisonment for which they could be sentenced if convicted of the offence charged.

The Court also directed that the under trial prisoners, who are accused of multiple offences and who have already been in jail for the maximum term for which they could be sentenced on conviction, even if the sentences awarded to them were consecutive and not concurrent, should be released forthwith, since their continued detention clearly violates not only human dignity but also their Fundamental Right under Art. 21 of the Constitution.

The Supreme Court has taken a big innovative step forward in humanizing the administration of criminal justice by suggesting that free legal aid be provided by the State to poor prisoners facing a prison sentence.

Case 4: Keshavananda Bharati vs. State of Kerala (1973)

The State of Kerala passed the Kerala Land Reforms Act, 1963. This Act affected the interest of the petitioner, Keshavananda Bharati, Swamiji of a mutt. So he filed a writ petition before the Supreme Court under Article 32 of the constitution, contending that his fundamental rights under Articles 14,19(1)(f), 25, 26 and 31 were violated by the Kerala Land Reforms Act.

While the case was pending, the parliament passed three constitutional Amendments, viz., 24th, 25th & 29th Amendments. The constitution Twenty-fourth Amendment repealed article 19(1)(f) which read "to acquire, hold and dispose of property". It also repealed Article 31, i.e., compulsory acquisition of property. It made several other changes. It also included the Kerala Land Reforms Act in the ninth schedule, thereby making them immune from attack on the ground of fundamental rights. As a result, the fundamental right to property was deleted from the constitution.

The petitioner felt that, by these Amendments, he would lose the case in the court. So, he amended his writ petition before the Supreme Court, & challenged the validity of 24th, 25th & 29th Amendments. He contended that though the power of the parliament to amend was wide, it was not unlimited. The power to amend under Article 368 should not empower the parliament to destroy the basic features of the constitution.

The Supreme Court's judgment in this case is as follows:

(*i*) The constitution Twenty-fourth (Amendment) Act, 1971, Section 2(a)(b) of the constitution Twenty-fifth (Amendment) Act, and the constitution Twenty-ninth (Amendment) Act are valid.

(*ii*) The decision of the majority in Golaknath's case that the word 'Law' in Article 13(2) included Amendments to the constitution & the Article operated as a limitation upon the power to amend the constitution under Article 368 is erroneous, and so, is overruled.

(*iii*) The power of Amendment includes within itself the power to add, alter or repeal the various Articles of the constitution, including those relating to fundamental rights.

(*iv*) There is no power to amend or alter the basic structure of the constitution.

(*v*) The First part of the Article 31-C is valid, and the second part of the Article 31-C laying down "no law containing a declaration that if it is for giving effect to such policy shall be called in question in any court on the ground that it doesn't give effect to such policy" is invalid.

(*vi*) There is no inherent or implied limitations on the power of Amendment under Article 368.

Case 5: Air India vs. Nergesh Meerza (1981)

A regulation made by Air India, a statutory corporation, fixed the normal age of retirement of air hostesses at 35 years but authorized the managing director to extend the same to 45 years at his option subject to other conditions being satisfied. The regulation was held bad as it armed the managing director with uncanalized and unguided discretion to extend the age of retirement of any air hostess. No guidelines, principles or norms were laid down subject to which the power was to be exercised. Nor was there any procedural safeguard available to an air hostess who was denied extension.

A regulation providing for termination of service of an airhostess in Air India on her first pregnancy has been held to be arbitrary and abhorrent to the notions of a civilized society.

Case 6: Visakha vs. State of Rajasthan (1997)

The Supreme Court has declared sexual harassment of a working woman at her place of work as amounting to violation of rights of gender equality and right to life and liberty which is a clear violation of Articles 14, 15 and 21 of the Constitution. Article 21 guarantees right to life with dignity. Accordingly the Court has observed in this connection: "the meaning and content of the Fundamental Rights guaranteed in the constitution of India are of sufficient amplitude to encompass all the facets of gender equality including prevention of sexual harassment or abuse".

Sexual harassment also violates the victim's fundamental right under Article 19(1)(g) "to practice any profession or to carry out any occupation, trade or business". Thus Article 32 is attracted.

In the absence of any domestic law relating to sexual harassment in India, the Supreme Court has itself laid down under Article 32 some directions for prevention of such harassment. These directions are binding and enforceable and are required to be strictly observed in all work places until suitable legislation is enacted to occupy the field.

Case 7: M.R. Balaji vs. State of Mysore (1963)

An order of the Mysore Government issued under Article 15(4) reserved seats for admission to the state Medical and Engineering colleges for Backward classes (28%) and 'more' Backward classes (22%). This was in addition to the reservation of seats for SCs (15%) and for STs (3%). Backward and more backward classes were designated on the basis of 'castes' and 'communities'.

The Supreme Court characterized Article 15(4) as an exception to Article 15(1) [as well as to Article 29(2)]. The court declared the order bad on several grounds in this case.

- The first defect in the Mysore order was that it was based solely on caste without regard to other relevant factors and this was not permissible under Article 15(4)
- Secondly, the test adopted by the state to measure educational backwardness was the basis of the average of student population in the last three high school classes of all high schools in the state in relation to a thousand citizens of that community. This average for the whole state was 6.9 per thousand. The vice of the Mysore order was that it included in the list of backward classes, castes or communities whose average was slightly above, or very near or just below the state average (e.g., Lingayats (7.1) were mentioned in BC list).
- Thirdly, the court declared that Article 15(4) does not envisage classification between backward and more backward classes as was made by the Mysore order.

In Balaji case, the Supreme Court could sense the danger in treating 'caste' as the sole criterion for determining social and educational backwardness. The importance of the judgment lies in realistically appraising the situation when the court said that economic backwardness would provide a more reliable yardstick for determining social backwardness because more often educational backwardness is the outcome of social backwardness. The court drew distinction between 'caste' and 'class'. An attempt at finding a new basis for ascertaining social and educational backwardness in place of caste is reflected in the Balaji decision.

The court also ruled that reservation under Article 15(4) should be reasonable. It should not be such as to defeat or nullify the main rule of equality enshrined in Article 15(1). While it would not be possible to predicate the exact permissible percentage of reservation, it can be stated in a general and broad way that it ought to be less than 50%.

Case 8: Indra Sawhney vs. Union of India (1992) (Mandal Commission Case)

The Supreme Court has taken cognizance of many complex but very momentous questions having a bearing on the future welfare and stability of the Indian society.

- The overall reservation in a year is limited to a maximum of 50%.
- Amongst the classes granted reservation, those who have been benefited from reservation and have thus improved their social status (called the 'creamy layer' by the court), should not be allowed to benefit from reservation over and over again. This means that the benefit of reservation should not be misappropriated by the upper crust but that the benefit of reservation should be allowed to filter down to the lowliest so that they may benefit from reservation to

improve their position. The court has said that if a member of IAS, IPS or any other All India Service, his social status rises; he is no longer socially disadvantaged. This means that, in effect, a family can avail of the reservation only once.

- An element of merit has been introduced into the scheme of reservation.
  - Promotions are to be merit based and are to be excluded from the reservation rule.
  - Certain posts are to be excluded from the reservation rule and recruitment to such posts is to be merit based.

Minimum standards have to be laid for recruitment to the reserved posts.

Case 9: Bijoe Emmanuel Vs. State of Kerala (1987)

The Director of Public Instruction, Kerala issued a circular instructing the students of all schools to sing National Anthem in their schools. Three students belonging to Jehovah's witnesses were expelled as they did not sing the National Anthem. A writ was filed by Bijoe Emmanuel on behalf of the three students in Kerala High Court, questioning the validity of the school management's expulsion order and also the circular of the Director of Public Instruction. The Kerala High Court dismissed the writ petition and upheld the expulsion. It held that it was every citizen's fundamental duty to respect the national integrity and to sing the National Anthem.

The Supreme Court reversed the judgment of the Kerala High Court and gave its judgment in favour of the appellant. The Court ruled that Jehovah's witnesses constitute a religious denomination. Compelling a student belonging to the Jehovah's witnesses to join in the singing of National Anthem despite his "genuine conscientious religious objection', would contravene the right guaranteed by Arts. 19(1)(a) and 25(1). The Court has noted that Jehovah's witnesses wherever they are do not sing the National Anthem, though they show respect to it by standing up whenever it is sung. They truly and conscientiously believe that their religion does not permit the singing of the National Anthem.

The Court has also held it a violation of Article 19(1)(a) to punish a student for not singing the National Anthem. Thus, the negative right, the right to remain silent has been implied in the freedom of speech guaranteed by Article 19(1)(a). As regards Article 51-A(a) imposing fundamental duties on citizens of India, the Court said. "It is true Article 51-A(a) enjoins a duty on every citizen of India to abide by the Constitution and respect its ideals and institutions, the National Flag and National Anthem".

Proper respect is shown to the National Anthem by standing up when it is sung. It will not be right to say that disrespect is shown by not joining in singing.

Case 10: People's Union for Democratic Rights vs. Union of India (1982) (Asiad case)

The Supreme Court has given an expansive significance to the term "forced labour" used in Art. 23(1) in a series of cases beginning with the Asiad case in 1982. The Court has insisted that Art. 23 is intended to abolish every form of forced labour even if it has origin in a contract. The Court insisted that every form of forced labour is within the inhibition of Art. 23 & it makes no difference whether the person who is forced to give his labour or service to another is remunerated or not. Even if a person has contracted with another to perform service and there is consideration for such service, "he cannot be forced, by compulsion of law or otherwise to perform such service, as that would be forced labour."

Even payment of wages less than the minimum wages would be regarded as forced labour. This case was brought before the Supreme Court under Art. 32 by an organization devoted to the protection of democratic rights of the people complaining of the breaches of the workers engaged in the construction of the Asiad projects.

Case 11: M.C. Mehta vs. Union of India (1987)

A petition was filed under Article 32 of the constitution by an advocate bringing the pollution of the River Ganges to the notice of the Court. This was caused by the discharge of effluents into the Ganga by the tanneries at Jajmau, in Kanpur, UP. The petition invoked Articles 21, 48A & 51 of the constitution together with the Water (Prevention and Control of Pollution) Act, 1974.

Referring to the Environment (Protection) Act, 1986 as well as the Water Act, the Court noted that nothing had been done to stop this public nuisance. The tanneries which had not taken minimum steps for the primary treatment of industrial effluents were ordered to be closed. This was done despite the unemployment and loss of revenue it would cause as the Court stated that life, health and ecology have greater importance.

Case 12(a): M.C. Mehta vs. State of Tamilnadu (1996)

The question of employment of child labour has been brought to the attention of the Supreme Court in several cases by way of Public Interest Litigation. In this case, the Court has considered the Constitutional perspectives of the abolition of the child labour in the notorious Sivakasi Match industries. The court has issued detailed directions to eradicate the practice of employing children below the age of 14 years in this hazardous industry. The Court has insisted that the employees must comply with the provisions of the child labour (prohibition and regulation) Act. The Court has emphasized that abolition of child labour is definitely a matter of great public concern and significance. The Court laid down the exhaustive guidelines for the education of children and for setting up a child labour rehabilitation welfare fund. Other industries in respect of which the directions were given are diamond polishing, glass industry, brassware industry, lock making industry and slate industry.

Case 12(b): M.C. Mehta vs. Union of India (1997)

In this case, the Supreme Court dealt with the problem of pollution and deterioration and damage to the Taj Mahal due to the establishment of 292 industries located and operated in Agra. The Court referred to Arts. 21, 48-A, 51-A (g) and 47 and directed that these industries should change over to natural gas as an industrial fuel and if they cannot get gas connections they should stop functioning with the aid of coke/coal. Two principles, viz., "Precautionary Principle" and the "Polluter pays Principle" for sustainable development have been developed by the Supreme Court. The Precautionary principle means that the State Government and the concerned statutory authorities must anticipate, prevent and attack causes of environmental degradation. The Polluter pays principle means that the absolute liability for harm to the environment extends not only to compensate the victims of pollution but also the cost of restoring the environmental degradation.

Case 13: Murali S. Deora vs. Union of India (2002)

Consequent to this case, the Supreme Court prohibited smoking in public places & issued direction to the Union of India, State Government and Union Territories to take effective steps to ensure prohibition in public places. The court held that there is no reason to compel non-smokers to be helpless victims of air pollution which is injurious.

Case 14: Unnikrishnan vs. State of Andhra Pradesh (1993)

The Supreme Court has ruled that establishing educational institutions cannot be regarded as trace or commerce falling under Article 19(1)(g). Imparting education cannot be allowed to become commerce. Trade or business normally connotes an activity carried on for a profit motive. Imparting of education has never been regarded as commerce in India. Private educational institutions are a necessity of the day as the Government alone cannot meet the demand for education particularly in the sector of medical and technical education which calls for huge outlays. In this case, the Court was faced with the question—how to encourage private educational institutions without allowing them to commercialize education.

The Court has reiterated the proposition that having regard to the fundamental significance of education to the life of an individual and the nation, the right to education is implicit in, and flows from the right to life guaranteed by Article 21. The parameters of this right, which is not absolute, have to be determined in the light of the Directive Principles contained in Articles 43, 45 & 46. The Court has now limited the state obligation to provide educational facilities as follows:

(i) Every citizen has a right to free education until he completes the age of 14 years.
(ii) Beyond that stage, the State obligation to provide education is subject to the limits of the economic capacity and development of the State. While denouncing the levy of capitation fee by certain professional colleges the Court has however accepted that unaided private educational institutions can charge higher tuition fee.

The Supreme Court held that Fundamental Rights and Directive Principles are supplementary and complementary to each other and that the provisions in Part III (Fundamental Rights) should be interpreted having regard to the preamble and the Directive Principles of State Policy.

Case 15: TMA Pai Foundation vs. State of Karnataka (2002)

In this case some of the major questions pending decision before the Supreme Court are:

- What are the indicia for treating an institution as a minority educational institution?
- Whether the State or the affiliating University can regulate admission of students to minority educational institutions?
- Whether the ratio in St. Stephen's College case (50%) is correct?
- Whether the ruling in Unnikrishnan case requires reconsideration/modification?
- What is the meaning of the expressions "Education" and "Educational Institutions" in various provisions of the Constitution? Is the right to establish and administer educational institutions guaranteed under the Constitution?

After a long wait an 11-judge bench of the Supreme Court heard and decided the matter in 2002. It was held.

1. The right to establish and administer educational institutions is guaranteed to all citizens [19(1)(g) and 26] and to minorities specifically under Article 30. These rights are not limited to minorities and are available to all persons.
2. The State is to be regarded as the unit for determining both 'linguistic minority' as well as 'religious minority'.
3. The question whether a sect or denomination of a religion can claim minority status even though followers of that religion are in minority was left unanswered.
4. The question as to what are the criteria for treating an educational institution as minority institution was left open.
5. The rights of minorities under Art. 30 cover professional institutions.
6. Admission of students to unaided minority institutions cannot be regulated by the State or a University but it can provide the qualifications and minimum conditions of eligibility in the interest of academic interests.

7. An aided minority educational institution has the right to admit students belonging to the minority but it may be required by the State Government to admit a reasonable number of non-minority students. Reasonable number would depend on the type of institution, courses being run and educational needs of the minorities.
8. Among the minority group admissions must be on merit.
9. In case of aided professional institutions the State may prescribe that only those persons may be admitted who have passed a common entrance test.
10. A minority institution may have its own procedure and method of admission but the procedure must be fair and transparent. Selection in professional and higher education colleges should be based on merit.
11. The state can provide that in aided institutions consideration is shown to weaker sections.
12. In case of unaided institutions the controls should be minimal. Conditions of recognition and affiliation by or to a Board or University have to be complied. But the appointment of teaching and non-teaching staff and control over them will vest in the management. The state may frame regulations prescribing the minimum qualification of a teacher or Principal and also in regard to service conditions.
13. Unaided institution can charge any fees but no institution can charge capitation fee.
14. The basic ratio of St. Stephen's College is correct but rigid percentage cannot be stipulated.
15. The (partly overruled) scheme framed in Unnikrishnan case is unconstitutional. But the principle that there should be no capitation fee or profiteering is correct (partly overruled).

Case 16: ADM Jabalpur vs. S. Shukla (1976)

The Supreme Court held that in view of the Presidential order (PO) of 1975 issued under Article 359 suspending the right of access to the courts for the enforcement of rights of any person under Articles 14, 21 and 22 generally, no person had any locus standi to move any petition before a High Court under Article 226 for a writ of habeas corpus or any other writ, to challenge the legality of detention order on any ground whatsoever.

- Article 21 was the 'sole repository' of the rights to life and personal liberty against the State. Any claim to a writ of habeas corpus to challenge detention on any ground amounted to enforcement of the right of personal liberty under Article 21, the enforcement of which had been suspended by the PO under Article 359.
- Article 21 contained the words 'Procedure established by law'. So, when a person complained that his detention was not in accordance with MISA (Maintenance of Internal Security Act), he was in substance complaining of violation of Article 21, which he could not do in view of the PO.
- The PO of 1975 was unconditional and much broader in scope than the PO issued in 1962, which was conditional and was confined only to the defence of India Act or the rules made there under. Therefore the cases under earlier emergency of preventive detention were not relevant under the PO of 1975.

Thus the Shukla case made the emergency of 1975 most draconian of all the emergencies so for under Article 352 so far as the people of India were concerned.

Case 17: Church of God (Full Gospel) in India vs. KKRMC Welfare Association (2000)

The question of controlling noise pollution has become embroiled with the question of religious freedom guaranteed by the Articles 25 and 26. Can a church claim the freedom to relay prayers on the loudspeakers causing noise pollution and nuisance to the residents? The Supreme Court has ruled in this case, that the question of religious freedom does not arise as no religion requires that prayers be performed through voice amplifiers. The Court directed that the guidelines framed by the Government under the relevant rules framed under Environment Protection Act, 1986 must be followed by the concerned authorities. Any such practice use of loudspeaker by a particular community should not affect the rights of others.

References

- Dr. Durga Das Basu, "Introduction to the Constitution of India", 19th Edition Reprint, Wadhwa Nagpur, 2005.
- Brij Kishore Sharma, "Introduction to the Constitution of India", 2nd Edition, Prentice-Hall of India, New Delhi, 2004.
- M.V. Pylee, "An Introduction to the Constitution of India", Vikas Publishing, 2002.
- Charles E. Harris, et. al., "Engineering Ethics", Thompson Asia, 2003.
- Mike W. Martin & Roland, "Ethics in Engineering", 2002.
- R.V. Badi, "Indian Constitution", 1st Edition, Vrinda Publications, Delhi, 2005.
- B.S. Lingaraj, "Constitution of India and Professional Ethics", 1st Edition, Vidyanidhi Prakashana, Gadag, 2006.
- Umapathi. K.L. & Ramesh. L.C., "The Constitution of India & Professional Ethics", 2nd Edition, Elite Publishers, Mangalore, 2006.
- Merunandan. K.B. & Naveed Ahmed, "Multiple Choice Questions on the Constitution of India", 1st Edition, Meragu Publications, Bangalore, 2006.
- Internet Material.

UNSOLVED SAMPLE QUESTION PAPER–I

06CIP18/28

USN | | | | | | | | | | |

Test Booklet Version: D

CONSTITUTION OF INDIA AND PROFESSIONAL ETHICS

Time: 2 hrs. **Max. Marks: 50**

INSTRUCTIONS TO THE CANDIDATES

1. Use only **Black ballpoint pen** for writing/darkening the circles.
2. Correctly enter your USN at the appropriate place on the **OMR** sheet supplied.
3. Correctly enter **your name (as it appeared on your earlier marks sheets)** and put your signature at the appropriate place on the **OMR** sheet.
4. **For each question, after selecting your answer, darken the appropriate circle corresponding to the same question number on the OMR sheet.**
5. Marking two circles for the same question makes the answer invalid.
6. **Damaging/overwriting, using whiteners** on the **OMR** sheet are strictly prohibited: whole answer sheet **(OMR sheet)** will be rejected.
7. **All questions are compulsory and carry equal marks.**

1. The Speaker of the Lok Sabha

(a) is appointed by the President.
(b) is elected by the members of the Parliament.
(c) is elected by the members of the Lok Sabha.
(d) none of the above.

2. Which of the following is the guardian of the fundamental rights of the citizens?

(a) The Supreme Court.
(b) The President.
(c) The Parliament.
(d) The Lok Sabha.

3. The President of India has power to issue ordinances when

(a) there is a national emergency.
(b) the Lok Sabha has been dissolved.
(c) the Government wants immediate legislation.
(d) the Parliament is not in session.

4. The Indian judiciary is a

(a) highest law-making body.
(b) single and integrated judicial system.
(c) dependent judicial system.
(d) none of the above.

5. Which of the following falls under the original jurisdiction of the Supreme Court?

(a) Disputes relating to the civil matters.
(b) Disputes relating to the criminal matters.
(c) Disputes between two citizens belonging to two different states.
(d) Disputes between the two states of the Indian union.

6. The Supreme Court of India can review

(a) its own orders or judgments.
(b) the orders issued by the executive.
(c) the laws passed by the Legislature.
(d) both (a) and (b).

7. All the union ministers sail and swim together. The entire ministry has to resign if it loses the confidence of the

(a) President of India.
(b) Lok Sabha.
(c) Rajya Sabha.
(d) None of the above.

8. The ministers hold office during the pleasure of the President which in fact means during the pleasure of

(a) the Parliament.
(b) the Lok Sabha.
(c) the Prime Minister.
(d) none of the above.

9. The Governor in the state plays a dual role as an agent of the President and

(a) as the agent of Chief Minister in the state.
(b) as the agent of Chief Justice of India.
(c) as the constitutional head of the state.
(d) as the agent of the Prime Minister.

10. Which of the following contains largest number of subjects?

(a) State list.
(b) Concurrent list.
(c) Union list.
(d) None of the above.

11. "The ideal fuel for modern living" is an example of

(a) trade secret.
(b) patent.
(c) copyright.
(d) trade mark.

12. According to the Marriage Act of 1954, the age is fixed at 21 years for the men and .... for women

(a) 15 years.
(b) 18 years.
(c) 21 years.
(d) 25 years.

13. The state legislative assembly is prorogued by

(a) The Chief Minister.
(b) The Governor.
(c) The Speaker of the assembly.
(d) None of the above.

14. The public is put to increased risk by allowing increased number of deviations from specified standards of safety and acceptable risk is known as

(a) normal accident.
(b) normalizing deviance.
(c) risk assessment.
(d) overestimated risk.

15. The Chief Justice and other Judges of the other state High Courts hold office until they attain the age of

(a) 58 years.
(b) 60 years.
(c) 62 years.
(d) 65 years.

16. An integral part of the Parliament is

(a) The President of India.
(b) The Chief Justice of India.
(c) The Prime Minister of India.
(d) The Election Commissioner.

17. $\frac{1}{3}$rd of the members of the Rajya Sabha retire

(a) every year.
(b) every two years.
(c) every three years.
(d) none of the above.

18. Chief Justice and other Judges of the Supreme Court hold office until they attain the age of

(a) 50 years.
(b) 55 years.
(c) 60 years.
(d) 65 years.

19. The Election Commissioners are appointed by

(a) The President.
(b) The Prime Minister.
(c) The Chief Justice of India.
(d) The Vice-President.

20. A compound measure of the probability and magnitude of adverse effect is known as

(a) compensation.
(b) benefit.
(c) risk.
(d) accident.

21. The Indian constitution is

(a) based on conventions.
(b) a brief document.
(c) an evolved constitution.
(d) written and bulky document.

22. The constituent assembly adopted the Indian constitution on

(a) August 15, 1947.
(b) November 26, 1949.
(c) January 26, 1950.
(d) January 26, 1948.

23. The Government of India Act 1935, provided for

(a) dyarchy at the center.
(b) establishment of federal court.
(c) provincial autonomy.
(d) all of the above.

24. India is a sovereign, socialist, secular, democratic, republic. This expression occurs in

(a) fundamental rights.
(b) citizenship.
(c) preamble.
(d) directive principles.

25. Engineers can use codes of ethics as guidelines to

(a) resolve the conflicts.
(b) formulate the problem.
(c) shift the responsibility.
(d) overcome the work pressure.

26. The ultimate source of authority in India

(a) The people.
(b) The Government.
(c) The Constitution.
(d) The Parliament.

27. The Constitution of India declares India as

(a) a unitary state.
(b) a federation.
(c) a quasi-federal state.
(d) a union of states.

28. The Constitution of India is

(a) unitary in form but federal in spirit.
(b) unitary with strong federal bias.
(c) is full of strong unitary features.
(d) federal in form but unitary in spirit.

29. The President of the constituent assembly of India was

(a) Pandit Jawaharlal Nehru.
(d) Dr. Babu Rajendra Prasad.
(c) Mahatma Mohandas K. Gandhi.
(d) Dr. B.R. Ambedkar.

30. No code will give .... to get solutions for ethical problems.
(a) guidelines.
(b) set of ideas.
(c) an algorithm.
(d) ethical standards.

31. In the Indian constitution, the fundamental rights
(a) were added by the first amendment.
(b) were added by the 42nd amendment.
(c) formed a part of the original constitution.
(d) none of the above.

32. Which of the following is not considered as the aim of engineering ethics?
(a) Moral imagination.
(b) Identification of ethical issues.
(c) Development of analytical skills.
(d) Shifting of responsibility.

33. The fundamental rights granted by the Indian constitution to its citizens cannot be suspended
(a) except by an order of the President during national emergency.
(b) except through an order of the President during war.
(c) except by an order of the Supreme Court.
(d) under any circumstances.

34. Which of the following is no longer a fundamental right?
(a) Right to liberty.
(b) Right to equality.
(c) Right to freedom of religion.
(d) Right to property.

35. In .... concept of responsibility, an attention is paid to those who are at the risk of being harmed.
(a) minimalist.
(b) reasonable care.
(c) good works views.
(d) all of the above.

36. The Constitution of India says 'untouchability' is abolished and its practice in any form is prohibited. This is provided under
(a) right to equality.
(b) right to liberty.
(c) right against exploitation.
(d) right to constitutional remedies.

37. The main purpose of including directive principles of state policy in the constitution of India is

(a) to check the arbitrary action of the government.
(b) to establish a secular state.
(c) to establish a welfare state.
(d) to provide opportunities for the development.

38. Which of the following writ issued by the Supreme Court if it sends an order to restrain a person from acting in an office to which he is not entitled?

(a) Certiorari.
(b) Quo Warranto.
(c) Habeas corpus.
(d) Prohibition.

39. No person who is arrested shall be detained in custody without being informed

(a) of the time when he will be produced before the magistrate.
(b) on the grounds for such arrest.
(c) of the orders of the court.
(d) none of the above.

40. Fear is .... to responsibility.

(a) a way to shift.
(b) an impediment.
(c) a way to corrupt.
(d) both (a) and (c).

41. As applied to engineering research and testing, retaining the data to draw a non-contradictory statement, discarding the rest is called

(a) cooking.
(b) trimming.
(c) scanning.
(d) skimming.

42. Fundamental duties were incorporated in the constitution by the ....

(a) 42nd Amendment Act, 1976.
(b) 44th Amendment Act, 1978.
(c) 45th Amendment Act, 1980.
(d) 46th Amendment Act, 1982.

43. The President of India may from time to time

(a) dissolve the Rajya Sabha.
(b) adjourn the Rajya Sabha.
(c) dissolve the Lok Sabha.
(d) adjourn the Lok Sabha.

44. President's rule can be imposed in the states

(a) during the national emergency.
(b) during general elections.
(c) on failure of the constitutional machinery in a state.
(d) all of the above.

45. Which of the following is not the conflict of interest as applied to making professional judgement?

(a) Virtual.
(b) Actual.
(c) Apparent.
(d) Potential.

46. The minimum age prescribed for the membership of the Rajya Sabha is

(a) 25 years.
(b) 30 years.
(c) 35 years.
(d) 40 years.

47. Which of the following is not done by the President?

(a) Prorogation of the Houses of Parliament.
(b) Summoning the Houses of Parliament to meet.
(c) Adjournment of the Houses of Parliament.
(d) Dissolving the Lok Sabha.

48. No person can contest elections for the membership of the Lok Sabha unless he is a citizen of India and has completed the age of

(a) 21 years.
(b) 22 years.
(c) 24 years.
(d) 25 years.

49. The ministers of the Union Cabinet are answerable to

(a) The Prime Minister.
(b) The Lok Sabha.
(c) The President.
(d) The Vice-President.

50. The executive power of the state is vested in

(a) The Governor.
(b) The State Legislature.
(c) The Chief Minister.
(d) None of the above.

UNSOLVED SAMPLE QUESTION PAPER –II

CIP71/81

USN | | | | | | | | | | **Test Booklet No. : C**

CONSTITUTION OF INDIA AND PROFESSIONAL ETHICS

Time: 3 hrs. **Max. Marks: 100**

INSTRUCTIONS TO THE CANDIDATES

1. Use only **Black ballpoint pen** for writing/darkening the circles.
2. Correctly enter your USN at the appropriate place on the **OMR** sheet supplied.
3. Correctly enter **your name (as it appeared on your earlier marks sheets)** and put your signature at the appropriate place on the **OMR** sheet.
4. Enter the **serial number** of question paper booklet supplied to you at the required place in the **OMR** sheet.
5. **For each question, after selecting your answer, darken the appropriate circle corresponding to the same question number on the OMR sheet.**
6. Marking two circles for the same question makes the answer invalid.
7. **Damaging/overwriting, using whiteners** on the **OMR** sheet are strictly prohibited: whole answer sheet **(OMR sheet)** will be rejected.
8. **All questions are compulsory and carry equal marks.**

1. **It is not one of the fundamental duties of every citizen**
   (a) to develop scientific temper.
   (b) to respect the judiciary and abide by its direction.
   (c) to strive towards excellence in all spheres of life.
   (d) to abjure violence.

2. **The President need not act on the advice of council of ministers in appointing**
   (a) The Comptroller and Auditor General of India.
   (b) The Finance Commission.
   (c) The Prime Minister of India.
   (d) The Attorney General of India.

3. **The President should submit his resignation in writing addressed to**
   (a) The Speaker of Lok Sabha.
   (b) Chief Justice of India.
   (c) The Prime Minister of India.
   (d) None of the above.

4. **Any dispute in connection with the election of vice-president of India**
   (a) may be filed in the High Court.
   (b) must be filed in the Supreme Court.
   (c) should be referred to Election Commission.
   (d) may be filed in the Supreme Court.

5. **Parliament consists of**
   (a) Rajya Sabha and Lok Sabha.
   (b) Rajya Sabha, Lok Sabha and the President of India.
   (c) Rajya Sabha, Lok Sabha, President and Vice President of India.
   (d) Rajya Sabha, Lok Sabha and Speaker of Lok Sabha.

6. **A person cannot be appointed as minister of state, unless he is**
   (a) member of Lok Sabha.
   (b) member of Rajya Sabha.
   (c) member of Legislative Assembly of any state.
   (d) none of the above.

7. **The Vice-President of India is elected by the**
   (a) members of Lok Sabha.
   (b) members of Lok Sabha and elected members of state assemblies.
   (c) members of Lok Sabha, elected members of state assemblies and members of Legislative Councils.
   (d) none of the above.

8. The Vice-President of India may be impeached by
(a) Lok Sabha.
(b) Rajya Sabha.
(c) only by Rajya Sabha.
(d) none of the above.

9. A person is not disqualified to contest for the election to Lok Sabha, if he
(a) is guilty of corrupt practices in relation to an election.
(b) is convicted for an offence and imprisoned for minimum one year.
(c) has failed to lodge the accounts of election expenses.
(d) has been dismissed from government service.

10. A person to be appointed to the post of governor of a state must have completed the age of
(a) 25 years.
(b) 30 years.
(c) 45 years.
(d) none of the above.

11. Governor has no power to appoint
(a) a Judge of High Court.
(b) Chief Minister.
(c) Cabinet Minister.
(d) Advocate General.

12. Every state legislature in India has
(a) Legislative Assembly and Legislative Council.
(b) no Legislative Assembly and Legislative Council.
(c) only Legislative Assembly.
(d) none of the above.

13. Governor shall nominate to the Legislative Council
(a) 12 members.
(b) 7 members.
(c) 5 members.
(d) none of the above.

14. A retired judge of the Supreme Court
(a) may be requested to sit and act as a judge of the Supreme Court.
(b) once retired, he cannot be requested to sit and act as judge of the Supreme Court.
(c) can practice as an advocate in the Supreme Court.
(d) can practice as an advocate only in High Court.

15. The Supreme Court has original jurisdiction in a dispute between
(a) The Lok Sabha and the Rajya Sabha.
(b) The Prime Minister and Chief Minister of any state.
(c) The President of India and Governor of any state.
(d) none of the above.

16. One of the tests of valid classification under Art. 14 is
(a) It must be based on social and educational standard.
(b) It must be based on principles of natural and social justice.
(c) It must be based on intelligible differentia.
(d) It must be based on directive principles of state policy.

17. Supreme Court permits to appeal by special leave
(a) when the time fixed to appeal against the judgment of the High Court has expired.
(b) when the judgment given by the High Court relates to property worth more than 50 lakhs.
(c) when the judgment given by the High Court relates to a person who is non-Indian.
(d) none of the above.

18. The Indian Constitution envisages
(a) five types emergencies.
(b) two types emergencies.
(c) only one type emergency.
(d) three types of emergencies.

19. To continue the National Emergency declared on the ground of armed rebellion
(a) a resolution must be passed by the Lok Sabha by simple majority.
(b) a resolution must be passed by both the Houses of Parliament by simple majority.
(c) a decision must be taken in the cabinet and it must be approved by the President.
(d) none of the above.

20. During National Emergency, the following Article cannot be suspended:
(a) Art. 17.
(b) Art. 18.
(c) Art. 19.
(d) Art. 20.

21. State emergency may be declared on the ground of failure of
(a) executive machinery in the state.
(b) total break down of administrative machinery in the state.
(c) failure of administrative machinery in the state.
(d) failure of constitutional machinery in the state.

22. The duration of state emergency in the first instance is
(a) one month.
(b) two months.
(c) six months.
(d) one year.

23. When the proclamation of financial emergency is approved by the resolution of both the Houses of Parliament, it continues for
(a) another two months.
(b) another six months.
(c) another one year.
(d) indefinitely.

24. The Election Commission does not perform
(a) counting of votes.
(b) to advice the Prime Minister in regard to the question whether a Member of Parliament has been subject to any disqualification.
(c) preparation of electoral rolls.
(d) conduct of elections.

25. When a person is detained under law of detention
(a) a charge sheet should be filed against him within 60 days.
(b) he should be tried in proper court within 90 days.
(c) an advisory board must be constituted within three months.
(d) he cannot be detained more than six months in any case.

26. Original jurisdiction of the Supreme Court relates to
(a) writs directly filed in relating to constitutional matters.
(b) criminal complaints directly filed in the Supreme Court.
(c) election petitions relatings to President, Vice-President or Prime Minister of India, directly filed in the Supreme Court.
(d) none of the above.

27. This is not one of the powers of Chief Minister
(a) formation of Government.
(b) control over the Ministers.
(c) advisor to the Governor.
(d) control over lower judiciary in the state.

28. Respite relates to
(a) powers of Election Commission.
(b) powers of Lok Sabha Speaker.
(c) powers of President.
(d) national emergency declared on the basis of armed rebellion.

29. The Chief Election Commissioner is appointed by

(a) The Prime Minister.
(b) The President.
(c) The Prime Minister in consultation with Council of Ministers.
(d) The Prime Minister in consultation with Chief Justice of India.

30. Governor will act on the advice of Council of Ministers while

(a) dissolving the Legislative Assembly.
(b) appointing the chairman of the State Public Service Commission.
(c) recommending for President's Rule in the state.
(d) returning a bill for reconsideration.

31. The number of ministers in the Central government is fixed by

(a) The President.
(b) The Prime Minister.
(c) The Parliament.
(d) none of the above.

32. It is not the duty of every citizen.

(a) respect the National Anthem.
(b) adopt practice, derogatory to the dignity of women.
(c) to develop the scientific temper.
(d) to abjure violence.

33. The Vice-President is having power

(a) to assent to the bills originated and passed by Rajya Sabha.
(b) to nominate two Anglo-Indian members to Rajya Sabha.
(c) return any bill passed by Rajya Sabha to reconsider.
(d) none of the above.

34. The President shall be elected by the members of electoral college consisting of

(a) all the members of Lok Sabha.
(b) all the members of Rajya Sabha.
(c) all the members of Lok Sabha, Rajya Sabha and elected members of Legislative Assemblies.
(d) none of the above.

35. Restriction can be imposed on the access to shops, hotels on the ground of

(a) place of birth.
(b) place of residence.
(c) sex.
(d) caste.

36. The protection given against self-incrimination is confined to

(a) only constitutional cases.
(b) only cases relating to fundamental rights.
(c) civil matters.
(d) none of the above.

37. There is no any provision in the constitution to protect the rights of

(a) religious minority.
(b) communal minority.
(c) linguistic minority.
(d) none of the above.

38. The right to freedom of Assembly is subject to reasonable restriction in the interest of

(a) law and order in the society.
(b) public property.
(c) trade, commerce, and business.
(d) the Sovereignty and Integrity of India.

39. Reasonable restriction cannot be imposed on the right to freedom of Association on the ground of

(a) Sovereignty and Integrity of India.
(b) public order.
(c) public morality.
(d) incitement to an offence.

40. The final draft of the Indian Constitution was signed by

(a) Dr. B.R. Ambedkar, who was the Chairman of the Drafting Committee of Indian Constitution.
(b) all the members of the Drafting Committee.
(c) all the members of the Constituent Assembly.
(d) none of the above.

41. To declare National Emergency on the basis of external aggression, threatening the security of India, a decision must be taken by the

(a) members of Lok Sabha.
(b) members of Rajya Sabha.
(c) members of Lok Sabha and Rajya Sabha.
(d) Union Cabinet.

42. Reducing the amount of sentence without changing the character of punishment is called

(a) Reprieve.
(b) Respite.
(c) Remission.
(d) Commutation.

43. The Vice-President of India

(a) cannot sign on any bill passed by the Parliament.
(b) promulgate ordinances only in urgent matters.
(c) can seek the advice of the Supreme Court except any matter connected with the security of the state.
(d) none of the above.

44. The oath is administered to Vice-President of India before assuming his office by the

(a) Chief Justice of India.
(b) President of India.
(c) Prime Minister of India.
(d) Speaker of Lok Sabha.

45. A Cabinet Minister is appointed by the President of India

(a) on the recommendations of Council of Ministers.
(b) on the recommendations of Prime Minister made with the prior approval of Union Cabinet.
(c) on the recommendations of Prime Minister made with the prior approval of Party-President.
(d) none of the above.

46. To Lok Sabha

(a) one anglo-Indian member is nominated.
(b) two anglo-Indian members are nominated.
(c) anglo-Indian members are not nominated.
(d) none of the above.

47. The Prime Minister is the link between

(a) The President and Council of Ministers.
(b) The President and both the Houses of Parliament.
(c) The Legislature and the Executive.
(d) India and Foreign States.

48. Compulsion to be a witness relates to

(a) legal obligation of a person to give evidence who has seen the crime being committed.
(b) forcing a person to give evidence in the court of law.
(c) reveal personal knowledge relating to the change.
(d) circumstances under which a government servant is bound to give proper evidence in the interest of nation.

49. An Advisory Board with reference to fundamental right refers to

(a) reservation in educational institutions.
(b) reservation in relation to services under the state.
(c) detention under the Preventive Detention laws.
(d) cultural and educational rights of minorities.

50. The Supreme Court can issue

(a) three types of writs.
(b) seven types of writs.
(c) five types of writs.
(d) six types of writs.

51. Professionals claim to be regulated by

(a) high moral standards and character.
(b) sound professional knowledge and skill required by extensive period of training.
(c) independent and objective judgment in discharging their duties.
(d) none of the above.

52. Professional codes of Ethics articulate

(a) clearly, the role of engineers in protecting the national interest, specially relating to public safety, health and welfare.
(b) in specific terms, the essential characteristics of engineering profession.
(c) shared standard of professional ethics.
(d) the unusual degree of autonomy possessed by engineers in the work-place.

53. Study of engineering ethics does not help in

(a) recognizing ethical issues.
(b) tolerating ambiguity.
(c) stimulating engineering skills.
(d) eliciting a sense of responsibility.

54. One of the characteristics of profession is that

(a) It demands hard and honest work.
(b) It needs extensive training.
(c) It is strictly regulated by the principles of morality and justice.
(d) It is based on integrity, honesty and public utility.

55. On the provision of professional services, professionals usually have

(a) self-interest.
(b) microscopic view.
(c) a monopoly.
(d) moral imagination.

56. One of the basic attitudes towards responsibility is

(a) reasonable care.
(b) absolute responsibility.
(c) strict responsibility.
(d) legal and ethical responsibility.

57. Minimalist view emphasizes

(a) a high standard of moral responsibility.
(b) both on moral and legal responsibility.
(c) a negative approach to responsibility.
(d) on due and reasonable care in performing functions.

58. This is not an impediment to responsibility

(a) failure to seek out the truth.
(b) uncritical acceptance of authority.
(c) fear.
(d) ignorance.

59. Microscopic vision

(a) is essential in Engineering Research and Testing.
(b) is essential to become a responsible engineer.
(c) is essential to adequately to promote the dissemination of information.
(d) none of the above.

60. Engineering codes of ethics emphasize the importance of engineers exercising

(a) Power and strict adherence to professional codes, whenever national interest is involved.
(b) Absolute discretion in rejecting works which are detrimental to the interest of society.
(c) Professional autonomy.
(d) High standard of engineering skill based on professional ethics.

61. This is not dishonesty in science and engineering

(a) forging.
(b) blending.
(c) trimming.
(d) cooking.

62. Biased professional opinion amounts to

(a) misusing the truth.

(b) deliberate deception.
(c) failure to adequately promote the dissemination of information.
(d) none of the above.

63. The following act amounts to misusing the truth:
(a) Retaining only those results that fit the theory and discard others.
(b) The smoothing of irregularities to make the data look extremely accurate and precise.
(c) Abusing client-professional confidentiality.
(d) Using intellectual property of others without proper permission or credit.

64. An engineer abuses client-professional confidentiality when he
(a) refuses to break confidentiality when the higher obligation to the public requires.
(b) fails to take proper care to protect the confidentiality.
(c) leaves the service illegally causing great loss to his employer.
(d) intentionally disobeys the express instruction given by the employer while discharging his duty.

65. Using the trade secrets of former employee amounts to
(a) misusing the truth.
(b) self-deception.
(c) forging.
(d) self-dishonesty.

66. Conflict of interest may be
(a) intentional.
(b) accidental.
(c) potential.
(d) imaginary.

67. According to Lawrence, one of the elements of risk is
(a) magnitude of adverse effect.
(b) defective technology.
(c) failure to take reasonable care.
(d) failure to assess the magnitude of risk.

68. One of the characteristics of high risk technology is
(a) complex designing.
(b) complex interaction.
(c) using outdated technology.
(d) unmindful experiment with new technology.

69. Fault tree is used
(a) to assess the risk.
(b) to assess the accuracy of the research work.

(c) in engineering testing.
(d) to trace the fault in engineering work.

70. Conflict of interest

(a) corrupts professional judgment.
(b) is an impediment to responsibility.
(c) hampers good works.
(d) none of the above.

71. Elections were held to form the constituent assembly to frame constitution for India in the year

(a) 1947.
(b) 1946.
(c) 1950.
(d) 1952.

72. Mountbatten plan refers to

(a) elect members to form constituent assembly.
(b) giving total independence to India by transferring power.
(c) partition of Punjab and Bengal provinces.
(d) permitting Muslim League to frame separate constitution for Pakistan.

73. The Preamble of the Constitution

(a) contained in the constitution, which came into force in 1950.
(b) was added to the constitution after the decision of Keshavanand Bharati case by the Supreme Court.
(c) was added to the constitution by making 42nd Amendment in 1976.
(d) was added to the constitution by making 24th Amendment.

74. Fundamental rights impose duties on

(a) all citizens.
(b) all citizens and non-citizens.
(c) all citizens, non-citizens and alien enemies.
(d) none of the above.

75. Fundamental rights are essential to

(a) unfold the capacities of human beings.
(b) keep a strong check on the working of Government machinery.
(c) to achieve the objectives mentioned in the preamble.
(d) none of the above.

76. There are no express limitations imposed on the following article

(a) Art. 16.
(b) Art. 17.

(c) Art. 18.
(d) Art. 19.

77. The rule of Right to Equality before law is not applicable to
(a) Chief Justice of Supreme Court of India.
(b) Prime Minister of India.
(c) Speaker of the Lok Sabha.
(d) None of the above.

78. The words "We the people" in the Preamble of Indian Constitution indicate that
(a) India is a republican polity.
(b) The Constitution was framed by the people who were elected by the Indian people.
(c) All the people of India took active part in framing the Constitution for India.
(d) None of the above.

79. Reservation at the promotional level in the state service
(a) is not all permitted.
(b) is permitted only for socially and educationally backward class people.
(c) is permitted only backward class people.
(d) none of the above.

80. The means test refers to find out
(a) The validity of classification made under Art. 14.
(b) The validity of reservation made under the government service.
(c) The validity of reservation made in educational institutions for socially and educationally backward class people.
(d) None of the above.

81. To protect the security of the state, the state can impose on the right of freedom of speech and expression
(a) Absolute restriction.
(b) Total restriction.
(c) Strict restriction.
(d) None of the above.

82. In relation to fundamental rights, public order relates to
(a) maintaining law and order.
(b) right to speech and expression.
(c) cultured and educational rights of the minority.
(d) human trafficking.

83. To require a newspaper to reduce its space for advertisements amounts to
(a) serious violation of right to freedom to carry on any trade or business.
(b) violation of right to freedom of speech and expression.
(c) violation of right to equality before the law.
(d) none of the above.

84. The state cannot put restriction on the freedom of formation of association on the ground of

(a) sovereignty and Integrity of India.
(b) public order.
(c) public morality.
(d) security of the state.

85. Prosecuting a government servant after making an enquiry and subsequently dismissing him from service amounts to

(a) double jeopardy.
(b) violation of right of equal protection of laws.
(c) violation of principles of natural justice.
(d) none of the above.

86. Compelling an accused person to give specimen signature amounts to

(a) violation of right to personal liberty.
(b) violation of rule of law.
(c) violation of right to equal protection of laws.
(d) none of the above.

87. Illegal telephone taping is violation of

(a) right to freedom of profession, trade and business.
(b) right to freedom of speech and expression.
(c) right to equal protection of laws.
(d) none of the above.

88. The right to life and personal liberty may be suspended during

(a) National Emergency declared on the ground of external aggression.
(b) National Emergency declared on the ground of security of the state.
(c) State Emergency declared on the ground of failure to maintain law and order in the state.
(d) None of the above.

89. The procedure prescribed to deprive the life or personal liberty must be

(a) in the interest of general public.
(b) to protect security of the state.
(c) reasonable, fair and just.
(d) to maintain the unity and integrity of the nation.

90. A person detained under law of preventive detention is having

(a) right to be produced before the nearest Magistrate within 24 hours of detention.
(b) right to consult his friends, and relatives.
(c) right not to be detained more than 48 hours, without the permission of the court.
(d) none of the above.

91. To detain a person under the law of preventive detention, the person must have committed an act

(a) affecting seriously the security of the state.
(b) for which the minimum punishment is life-imprisonment.
(c) which endangers the life of President, Vice-President or Chief Justice of India.
(d) none of the above.

92. Traffic in human beings is violation of

(a) right to life and personal liberty.
(b) right against exploitation.
(c) right to social justice.
(d) right to equal protection of laws.

93. With reference to Indian constitution, minority refers to

(a) persons belonging to S.C. and S.T.
(b) persons belonging to socially and educationally backward class.
(c) a small percentage of people who are economically and educationally backward.
(d) none of the above.

94. When an inferior court acts contrary to the rules of natural justice, the superior court issues a

(a) writ of Mandamus.
(b) writ of Prohibition.
(c) writ of Quo-Warranto.
(d) none of the above.

95. Writ of Quo-Warranto is issued

(a) against an inferior court, exceeding its jurisdiction.
(b) against a person, to prevent illegal assumption of any private office.
(c) quash an order issued by the lower court without jurisdiction.
(d) none of the above.

96. A public authority is directed to discharge public duty by issuing a writ of

(a) Habeas Corpus.
(b) Certiorari.
(c) Mandamus.
(d) Quo-Warrants.

97. To file Public Interest Litigation

(a) Locus standi is not necessary.
(b) The person filing the P.I.L. must have direct interest in the litigation.
(c) The person filing the litigation should have substantial interest in the litigation.
(d) The person filing the litigation must have suffered some monetary loss.

98. The directive principles of the state policy direct the state to secure all the citizens

(a) common civil code.
(b) uniform civil code.
(c) modern civil code.
(d) practicable and workable civil code.

99. The directive principles of state policy direct the state to improve

(a) standard of education.
(b) standard of public health.
(c) judicial system.
(d) law and order conditions.

100. The directive principles of state policy do not direct the state to meet

(a) social reforms.
(b) economic reforms.
(c) political reforms.
(d) cultural reforms.

ANSWERS TO UNSOLVED SAMPLE QUESTION PAPER–I

1. (c)	2. (b)	3. (d)	4. (a)	5. (d)	6. (c)	7. (b)	8. (c)
9. (c)	10. (c)	11. (c)	12. (b)	13. (b)	14. (b)	15. (c)	16. (a)
17. (b)	18. (d)	19. (a)	20. (c)	21. (d)	22. (b)	23. (d)	24. (c)
25. (a)	26. (c)	27. (d)	28. (d)	29. (b)	30. (c)	31. (c)	32. (d)
33. (a)	34. (d)	35. (b)	36. (a)	37. (c)	38. (c)	39. (a)	40. (b)
41. (a)	42. (a)	43. (c)	44. (c)	45. (a)	46. (b)	47. (c)	48. (d)
49. (a)	50. (c)						

ANSWERS TO UNSOLVED SAMPLE QUESTION PAPER–II

1. (b)	2. (c)	3. (b)	4. (d)	5. (b)	6. (d)	7. (d)	8. (d)
9. (a)	10. (d)	11. (a)	12. (a)	13. (d)	14. (a)	15. (d)	16. (c)
17. (d)	18. (d)	19. (b)	20. (d)	21. (d)	22. (b)	23. (d)	24. (b)
25. (c)	26. (d)	27. (c)	28. (c)	29. (b)	30. (c)	31. (c)	32. (b)
33. (d)	34. (d)	35. (d)	36. (d)	37. (b)	38. (d)	39. (d)	40. (a)
41. (d)	42. (c)	43. (d)	44. (a)	45. (b)	46. (b)	47. (a)	48. (a)
49. (c)	50. (c)	51. (c)	52. (a)	53. (c)	54. (d)	55. (d)	56. (a)
57. (b)	58. (a)	59. (d)	60. (a)	61. (b)	62. (d)	63. (c)	64. (d)
65. (d)	66. (c)	67. (d)	68. (b)	69. (a)	70. (d)	71. (a)	72. (c)
73. (c)	74. (a)	75. (a)	76. (c)	77. (d)	78. (a)	79. (a)	80. (d)
81. (d)	82. (b)	83. (d)	84. (d)	85. (d)	86. (d)	87. (b)	88. (a)
89. (c)	90. (a)	91. (a)	92. (b)	93. (d)	94. (b)	95. (d)	96. (c)
97. (c)	98. (b)	99. (b)	100. (d)				